New Frontiers in Regional Science: Asian Perspectives

Volume 51

More information about this series at http://www.springer.com/series/13039

Adrián de León-Arias • Patricio Aroca
Editors

NAFTA's Impact on Mexico's Regional Development

Springer

Editors
Adrián de León-Arias
University of Guadalajara
Zapopan, Jalisco, Mexico

Patricio Aroca
CEPR, Business School
Universidad Adolfo Ibáñez
Viña del Mar, Chile

ISSN 2199-5974 ISSN 2199-5982 (electronic)
New Frontiers in Regional Science: Asian Perspectives
ISBN 978-981-16-3167-2 ISBN 978-981-16-3168-9 (eBook)
https://doi.org/10.1007/978-981-16-3168-9

This Springer imprint is published by the registered company Springer Nature Singapore Pte Ltd.
The registered company address is: 152 Beach Road, #21-01/04 Gateway East, Singapore 189721, Singapore

Introducción

In this book, the dynamics of continuity and change in economic activity across Mexican regions and the overall regional development are analyzed along the last thirty years (1980–2020). This subject is of interest in the literature on regional economic development, while the Mexican case, through its history since Colonial times, has been clearly polarized and, more recently, challenged with trade opening, mostly with the USA, since the late 1980s, and afterwards with the North American Free Trade Agreements (NAFTA and USMCA), as well as a more protagonist role of the local and regional economic agents in their economic development strategies. In this respect, this volume looks for an explanation of the diversity of regional patterns as a result from trade integration and local dynamics with emphasis in different perspectives and Mexican regions and the U.S. Southern States.

In the way about how regional economic development in Mexico under trade integration and local developments are analyzed, this book is oriented to readers interested in academic fields related to examine geographical space and economics such as new economic geography, geographical economics, (proper) economic geography as well as to international economics, regional economic development, and Mexican economy, additionally, a couple of chapters deals with input–output explorations.

Moreover, this book is of interest to academic and professional researchers in those fields in order to be acquainted to recent contributions in regional economic development as stepping stone to generate a more general framework to analyze the impacts of recent developments in regional trade integration, such a Brexit or USMCA, looking for the impacts of such developments in subnational economies.

This book is an excellent reference for policymakers at national and subnational levels, while this book would help to identify areas of interest to policy implementation to encourage the dynamics of regional development as well as graduate students in those fields while gives an updated review to this day of the themes presented which can be useful for thesis research.

It is relevant to note that regional economic development in Mexico is a significant case which, in particular, after the implementation of NAFTA, has been subject of international academic attention in fields such as regional economics, new geographical economics, (proper) economic geography, among others, because dynamics of that development pattern became an excellent laboratory, altogether with the European Union case, to analyze economic or trade integration in a context of imperfect competition, spatial agglomerations of economic activity, divergent geographical patterns of endogenous growth, as well as industrialization strategies and evolutionary patterns.

Furthermore, in the 1990s decade, the trade and investment globalization wave, as well as, the expansion of regional trade agreements took the attention of economic researchers on the evaluation of the benefits and costs of such international cooperation strategies and related to the research topics of this book, about their subnational impact, that is, taking into consideration the relevance of the impact of such trade agreements on regions inside nations.

In the series of issues mentioned above, for the case of Mexican regional economic development, relevant contributions were Livas and Krugman (1992), as well as Hanson (1994) which, taking into consideration agglomeration economies and geographical (economic) distance, topics related to new geographical economics, in a context where Mexico city that concentrated industrial activities was located relatively far from the USA, while cities with recent industrialization, at that time, and geographical close to the USA could take advantage of agglomeration economics generated by closeness to the new central market, the American economy. This and other more general hypothesis were evaluated in a growing literature.

While previously mentioned research focused on regional development under trade liberalization mostly related to location, other economists extended these regional evolutions in a perspective more dynamic, related to economic growth, with an emphasis on productivity, see, for instance, Esquivel (1999), De León Arias (1999), and Aroca González et al. (2005). In these works, they observed that, if well employment and economic activity was growing in the Northern Border in relation to Mexico city, altogether with some states located geographically around that city, labor productivity growth was accelerated in regions as Central Mexico rather than in the Northern Border region. Then, more availability of human capital, infrastructure, and capacity to generate knowledge spillovers was identified as significant growth factors in explaining productivity growth in a regional perspective in Mexico. Nonetheless, these studies showed that regional economic growth could be described not only through reception of trade and foreign investment but also in terms of the endogenous characteristics of the regions.

The historical dynamic role of those endogenous factors in Northern and Central Mexico regions under international trade integration has been validated by analytical contributions of the so-called proper economic geography, in particular following the recommendation of Garretsen and Martin (2010) of linking new economic geography and history. In the research presented in this book, geographical space becomes endogenous and function of the process being explained.

In some way, collaborations presented in this book in their analytic dimension follow a couple foundational perspective pointed out by Ohlin [1967 (1933)]: (1) in explaining regional industrial activity taking into consideration the varying supply of productive factors in different places and where some factors are freely mobile and others not, moreover those factors "placed in the group called nature" are completely immobile Ohlin (Ibid, p. 2). And (2) following this argument, Ohlin, in appendix II to his original book, also pointed out the role of productive conditions and analysis of development through the time (Ohlin, Ibid, p.314) as conditions of analysis of regional development.

It may be relevant to note that in some chapters of this book, there is call for explanation where "*history matters*" and where this expression indicates that current and future economic outcomes are strongly influenced by past events—hence, analysts often observe heterogeneous and path-dependent developmental trajectories across economic growth patterns, which can be better understood by illuminating differences in starting conditions, past successes and failures, or lasting institutional features. In this general form, the guideline history matters can be applied to a variety of regional economic development experiences.

In the same perspective, collaborations in this book also—some kind—follow recent debate about the role of historical dynamics in the new geography economics (NGE) or geographical economics, collaborations in this book are close to the so-called proper economic geography (PEG), as defined by Martin (1999) while most of them involve a commitment to study regions where local specificity matters and taking into consideration the role of historical-institutional factors in the development of those regions and giving history and geography a central role in their explanation.

Additionally, research reported in this book continues the contributions of a large group of Mexican and other countries' researchers who have taken advantage of the case of Mexico´s regional development under NAFTA, as far as it showed a feedback between internal or endogenous factors and trade flows and FDI from an analytical and historical point of view. For a review of these contributions, see De León Arias and Llamosas (2016) and De León Arias (2019).

Most of the collaborators in this book are researchers who have been analyzing on Mexico and US Southern border regional economic development since 1990s and advanced their investigations in the context of expectation and results for those regions from the Mexico´s free trade agreements. In this book, they were asked for long run regional economic development exploration based on their expertise developed in previous research. In the following, abstract of the chapters is presented.

In the chapter "**A Review of Regional Development, Disparities, and Public Policies in Mexico: Reflections on an Environment of Strategic Reconfigurations**" by Alejandra Trejo, *Colegio de Mexico*, taking into account the context of a recent turbulent world dynamics with geopolitical change and the reversal of major trends appears to be underpinning a return to protectionism as a strategic political tool. In addition to that international changes, author added that Mexico is facing internal political rearrangement in which particular visions of the national model are being adopted; therefore, these national and international adjustments offer an opportunity for a broad discussion of the Mexican development paradigm and its regional impacts. This chapter then contributes to the debate on regional economic development in Mexico and reflects on some of its main dilemmas. After a succinct review from a historical perspective, a more detailed account is provided of regional development and spatial disparities in the opening up and liberalization phase. She also discusses key elements in the evolution of planning and regional policy in the country throughout the twentieth century and to date. The work concludes with four reflections about Mexico's regional development perspectives and challenges.

In the chapter **"Regional Advantages: Why U.S.–Mexico Trade Is Robust and Permanent,"** James Gerber, *SDSU Emeritus professor*, observed that while Mexico and the USA have the second largest bilateral trade relationship in the world, after only U.S.–Canadian trade, and the free trade agreement facilitates the flow of goods and services, there are other factors which are also important enough that an abrogation of the agreement would not likely alter the volume of trade in a significant way. In particular, according to professor Gerber, Mexico–U.S trade is driven by five factors in addition to the effects of the trade agreement. First, the proximity of the USA and Mexico reduces transportation costs. Second, the size of both the USA and Mexican economies creates a large demand for each other's goods and services. Third, economic policy reforms in Mexico and the USA encouraged closer trade ties, particularly in the border region where Mexico's export processing zone was deeply integrated with the American economy. Fourth, new information and communication technologies led to the development of cross-border value chains that further integrated manufacturing systems. And fifth, state and local efforts along the border have strengthened cross-border economic ties.

In the chapter **"Regional Economic Development in Mexico: Past, Present, and Future,"** Rafael Garduño, *Universidad Panamericana-Aguascalientes*, analyzes factors such as climate, security, production, specialization, trade, infrastructure, and investment and their effect on the Regional Economic Development in Mexico in the last years with focus in the regional concentration of economic activity, production efficiency, and economic growth.

In the chapter **"Identification and Spatial Hierarchy of Industrial Conglomerates with Census Data. A Suggested Procedure and Application to the Mexican Case of Study"** professor Jesús A. Treviño Cantú, *Universidad de Nuevo León*, develops a new methodological combination and sequence of existing techniques of spatial analysis to identify industrial conglomerates and set up their spatial hierarchy. While the word "conglomerate" refers to the fusion of concentration and agglomeration processes of magnitude or intensity, in this contribution, concentration is the occurrence of high global values, regardless of their location. Conversely, agglomeration is the concentration of adjacent high local values. Both agglomeration and concentration create conglomerates of magnitude or intensity when they are merged through a geographical overlay procedure. While magnitude refers to size, intensity refers to importance of the studied variable. For the first time in the study of the spatial pattern of manufactures, the spatial hierarchy is obtained by overlaying conglomerated and non-conglomerated high values of magnitude and intensity.

Potential benefits of the suggested procedure for an area-based public policy are illustrated by assessing industrial employment in 2,352 and 2,457 Mexican municipalities in 1998 and 2013, respectively. The procedure in this study may easily be extended to identify spatial patterns of diseases, crime, poverty, aging population, pollution, or environmental justice in different areas or countries.

In the chapter, **"Regional characteristics of labor productivity in Mexico's manufacturing sector,"** professor Eduardo Mendoza, *Colegio de la Frontera Norte*, studies labor productivity in the manufacturing sector of Mexico for the period 2007–2020/01. In particular, an analysis of the structure and trends of labor productivity at the state level is studied. Results show that labor productivity at the regional level has shown an uneven growth. In addition, the study discusses the determinants of labor productivity in Mexico and establishes an econometric model to explore the impact of the determinants of labor productivity such as foreign direct investment, schooling, and gross capital formation which have positive effects on labor productivity growth.

In the chapter **"Value Added in Exports under NAFTA: A Binational Input–Output Model,"** professors Noé Arón Fuentes, Alejandro Brugués, Gabriel González-König, *Colegio de la Frontera Norte*, highlight the stylized fact that Mexico has had a significant gross trade surplus with the USA during the NAFTA period, proving the existence of a notable deficit for Mexico in terms of the added value incorporated in this trade. The value-added flow in Mexico's gross exports to the USA only reaches 164.4 billion, while the domestic content of the USA gross exports is 188.7 billion. In the disaggregation of added value, the great difference between domestic and foreign components incorporated in exports stands out, while for the USA the foreign added value in its exports reaches 2.5 billion for the case of Mexico, this concept is 50.2 billion, which is more than 20 times the amount it represents for the USA. A conclusion that derives directly from this last aspect is that during NAFTA an important part of the income from Mexican exports goes to remunerate productive factors used in the USA.

Edgardo Ayala and Joana Chapa in the chapter **"Structural Change in the Exports and Foreign Direct Investment of the Southeast Gulf Mexican States"** presents a combination of econometric and multi-sectoral techniques to show that NAFTA has not only beneficiated northern states in Mexico, but also to the south region of Mexico. A structural break in manufacturing exports and foreign direct investment is found in the Southeast Gulf of Mexico, which encompasses the states of Veracruz, Tabasco, Campeche, Quintana Roo, and Yucatán, most likely caused by those major liberalization reforms. Manufacturing exports might increase by 48.3% of pre-NAFTA levels, whereas FDI rose by 71.6%. The increment in manufacturing exports is linked to a rise of 1.0% in gross value added and 1.7% in employment of the region. Meanwhile, FDI expansion likely contributed with an additional increment of value added and employment of 1%.

While chapter contributions in this volume were written during 2020 and March 2021, new issues were developed along, such as some institutional consolidation from the *old* NAFTA to the *new* USMCA, and the regional policy in the new federal administration, both of them were somehow already taken into account in some of the chapters, but not so the impact of COVID-19 which surely remains as a question to be not only as a subject of study but also a social and economic challenge.

Regarding regional policy in the new federal administration which began in the late 2018, one of the challenges in the near future is improving the design and evaluation of the significant efforts in terms of public investment directed to Mexican South. In particular, Federal Government has implemented large infrastructure projects for that region.

Mexican South has been the Mexican lagged region in terms of economic development for the long time. Aroca González et al. (2002) evaluated the effect of the trade opening of economy at large in the 1990s on this region and identified such policy as insufficient as development strategy.

Another emergent area of interest in current regional inquiry is, of course, the design of methodologies in evaluating the regional impact of COVID-19. The analysis of the impact of such virus has become a relevant topic of research in all areas, where regional impact is not the exception. While that inquiry at this time (March, 2021) is mostly in process, there are investigations which are looking for learning from identified impacts by previous virus contagious like SARS (in this respect, see SOUTHGN.COM 2020).

Among some other relevant research methodological approach is Bonet-Morón et al. (2020) who developed an input–output formulation for analyzing the regional economic impact of COVID-19 in Colombia. There is also an investigation on the evaluation of the economic cost of the closing of no essentials activities by means of a multisectorial and regional analysis with SAM models (Dávila-Flores y Valdés-Ibarra 2021).

Niembro and Cala (2020) identified the magnitude of the regional impacts, including related issue of informal labor and self-employment for the Argentina case by building an index of territorial economic impact by COVID-19.

Of methodological interest in the recent literature on the economic impact of COVID-19 is the analysis based on data at granular level in real time using anonymized data from private companies. Even more in the case of regional research these studies can be extended to key locational indicators disaggregated by ZIP code industry income group and business size. See Chetty et al. (2020).

In general, the analysis of impact of COVID-19 on economies has renewed the inquiry from a regional and urban perspective as pointed out by Hadjimichalis (2020) for the European Union but it can be appreciated to any national economy.

Additionally, it is interesting to note that besides the perception of deep insecurity and crime which have been extended in Mexico in recent decades, however, in these chapters presented few references to the issues of crime and insecurity, that it may be of interest for researching in the future.

Regional inmediate experiences in Mexico after national debates on the transition from NAFTA to USMCA and during year 2020 under the Covid-19 impact have recovered the concept of regional resilence while regional conditions show persistence of growth patters and a relevant flexibility on part of regional governments, firms and socities.

As editors of this volume we would thank to all and each one of the chapter´s authors and their institutions the generosity in sharing their recent research through this book. Additionally, to the COES (Center for Conflict and Cohesion Studies) whose supports are gratefully acknowledged. To professor Selene Vielmas for dedicated editorial and administrative labor to make this work possible.

Universidad Adolfo Ibáñez, Santiago, Chile — Patricio Aroca
Universidad de Guadalajara-CUCEA, Guadalajara, Mexico — Adrián de León-Arias
11 pm 28 de marzo 2021

References

Aroca González P, Maloney WF (2005) Migration, trade, and foreign direct investment in Mexico. World Bank Econ Rev 19(3): 449-472. https://doi.org/10.1093/wber/lhi017

Aroca Gonzalez P, Maloney WF (2005) Migration, trade, and foreign direct investment in Mexico. Policy research working paper; No. 3601. World Bank, Washington, DC. © World Bank. https://openknowledge.worldbank.org/handle/10986/8930 License: CC BY 3.0 IGO

Aroca González P, Maloney WF, Bosch Mossi M (2003) Is NAFTA Polarizing Mexico? or El Sur Tambien Existe? Spatial Dimensions of Mexico's Post-Liberalization Growth. Or El Sur Tambien Existe

Aroca González P, Bosch M, Maloney WF (2005) Spatial dimensions of trade liberalization and economic convergence: Mexico 1985–2002. World Bank Econ Rev 19(3):345-378

Baggio JA, Brown K, Hellebrandt D (2015) Boundary object or bridging concept? A citation network analysis of resilience. Ecol Soc 20(2). https://doi.org/10.5751/ES-07484-200202

Bonet-Morón J, Ricciulli-Marín D, Pérez-Valbuena GJ, Galvis-Aponte LA, Haddad EA, Araújo IF, Perobelli FS (2020) Regional economic impact of COVID-19 in Colombia: an input-output approach. Reg Sci Policy Pract 12(6): 1123-1150. https://doi.org/10.1111/rsp3.12320

Chetty R, Friedman J, Hendren N, Stepner M (2020) The economic impacts of COVID-19: evidence from a new public database built from private sector data. Opport Insights. Retrieved https://fairmodel.econ.yale.edu/ec438/chetty1.pdf

Dávila-Flores A, Valdés-Ibarra M (2021) México. Costos económicos del cierre de las actividades "no esenciales" por la pandemia Covid-19. Análisis multisectorial y regional con modelos SAM. Economía: Teoría y Práctica. Nueva época, (Núm. Especial): 15–44. https://doi.org/10.24275/ETYPUAM/NE/E052020/Davila

De León Arias A (1999) Trade liberalization and endogenous growth. Ph.D. dissertation. University of Notre Dame, Notre Dame

De León Arias A (2019) El Desarrollo Económico Regional en México. Universidad de Guadalajara

De León Arias A, Llamosas IJ (2016) Trade liberalization and regional productivity growth: Some lessons from Mexico's Northern Border manufacturing after

20 years. Ensayos sobre Política Económica 34(79):40–50. https://doi.org/10.1016/j.espe.2016.02.001

Esquivel G (1999) Convergencia regional en México. El Trimestre Económico 66 (264(4)):725–761

Garretsen H, Martin R (2010) Rethinking (new) economic geography models: taking geography and history more seriously. Spat Econ Anal 5(2):127–160. https://doi.org/10.1080/17421771993730729

Gong H, Hassink R, Tan J, Huang D (2020) Regional resilience in times of a pandemic crisis: the case of COVID-19 in China. Tijdschr Econ Soc Geogr 111 (3):497–512. https://doi.org/10.1111/tesg.12447

González Laxe F, Arnesto Pina JF, Lago-Peñas S, Sanchez-Fernandez P (2020) Impacto económico del COVID-19 en una economía regional: El caso del confinamiento para Galicia 1(1/2020):1–18. https://mpra.ub.uni-muenchen.de/100002/

Hadjimichalis C (2020) An uncertain future for the post-Brexit, post-COVID-19 European Union. Eur Urban Reg Stud 28(1):8–13. https://doi.org/10.1177/0969776420968961

Hassink R (2010) Regional resilience: a promising concept to explain differences in regional economic adaptability? Camb J Reg Econ Soc 3(1):45–58. https://doi.org/10.1093/cjres/rsp033

Hanson G (1994) Regional adjustment to trade liberalization (Working Paper No. 4713). Retrieved: National Bureau of Economic Research website: http://www.nber.org/papers/w4713

Livas E, Krugman P (1992) Trade policy and the third world metropolis (Working Paper No. w4238). Retrieved: National Bureau of Economic Research website: http://www.nber.org/papers/w4238.pdf

Martin R (1999) Critical survey. The new 'geographical turn' in economics: some critical reflections. Camb J Econ (23):65–91. doi:https://doi.org/10.1093/cje/23.1.65

Martin R (2018) Shocking aspects of regional development: towards an economic geography of resilience. In: Clark G, Gertler M, Feldman MP, Wójcik D (eds) The new Oxford handbook of economic geography. Oxford University Press, Oxford, pp 839-864

Martin R (2021) Putting the case for a pluralistic economic geography. J Econ Geogr 21(1):1–28. https://doi.org/10.1093/jeg/ibaa025

Martin R, Sunley P (2020) Regional economic resilience: evolution and evaluation. In: Bristow G, Healy A (eds) Handbook on regional economic resilience. Edward Elgar, Cheltenham, pp 10–35

Martin R, Sunley P, Gardiner B, Tyler P (2016) How regions react to recessions: resilience and the role of economic structure. Reg Stud 50(4):561–585. https://doi.org/10.1080/00343404.2015.1136410

Mendoza E (2002) Agglomeration economies and urban manufacturing growth in the northern border cities of Mexico. Econ Mexicana Nueva Epoca 1(9):8. http://hdl.handle.net/11651/4085

Niembro A, Cala CD (2020) A fist exploratory analysis of the regional economic impact of COVID-19 in Argentina. (Documento de Discusión Agosto 2020). Retrieved: http://nulan.mdp.edu.ar/id/eprint/3376
Ohlin B (1967|1933) International and interregional trade. Cambridge, MA: Harvard University Press.
SOUTHGN.COM (2020) How did the lessons learned from SARS 17 years ago Become Guankdong's Armor against the COVID-19? Retrieved: http://news.southcn.com
Thorén H (2014) Resilience as a unifying concept. Int Stud Philos Sci 28 (3):303–324. https://doi.org/10.1080/02698595.2014.953343
Trejo A (2017) Localización manufacturera, apertura comercial y disparidades regionales en México: organización económico-espacial bajo un nuevo modelo de desarrollo. El Colegio de México, Centro de Estudios Demográficos, Urbanos y Ambientales, México

Contents

About the Editors

Adrián de León-Arias Professor and Researcher, Universidad de Guadalajara (Mexico). 2019, Senior Research Scholar at ILAS, Columbia University (New York). Research interest: Mexico´s regional economic development; Growth and Development in Mexico; US-Mexico Relations (Migration and Trade).

Patricio Aroca Universidad Adolfo Ibáñez, Viña del Mar, Chile, and Visiting Associate Professor, University of Illinois. He is specialized in econometrics, natural resources and regional economics, and more specifically works with Input-Output analysis, Spatial Econometrics, Regional Growth and Labor Interregional Migration.

A Review of Regional Development, Disparities, and Public Policies in Mexico: Reflections on an Environment of Strategic Reconfigurations

Alejandra Trejo-Nieto

Abstract Recent turbulent world dynamics with geopolitical change and the reversal of major trends appear to be underpinning a return to protectionism as a strategic political tool. In addition to political reconfiguration at the international level, Mexico is facing internal political rearrangement in which particular visions of the national model are being adopted. These national and international adjustments offer an opportunity for a broad discussion of the Mexican development paradigm and its regional impacts. This chapter contributes to the debate on regional economic development in Mexico and reflects on some of its main dilemmas. After a succinct review from a historical perspective, a more detailed account is provided of regional development and spatial disparities in the opening up and liberalization phase. I also discuss key elements in the evolution of planning and regional policy in the country throughout the twentieth century and to date. The work concludes with four reflections about Mexico's regional development perspectives and challenges.

Keywords Regional development · Regional disparities · Territorial policy · Trade · Mexico

1 Introduction

Recently the dynamics of world geopolitical change and the reversal of major trends appear to be underpinning a return to protectionism as a strategic political tool. Britain's exit from the European Union (Brexit) and the United States interest in reversing the North American Free Trade Agreement (NAFTA), the emergence of

A. Trejo-Nieto (✉)
El Colegio de México, Centro de Estudios Demográficos Urbanos y Ambientales, Ciudad de México, Mexico
e-mail: abtrejo@colmex.mx; https://cedua.colmex.mx/personal-academico/trejo-nieto-alejandra-berenice

A. de León-Arias, P. Aroca (eds.), *NAFTA's Impact on Mexico's Regional Development*, New Frontiers in Regional Science: Asian Perspectives 51,
https://doi.org/10.1007/978-981-16-3168-9_1

new macroregional spaces and trade blocs, and other international geo-economic adjustments to such factors as China's increasing significance in the global economy all contribute to this turmoil. In addition, the current speed of change seems to have no precedent. Whether the opening up model, based on the integration of regional blocks, is lapsing and what new (or old) models and organizational structures in countries' commercial relationships and internal economies will replace it are significant questions. The debate about how Mexico and the world should be restructured is therefore very much alive. Despite the speed at which events are occurring, it is essential to examine their effects and implications systematically and continuously.

More than 30 years ago Mexico, like many other developing countries, took a radical turn in its economic policy. The exhaustion of the import substitution model coupled with the problem of external debt, which had become a serious obstacle to the country's stability, led to the implementation of a new economic model. This consisted of a set of policies including trade liberalization, privatization, and deregulation (Trejo 2017). The emphasis was on shrinking the scope and size of the government and trusting in the efficiency of free-market processes and private-sector activities. The economic model was based on the premise that the external sector's dynamism would mobilize all sectors of the economy. The state simply had to focus on maintaining the stability of its key macroeconomic variables to be able to offer a favorable environment for investment. The opening up of the Mexican economy led to a radical suppression of barriers to international trade. The first stage of this process, in the 1980s, was based on far-reaching unilateral liberalization followed by multilateral liberalization within the framework of the General Agreement on Tariffs and Trade (GATT). Later, NAFTA coming into force in 1994 revealed Mexico's aspiration to integrate itself into the global economy via favorable positioning in North America (Cárdenas 2015).

Trade liberalization and integration with North America were presented as powerful tools for the expansion of trade and foreign investment, the greater mobility of productive factors between Mexico and its partners, and economic growth and diminishing inequalities within Mexico: in short, for greater prosperity (ibid). Over the years much discussion has revolved around the question of how NAFTA triggered any positive social, economic, and territorial change given the opportunities it offered, and the challenges and pressures imposed by the international economic order.

Despite the positive effect on trade flows and investment, Mexico's liberalization brought about heterogeneous effects. In particular, opening up the markets had asymmetric impacts on economic opportunities, productive capacity, and outcomes. The regional effects and impacts of liberalization and NAFTA have been an issue of particular interest (Chamboux-Leroux 2001; Sanchez-Reaza and Jordaan 2002; Corona Jímenez 2003; Decuir-Viruez 2003; Dussel Peters 2003; Rodríguez-Pose and Sánchez-Reaza 2003; Jordaan and Sanchez-Reaza 2004; Aroca et al. 2005; Diaz Bautista 2005). There is evidence that Mexico has historically been characterized by important economic contrasts across its territory (Trejo Nieto 2020), and several authors have pointed out that these territorial imbalances persisted after the opening up of the economy and the country remained geographically fragmented in terms of its economic development (Mendoza-Velázquez et al. 2020; Díaz Dapena et al. 2017; Trejo 2017). Trejo (2017), for instance, points out that the geographic distribution of economic opportunities in recent decades has been irremediably linked to the export-oriented economic model. Initially, it gave rise to favorable conditions for the take-off or consolidation of industrial centers located mainly in the north of the country; subsequently, some economic de-concentration benefited cities and regions in the center-north and the Bajío, leaving the south of the country behind.

In addition to political reconfigurations at the international level, the country has recently been facing internal political rearrangement in which particular visions of the national model have been shifting (Villanueva Ulfgard and Villanueva 2020). Both national and international rearrangements have offered the possibility of a broad discussion about the Mexican development paradigm. For instance, the revision and renegotiation of NAFTA which began in 2017 presented the possibility of rethinking the opportunities and advantages that the agreement had offered as well as the difficulties inherent in the commercial and productive link between Mexico, the USA, and Canada. Perhaps without careful consideration of NAFTA's limitations and drawbacks, in June 2019 Mexico became the first country to ratify the US-Mexico-Canada Agreement (USMCA), a trade deal that replaced NAFTA but essentially remains with a few updates (Villarreal and Fergusson 2019). Meanwhile, a new national development program under a president who came to power in December 2018 has not defined a clear strategy for addressing regional development issues.

It is essential to continue the discussion and investigation of regional development processes and trajectories. A pending task is to accurately inform, from this debate, the necessary public action to be exercised regarding different programs and policies to close or reduce the gaps between the different areas of the country. This chapter adds to the debate on regional economic development in Mexico and reflects on its opportunities and challenges. The following section reviews regional development and disparities in Mexico from a historical perspective. Then I briefly outline the process of the liberalization of the Mexican economy, including the commercial integration of North America through the Free Trade Agreement that came into force in 1994 and was in a process of revision and renegotiation in 2018, suggesting some of its implications and results. Section 4 reviews regional development and spatial disparities in Mexico's opening up and liberalization phase. Then I discuss the evolution of planning and regional policy in Mexico throughout the twentieth century and to date. The work concludes with four reflections about the development perspectives of and challenges to Mexico's regions.

2 Regional Economic Disparities from a Historical Perspective

As discussed earlier, significant disparities are a historic feature of regional development in Mexico (Trejo Nieto 2020). The salient regional differences and socio-economic backwardness of large areas of the country date back to the territorial system under a colonial rule designed to exploit human, mineral, and agricultural resources for the benefit of the Crown and accelerate the flow of goods between the interior of the country, the capital, the port of Veracruz, and finally Spain (Ordóñez 2015). Mexico City, the capital of New Spain, located in the country's central region, became the dominant urban center. In addition to the capital of the viceroyalty the urban system included a variety of settlements: administrative and military cities (Guadalajara and Mérida), port cities (Veracruz, Acapulco, and Mazatlán), and mining centers (Guanajuato, Pachuca, Zacatecas, San Luis Potosí, and Taxco). The first decades of Mexico's return to independence saw a highly regionalized and weakly articulated urban system. The center of the country maintained its primacy due more to generalized weak economic and political power than to its dynamism. In subsequent decades the country saw few changes to its spatial organization apart from significant transformations in the delimitation of the national territory due to political conflict and internal and external disturbances: Mexico lost more than two million square kilometers in the north when Alta California, Texas, and Arizona were annexed to the USA (Kemper and Royce 1979). After several failed governmental attempts to alleviate the political and economic turmoil in the country, at the end of the nineteenth century the government of Porfirio Díaz sought to foster industrialization and promote urban development.[1] Although industrialization was in an incipient stage, it was strongly supported by foreign capital investment, mining exploitation, the construction of infrastructure—mainly a national railway system—and promotion of an exporting sector. Of these, the railway system was particularly relevant to territorial development and connection (ibid), improving access to markets by helping to reduce local and regional trade barriers (Unikel 1975). During this time public policy also addressed modernizing the legal framework for business and eliminating regional taxes on trade (Ordóñez 2015) such as the well-known *Alcabalas.*[2]

The rail network particularly benefited some areas of the country by connecting them to the national capital and the main ports. Mexico City, Guadalajara, Toluca, and Aguascalientes grew rapidly as commercial and industrial centers. Torreon underwent an outstanding transformation and became an important cotton production center due to the positive impact of the railroad, but Puebla, Morelia, Tlaxcala, Leon, and Guanajuato remained limited local or regional markets. The most prominent cities grew at twice the national rate, but Guadalajara, Monterrey, Merida, San

[1] A period known as Porfiriato.

[2] A provincial sales tax that was an important in molding the shape of interregional exchange in both colonial and postcolonial Mexico.

Luis Potosi, and Veracruz grew demographically faster than Mexico City and Monterrey became the chief industrial center (Kemper and Royce 1979).

Thus both in colonial Mexico and during the Porfiriato the center and north of the country and Veracruz became the main centers of economic activity. The revolution and post-revolution saw an era of armed conflict and rural and agrarian reform with strong economic and social differences between regions (Trejo 2017). Esquivel (1999) estimates that per capita income in Mexico City was approximately 9.4 times that in the state of Oaxaca. Beyond the legacies of colonial rule, the Porfiriato and the Revolution, contemporary territorial disparities were defined by factors related to the implementation of different industrialization models in the twentieth century.

The 1940s were a turning point in the process of industrialization and development. Like many developing countries, Mexico faced the problem of late industrialization as its economy was mainly based on processing and trading primary products. It implemented a protectionist import substitution strategy to promote the development of the domestic industrial sector, bringing about a sectoral shift from agriculture to manufacturing. Government measures in the industrialized closed economy model induced a strong transfer of resources to industrial activities, to the detriment of the primary sector, and public funds were channeled for the development of infrastructure favoring the main urban areas—Mexico City, Guadalajara, and Monterrey—and affecting economic and social development in the south of the country (Trejo 2017; BBVA Bancomer 2001).

A broad protectionist apparatus was instituted via a variety of commercial policy instruments to encourage national investment. Tariffs of up to 100% were imposed on several final consumption goods, especially durable consumption goods, and licensing requirements were established for more than two-thirds of total imports. With this commercial scheme underway the domestic market, which was concentrated in the center of the country, became the main destination for national production. In the 1960s the border industrialization program, a regional industrialization plan that used federal subsidies for the creation of infrastructure and industrial parks in different cities along the border with the USA, was established, activating the maquiladora program. The special tax regime for the maquiladoras allowed duty-free imports of the necessary machinery, parts, and raw materials from international outsourcing companies, mainly in the USA (Trejo 2017).

Rodríguez-Pose and Sánchez-Reaza (2003) identify a clear duality in the territorial pattern of the Mexican economy throughout the protected economy period. Economic activity was concentrated in the Federal District and the State of Mexico in the center of the country. Nuevo Leon and Jalisco were established as important economic poles. In the 1960s the maquiladora program entailed the establishment of industrial activity and some economic dynamism in several border cities. This resulted in two regional blocks: one prosperous, which included the center of the country and along the border with the USA, the other the periphery, which included the southern and southeastern states. These authors support the idea that the polarized geographical pattern of Mexico's economic development has a historical origin,

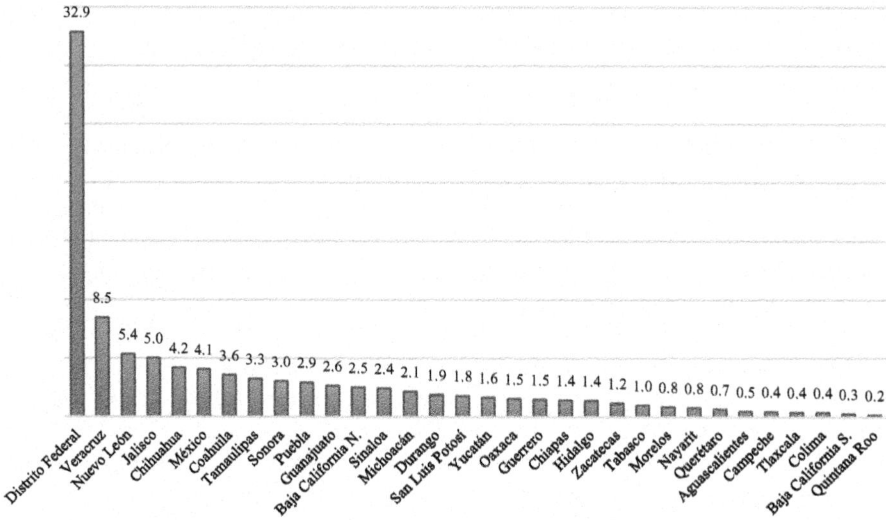

Fig. 1 Average State Contribution to National GDP, 1940–1970 (%)

and that the industrialization strategy activated mechanisms that aggravated the economic backwardness of the South and Southeast, whose economies had historically been based on exporting natural resources and primary products. Bassols (1993) perceives this duality as part of a very long and chaotic development pattern in which the primacy of the most developed region originated in the pre-colonial era.

Although concerns about the regional problem and development disparities arose in the first decades of the import substitution model, the primary objective in privileging national economic growth puts these issues in second place. In the 1960s the industrialization strategy revealed strongly centralizing effects, as reflected in the significant concentration of economic activity in Mexico City. In the 1970s explicit government attention was directed at the problem of the interregional imbalance (Janetti 1988). Figure 1 shows the average percentage of national Gross Domestic Product (GDP) across states between 1940 and 1970. Almost 33% of total GDP was concentrated in the Federal District, as Mexico City was previously called: almost four times more than in the second state. In 1960 the Federal District produced around 37% of the country's GDP.

There were dramatic differences between states' GDP per capita between 1940 and 1970, and these differences widened according to changes in the standard deviation. In 1940 the Federal District and Baja California had the highest per capita income, almost 20 times that of Oaxaca's. By 1970 there was a general increase in income per person, mainly in the states of Mexico, Jalisco, Nuevo León, and Sonora,

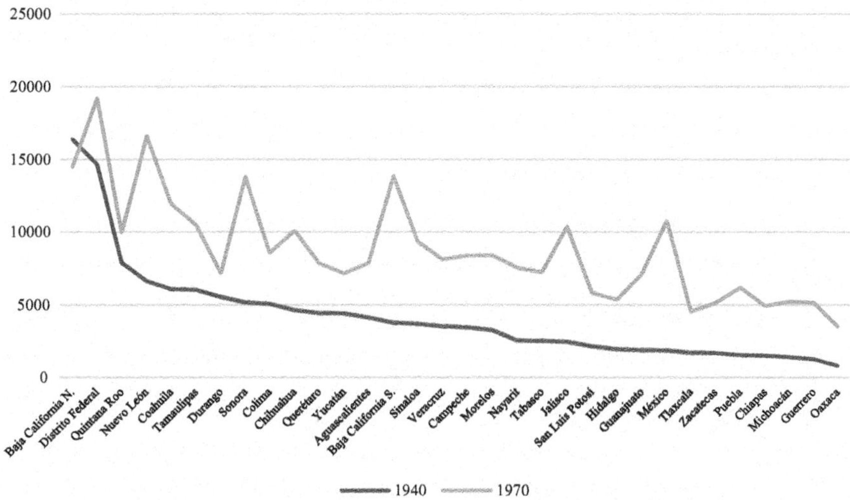

Mexican pesos, 1993 = 100

Fig. 2 GDP Per Capita by State in 1940 and 1970. (Based on German-Soto 2005)

leading to an important rearrangement in the ordering of the states according to GDP per capita, with Nuevo León second after the leading Federal District (Fig. 2).

Although the problem of regional disparities is long-standing, in the Mexican academic sector this strand of analysis underlining the problem of economic-spatial divergence started to gain relevance in the 1960s and 1970s. Unikel (1975, p. 143) states:

> Territorially speaking, socioeconomic development does not occur uniformly; it occurs with greater intensity in some places than in others, which creates regional inequalities. It is a worldwide phenomenon; in fact, there is no country, whether industrialized or not, [. . .] that does not present regional disparities in per capita income, in the standard of living of the population, and, in general, in the distribution of national wealth.

Other efforts to address regional and urban problems and carry out territorial delimitations in the country go back to works such as those of Bataillon (1967), Barkin (1972), and Unikel et al. (1976). These contributions paved the way for research and analysis of the development issue from a territorial point of view, triggering not only research but also teaching on regional and urban issues and the generation and systematization of subnational data and indicators. This awareness involved several actors comprising mainly academics from different disciplines, the National Statistics Office, and to some extent governments and public policymakers. Research on regional development and socioeconomic disparities in Mexico has since expanded significantly.

3 Liberalization of the Mexican Economy in the Reformist Agenda

There is a broad consensus that the Mexican economy went through a relatively successful stage of economic growth and industrial transition between 1945 and 1960, although at the end of this period some serious structural problems came to light in the import substitution model (Trejo 2017). The 1970s represented an exceptional stage during which the economy experienced sustained economic growth, interrupted by the balance of payments crisis in 1976. This crisis was stimulated by both deficit spending and increasing external debt, with the oil boom multiplying the size of public and private spending and external debt. The oil boom in 1978–1981 saw the recovery of the economic growth rate to the rates of previous decades before a combination of factors led to a debt crisis in the first quarter of 1982. At that time the financing of external deficits ceased abruptly when foreign banks, private lenders, and international financial institutions refused to issue new loans (Cárdenas 2015).

The debt crisis is a key explanatory factor in Mexico's accelerated transit to a liberalized and globalized economy. Banks and lenders accepted the reestablishment of credit and the programming of a new debt schedule under the condition that the government followed a series of structural adjustment measures. The rescue package included a complete program of deregulation, privatization, and economic liberalization. Once the stabilization program was implemented the economy entered a deep recession in which consumption, investment, and economic activity slowed considerably. From 1982, the economic policy had to be reformulated in unstable conditions. It was up to the government of President Miguel de la Madrid to undertake this change in national policy. The 1983–1988 National Development Plan highlighted the need to promote structural reforms favoring export-orientated industrialization and sustained economic growth (Poder Ejecutivo 1983).

Mexico's formal commitment to the International Monetary Fund (IMF) to rationalize its excessive import protection was the starting point of the open economy scheme. Formal dismantlement of its protectionist apparatus began when Mexico acceded to the GATT in 1986. Subsequently the government promoted an export-oriented program of industrialization that included incentives for non-oil exports, the restructuring and simplification of administrative procedures, greater access to credit, and the reduction of restrictions on the use of export earnings. In 1987, export taxes and other export controls were reduced and the government abandoned its previous efforts to limit foreign direct investment (FDI). The liberalization program led to a radical lowering of trade barriers to facilitate trade and investment flows (Cárdenas 2015). Figure 3 illustrates the three stages of development restructuring.

Some of the results of the first stage of structural adjustment in the 1980s included macroeconomic stabilization; an increase in the value of total exports at an average annual rate of approximately 9% between 1983 and 1993; an increase in the share of non-oil exports from 28 to 86%; and an average annual growth in manufacturing

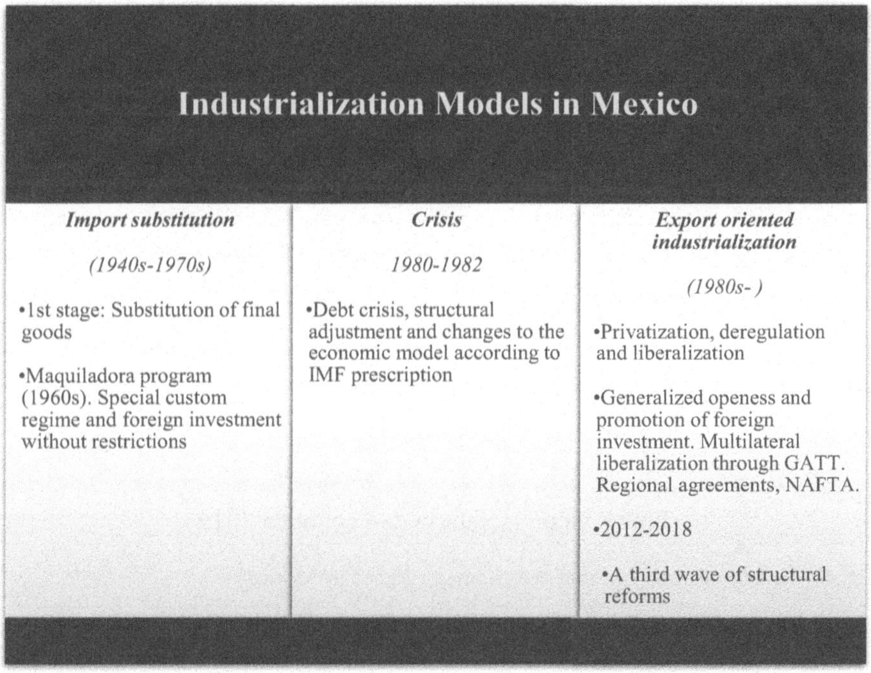

Fig. 3 Industrialization Strategies and Ruptures

exports of 25%. Manufacturing exports replaced oil as the main source of foreign exchange, and foreign direct investment grew substantially (Trejo 2017).

Structural reform intensified in the 1990s when Mexico signed NAFTA and reached free trade agreements with numerous countries to become one of the most open economies in the world (ibid). Tovar Landa (2016) points out that at the beginning of the liberalization stage based on trade agreements, the country eliminated the most favored nation tariffs on more than 1200 products. The simple average tariff remained at around 13%, but the weighted average tariff decreased from 7.8 to 2.7% in just 4 years between 1993 and 1997. Import permits were eliminated to be replaced by tariffs or quotas. By 2016 the country had signed 12 free trade agreements involving 46 countries (Fig. 4).

Trade reforms, and NAFTA in particular, were announced as powerful tools for the expansion of trade and investment, for the mobility of productive factors, for triggering economic growth, and for reducing inequalities (Trejo 2017). Trade and investment among NAFTA members became more dynamic. NAFTA also contributed to Mexico's recovery from the 1994 crisis and helped to generate conditions for macroeconomic stability over 20 years. Export growth accelerated and was sustained (Cárdenas 2015). However, the imported component in the total supply in the Mexican market also increased substantially. The significant burden of intermediate and capital goods within total imports was evidenced, demonstrating the structural

ProMexico, Secretaría de Economía 2015

Fig. 4 Map of Trade and Investment Agreements Signed by Mexico

deficiency in the production of such goods. Paradoxically, the countries that benefited from the expansion of Mexico's imports have been economies with which Mexico does not have trade agreements, such as China (Trejo 2017).

Over the decades numerous limitations to the development model emerged: low economic growth, enduring external dependence, continuous deficits in the trade account, and growing current account deficits (Cárdenas 2015). This was the obvious result of the abrupt opening up of the economy without the previous implementation of policies to help domestic companies overcome the initial disadvantages of exposure to international competition. Trade liberalization faced inefficient and non-competitive domestic producers that took advantage of privileged access to a captive national market against stronger foreign competition. The inability to operate under the new circumstances forced inefficient companies to close or reduce their operations. As the opening up of the Mexican economy resulted in unfavorable conditions for domestic companies a secondary export sector developed, characterized by fragility, dependence on maquiladora exports, and limited linkages with the rest of the economy. Exporting companies became dependent on the strategies of transnational corporations and the economic activity of the USA. At different times export dynamics responded to a greater extent to a weak domestic demand due to recessive processes and large devaluations of the Mexican currency. Although Mexico expanded its network of free trade and investment agreements it made no significant progress in export diversification. Instead, its success with the export-oriented model was limited to a small number of sectors, companies, and regions. In addition, structural dependence on intermediate and capital goods was not overcome (Trejo 2017).

4 The Regional Question and Spatial Disparities in the Openness and Trade Liberalization Era

As in other countries, globalization and its effects served as motivation for further research on regional development in Mexico. The country's problem was to reconcile a successful export-oriented development model with the wide economic and social imbalance between regions and between urban centers and to overcome the conditions of economic and demographic concentration that were preventing more balanced development during the import substitution industrialization. In the 1990s the export model affected urban-regional economic development by favoring certain sectors, cities, and regions of the country. Subsequent research agreed that opening up the economy had contributed to defining territorial patterns of economic location and regional growth causing significant uneven development. Some regions and cities became more dynamic and competitive, while others lagged.

Thus there is plenty of literature from various perspectives addressing Mexico's regional disparities and the impacts of globalization. Krugman and Livas (1996) discuss the effect of trade liberalization on Third World metropolises, focusing on Mexico and Mexico City. Hanson (1997, 1998) shows how trade reforms led to the rupture of the industrial nucleus in Mexico City and the relocation of manufacturing in states bordering the USA. Gamboa and Messmacher (2002), Rodriguez-Oreggia (2002), Sanchez-Reaza and Rodriguez-Pose (2002), Díaz Bautista (2003), Díaz Bautista and Mendoza (2004), Borraz and López-Córdova (2004), Rodrıguez-Oreggia (2005) and Calderon and Tykhonenko (2006) analyze disparities in growth and income inequality. Others, for example, Díaz Bautista and Mendoza (2004), address differences in labor productivity and wage gaps. Decuir-Viruez (2003), Rodríguez-Pose and Sánchez-Reaza (2003), Aroca et al. (2005), and Diaz Bautista (2005) analyze the relationship between regional growth trends in Mexico and trade reforms and convergence, while Esquivel et al. (2002), Chamboux-Leroux (2001), Sanchez-Reaza and Jordaan (2002), Corona Jímenez (2003), Dussel Peters (2003), Garza (2003), and Jordaan and Sanchez-Reaza (2004) provide explanations and accounts of how trade liberalization and the relocation of economic activity are linked. These studies on regional disparities in Mexico in the 1990s and the first decade of the 2000s shed valuable light on the connection between economic globalization, regional development, and disparities.

After more than 12 years of not being a central concern in Mexico's public agenda, the NAFTA debate went from being a subject of primarily academic attention to, once again, the media headlines. The revived interest in NAFTA was brought about by its renegotiation, the process of which even raised the possibility of its termination. According to Dussel (2018), it was worrying that after almost 25 years of the agreement there had been no public evaluation of NAFTA. An essential area in these evaluations had to be its regional impact.

Some recent diagnoses of regional economic growth, the agglomeration of industrial activity, welfare and human development, poverty, productivity, inequality, and marginalization in Mexico such as those by BBVA Bancomer (2001),

Delgadillo et al. (2001), Meixueiro and Moreno (2012), Garduño (2014), Viesti (2015), López (2016), and Trejo (2017) show that regional development remains unequal and polarized due to the concentration of economic dynamics in specific areas of the country. Although the opening up of the economy generated some dynamism in new industrial locations in the north and the Bajío, it also increased the divergence concerning the south, resulting in a relative convergence between the north, the center, and the Bajío and their divergence from the South.

Figure 5 shows the distribution of the percentage of national GDP across states from 1993–2016. In 1993, Mexico City contributed almost 24%, followed by the states of Mexico, Jalisco, Nuevo León, Veracruz, Chihuahua, Guanajuato, and Puebla, which altogether made up 62% of total GDP. In 2016 the distribution among this group of states had changed relatively little. The most relevant changes included a drop of 3.7 percentage points in Mexico City, an increase of 1.2 percentage points in Nuevo León, and of almost 1 percentage point in Chihuahua and Guanajuato; together the eight states contributed 61% of national GDP. Relatively more substantial increases occurred in Querétaro, Aguascalientes, Sonora, Coahuila, and Baja California, while Campeche, Guerrero, Oaxaca, and Chiapas saw the biggest drops. Production experienced a relative de-concentration due to the emergence of export platforms in sectors located in medium and small cities in the west and the north. This outlined an exogenous territorial model because the dynamics of successful regional and urban spaces was subject to the behavior of the export sector, which in turn was largely based on foreign direct investment, forging a pattern of concentration in a few states.

Controlling for population size, GDP per capita by state shows the differences in average income per person. The disparities have been widening over time. In 1993 GDP per capita in Mexico City was 5.4 times that in Chiapas state, which had the lowest average GDP. In 2016 GDP per capita in Mexico City was seven times higher than in Chiapas. Aguascalientes, Queretaro, Chihuahua, Sonora, and Coahuila improved their relative position in terms of GDP per capita, whereas Campeche and Quintana Roo observed a significant fall. Chiapas and Tabasco remained at practically the same levels of GDP per inhabitant at the beginning and end of the period. Figure 6 shows the growing regional disparity throughout the period, measured by the standard deviation in GDP per capita.

A strand of the literature that analyzes regional disparities and convergence also deal with the question of whether regional imbalances expand or contract during the economic cycle based on whether the economy is expanding or declining (Petrakos et al. 2005). This question is strongly related to attempts to verify Williamson's hypothesis related to the correlation between the level of national income and the scale of regional disparities (Petrakos and Saratsis 2000; Petrakos et al. 2005; Smętkowski 2014) and to testing Berry's idea (cited in Petrakos and Saratsis 2000; Petrakos et al. 2005) that high rates of economic growth are linked to increasing regional disparities. Evidence of this relationship is mixed, with some studies finding that a positive relationship between economic growth and disparities means that regional inequalities have a pro-cyclical character, increasing in periods of economic expansion and decreasing in periods of economic recession (Petrakos and Saratsis

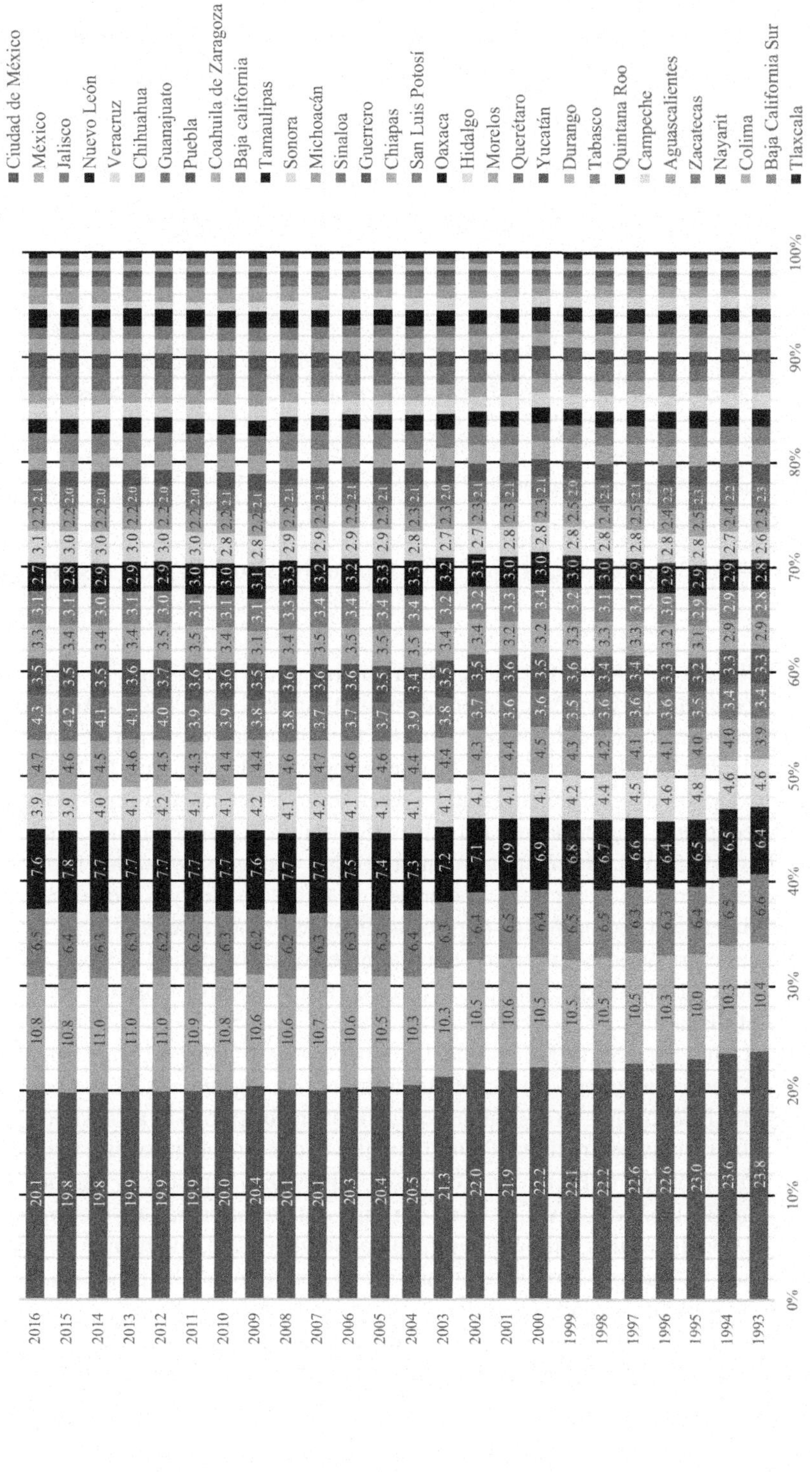

Fig. 5 Mexican States' Contribution to National GDP, 1993–2016 (%) (Based on German-Soto 2005)

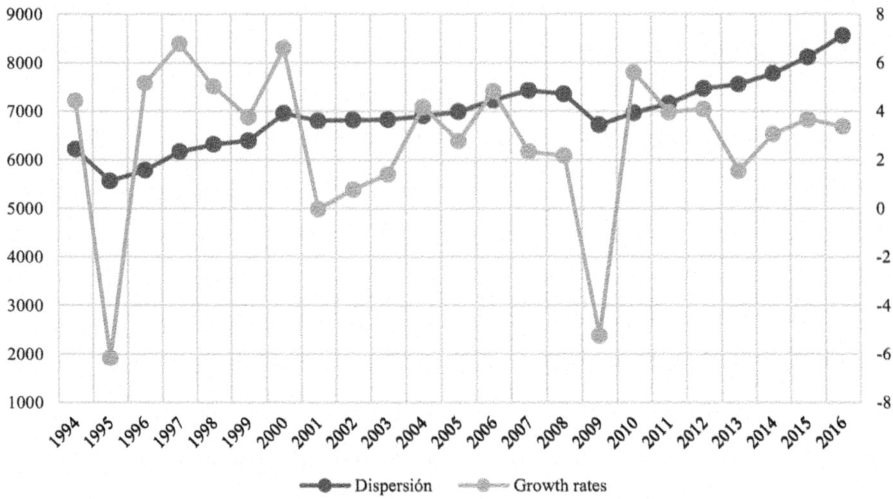

Dispersion: Standard Deviation of per capita GDP

Growth rates (%)

Fig. 6 GDP Growth and Regional Disparities in Mexico, 1993–2016 (Based on German-Soto 2005)

2000; Petrakos et al. 2005) and others finding an inverse relationship, i.e. economic growth associated with convergence or decreasing regional imbalances (Aokić et al. 2016) or no evidence of correlation between the dynamics of disparities and the economic cycle (Smętkowski 2014). Figure 6 includes the national GDP growth rates in Mexico to show the relationship between the evolution of regional disparities and macroeconomic performance. It reveals that critical episodes of national economic crisis (1995) and international economic crisis and recession (2001 and 2008) are linked to decreases in regional disparities, in line with Berry's idea of a direct relationship between decreasing disparities in times of economic crisis. Even though the statistical correlation between the two variables over the period is weak, with a correlation coefficient of 0.2, the relationship is positive, suggesting a pro-cyclical evolution of disparities.

Petrakos and Saratsis (2000) argue that in periods of recession metropolitan regions in Greece have been hit harder than the remaining regions of the country, thus reducing inequalities. In a similar vein, although Smętkowski (2014) does not find a correlation between national GDP dynamics and regional disparities in Central and Eastern European (CEE) countries, he observes that capital city regions and other regions in their close vicinity are forming functional areas or metropolitan regions and concludes that although regional convergence and divergence processes do not depend on macroeconomic dynamics alone, metropolization processes play a significant role in driving development and disparities.

In Mexico the distribution of economic activity and growth occurring mostly in some of the largest metropolitan areas of the country has been strongly guided by the location and operation strategies of exporting companies and FDI. The opening up of the economy and NAFTA engendered or reinforced international connections for some regions and cities following a logic primarily oriented towards trading with foreign markets. Led by its international trade, the country's regional structure became both more diverse and more polarized. While some regions emerged or consolidated as centers of economic development when inserted into export dynamics the traditionally most marginalized regions had access to fewer opportunities (Trejo 2017). Although it is simplistic to attribute any change in regional disparities exclusively to liberalization and NAFTA, it can be argued that regions that have successfully participated in the export activity have benefited from the economic dynamics produced by trade. In contrast, these regions have been more affected by the economic crisis which has produced a reduction in regional imbalances. Delgadillo et al. (2001) also suggest that although territorial imbalances in development reflect the presence of winning and losing regions in the opening process, they are also the result of accumulated advantages over time, as in the case of Mexico City. The possible advantages, of course, are diverse in nature, ranging from natural and geographical advantages to advantages built on the political, institutional, and social structures of each territory.

Trejo (2017) points out that not only variables related to the NAFTA (exports, FDI, and location close to the US border) have defined regional success in the country. Industrial and transport infrastructure, including that connecting production sites with internal markets; logistics, and transportation costs; public services; skilled labor; labor market stability; and local government incentives, e.g., employment programs and tax benefits, are all factors that encourage and attract economic activity to particular parts of the country. Viesti (2015) finds regional disparities to be closely related to differences in economic specialization; the size of the informal economy; the characteristics of local labor and human capital; the development of innovation; infrastructure; and physical geography. López (2016) highlights the importance of specialization and local public policy in triggering regional success. Meixueiro and Moreno (2012) identify transport infrastructure, the functioning of public services, regional development policy, human capital, and institutions as the main factors driving regional performance, and BBVA Bancomer (2001) refer to the limitations of regional development in terms of deficiencies in road infrastructure, regulatory barriers (transaction costs and business opening procedures), and gaps in the educational system.

The economic opening up, carried out primarily under the NAFTA framework, had unequal effects across Mexico to the extent that its benefits were concentrated in certain regions. However, internal structural factors have also fueled regional inequalities. Such factors include a deficient economic policy, particularly the abandonment of active industrial policy aimed at structural change in the manufacturing sector. Despite the acuteness of regional disparities, the State has continually abandoned its regionally-oriented policies. I discuss regional policy and planning in Mexico in next section.

5 Regional Planning and Policy in Mexico

Assessing the problems, challenges, and opportunities for regional development raises the unavoidable question of the role of the State and its public policies in fostering regional growth and competitiveness. Most of the regional development programs and policies implemented in Mexico have been motivated by the presence of the country's wide regional imbalances (Alba 1999). Yet throughout the twentieth century, regional policies were formulated and modified according to the priorities of industrial development and the specific circumstances of the moment. Firstly, the main objective was to equalize the uneven development of the regions, but globalization stimulated competition among territories to attract investment and increase international trade.

Post-revolutionary governments' efforts to achieve efficient planning and territorial ordering placed particular emphasis on the reorganization of agrarian space in a predominantly rural country. The Mexican State consolidated as the central governing organization for development, which was meant to be based on the industrialization and urbanization. Between the 1940s and the 1960s stimulating industrialization and national growth was considered the best mechanism for the automatic redistribution of benefits across economic sectors, regions, and the population (Trejo 2017). Development projects promoted in specific areas were seen as a catalyst of national growth. Among these projects were, for example, hydrological basins, irrigation works, and roads. In response to industrial concentration in the three main metropolitan areas of the country, in the 1960s and 1970s the development of industrial parks, industrial ports, and tourist centers became the predominant regional policy strategy (Alba 1999). Industrial parks were created in Ciudad Sahagun, Torreon, and Irapuato, and the Border Industrialization Program was established. Despite the apparently territorial emphasis of these policies, their implementation resulted in the creation of productive enclaves with little impact on regional development (Janetti 1988). Such initiatives took place within the framework of a decentralizing discourse to attain a more balanced regional system, but in practice the scope and achievements of regional development were limited due to the strong centralization that continued in practice. Given the persistent economic concentration in Mexico City, new programs tried to boost development in regions such as the Isthmus of Tehuantepec and Baja California. The stimulus to invest in preferential areas and industrial parks, the formulation of Public Investment Programs for Rural Development, the Committee for Economic Development, the National Commission for Regional and Urban Development, the General Coordination of the National Plan for Depressed Zones and Marginalized Groups, State Development Programs, and Comprehensive Rural Development Programs were part of the regional policy framework throughout the decade. However, the institutionalization of the territorial approach to development had few effective results (Alba 1999).

In the 1980s the State, under the so-called neoliberal model, dismantled all tools, programs, and structures linked to territorial planning. Paradoxically, the growing importance of subnational regions in the face of globalization processes was accompanied in the 1990s by weakening regional policy. By rethinking its public policy and reducing its role as a planner, the State largely delegated the shaping of urban and regional development to market forces. Still, there were some attempts to develop a regional and active industrial policy aiming to promote structural changes in strategic sectors and regions (Trejo 2017).

Characteristics of the period were Development Agreements (CUD) and State Development Planning Committees (Coplades), which served in a collaborative federal and state government approach to defining states' development priorities and investment needs. Also, some regional programs were developed under the 1983–1988 National Development Plan (Alba 1999). The National Program for Industrial Development and Foreign Trade (PRONAFICE) enacted in 1984 strategies for strengthening the domestic market and increasing the integration and efficiency of national firms to cope with global economic competition. For its part, in 1985 the Program for the Integral Promotion of Exports (PROFIEX) recommended specific policies for border areas and free zones to promote their integration with the rest of the country, although their full implementation was inhibited by limited financial resources. From then onwards industrial policy was reduced to action aimed at eliminating regulations, state monopolies, and tariffs within the framework of a free market and globally competitive economy. Under orthodox economic principles, a series of programs were formulated to strengthen FDI, some of which aimed to establish financial and fiscal incentives to promote the location of transnational companies in new or strategic sectors such as the automotive industry and the aeronautical industry, while others included measures to support other economic sectors such as electronics, software, and computing, and strategic industries such as electricity, telecommunications, oil, and natural gas. Also, cluster and pro-competitiveness policies were established. In general, however, active industrial policy ceased to be a central government priority (Trejo 2017).

Subsequent governmental programs did not have a comprehensive territorial and regional approach; isolated action has predominated, and policies have lacked continuity. Improvisation has been another characteristic of the regional policy process (Delgadillo et al. 2001), and regional development policy has been weakly articulated with economic policy. Figure 7 summarizes the main aspects of regional policy over the last five federal administrations.

Although industrial policies are normally seen as drivers of economic growth, they should also be viewed as tools for promoting structural and technological transformation and mechanisms for reducing inequality through public investment in infrastructure, education, and technology. Over recent decades regional development has demanded inclusive and efficient territorial and regional planning, but this has not been accompanied by strategic industrial policy to boost national economic growth, which has been minimal.

1988-1994: Reduced public resources for territorial planning and progressive dissolution of state intervention. Regional and territorial policy delegated to states and municipalities. Urban- and regional-oriented policies subsumed within the Ministry of Urban Development and Ecology, which later became the Ministry of Social Development (SEDESOL). National Urban Development Program had limited applicability. The 100 Medium Cities Program was established.

1994-2000: Different territorial programs formulated but their implementation subordinated to sectoral policies: 100 Cities Program, Development Program for Metropolitan Areas Outside the Capital, Program for territorial planning and urban development, Program for social participation in urban developmen, Border XXI Program, National Program of Attention to 250 Microregions, Megaproject .

2000-2006: Reorientation of territorial and regional development. A central office specifically for strategic planning and regional development. Megaprojects included the Interstate regional planning (or mesoregions program), the Puebla-Panama Plan, and projects for the development of industrial infrastructure, regional trusts and other regional programs.

2006-2012: Fewer resources and limited attention to program implementation. Continuation of some programs such as the Program for Priority Areas Development, the Habitat Program, and the Local Development Program, among others. The Mesoamerica Project replaced the Puebla-Panama Plan.

2012-2018: Renewed interest in territorial policy under the new Ministry of Agrarian, Territorial and Urban Development (SEDATU). The main regional plan was the Special Economic Zones as a strategy for development and industrialization in the south of the country, but the plan was canceled by the new president.

Fig. 7 Regional Policy Orientation (1988–2018)

6 Final Considerations: Towards the Future of Regional Development

Little progress is expected in regional and industrial policy under the government that came to power in 2018. The 2019–2024 National Development Plan lacks a comprehensive and articulated regional development program. Regional development plans include three specific projects: the Mayan Train, the Transistmic Corridor, and the North Border Free Zone. The Mayan Train is considered the federal government's most important infrastructure project, promoting sustainable development and multiplying the economic benefits of tourist activity in the Yucatan Peninsula by creating jobs. It will include a 1525-kilometer train route with 15 stations, passing through the states of Chiapas, Tabasco, Campeche, Yucatan, and Quintana Roo, interconnecting the main cities and tourist sites (DOF 2019a).

The Program for the Development of the Isthmus of Tehuantepec seeks to boost the growth of the regional economy in two of the country's most backward states, Oaxaca and Veracruz, by developing an Interoceanic Multimodal Corridor. The project plans to take advantage of the geographical position of the Isthmus to increase transport competitiveness and for the development of storage, packaging, and other logistics services. A gas pipeline will be built to supply domestic businesses and consumers; and free zones will be created to attract private investment. The project will be provided with infrastructure and supplied with energy, water, digital connectivity, and other basic services. VAT and income tax will be reduced and fuel will be sold at reduced prices in the 76 municipalities of Oaxaca and Veracruz involved in the project. The program includes the provision of educational services, housing, and infrastructure for research and technological development. Finally, the North Border Free Zone Program has already been implemented in the 43 municipalities bordering the USA. It offers benefits such as VAT reduced from 16 to 8%, a lower income tax of 20%, a better regional minimum wage, and the homologation of fuel prices with those of the USA.

Given the limited scope of and poor effects expected from regional economic policies, to conclude this Chap. 1 discusses some of the challenges for development in four major regions of the country: the northern border, the traditional center, the forgotten South, and the industrial Bajío. All four of these regions need efficient public policies, effective governance, and healthy public finances to strengthen Mexico's national and international position.

6.1 Border Competitiveness and the Relative Success of the Mexican North

The relative position of states and cities at the northern border was significantly redefined with the increasing opening up of the economy and the advantages of their proximity to Mexico's most important external market, the USA. The main international crossing points for goods, capital, and people are on the northern border and the success of the region in the North American market integration process has been celebrated. Powerful industrialization and relatively fast growth being the main attributes of this success (Trejo 2017). However, the North is highly complex. First, its local and regional economic agenda covers a wide variety of issues from international migration and international trade to FDI, employment, energy, etc. Its economy relies on the circulation of money related to money laundering, smuggling, and the trafficking of drugs, people, and weapons. Moreover, the northern border is very heterogeneous, with dynamic and productive areas as well as declining and stagnating areas. This heterogeneity in itself is a challenge that relativizes the country's regional success (Trejo 2013).

Cities in the North, especially those along the border, compete for investment and trade flows that generate economic benefits. The growing pressure on local economies to retain and attract FDI (especially from maquiladoras) and a complex network of social problems present an urgent need to rethink the issue of regional development. While different sub-regions and cities compete with one another they also face the task of jointly establishing themselves as an economically and socially efficient region. On the issue of competitiveness, the northern border is experiencing a series of difficulties that highlight the need to reach and maintain high levels of efficiency in a context of crisis and international competition. These difficulties include underutilization, supersaturation, deterioration, and lack of infrastructure. The many problems that arise from inadequate infrastructure include traffic jams, saturation, and congestion at a few crossing points while a considerable number of other border crossings are underutilized. In turn, infrastructure flaws are closely related to the inadequacy and poor quality of public services. In various areas the northern Mexican border exemplifies the insufficiency of general public services which is exacerbated by the growing migration.

These deficiencies reveal the need for fast, efficient, and safe crossings to facilitate commercial activity with the country's main trading partner, and investment attraction. A larger number of border crossings and fiscal precincts with greater capacity, more efficient administrative procedures, and more security are required. In addition to logistic services, physical infrastructure is a fundamental aspect of increased productive efficiency and competitiveness at the border: inter-metropolitan connectivity and the national road network that connects the country with the borders need substantial improvement.

The progress of globalization and liberalization in the most recent stages of capitalism has led to strong competition for foreign capital to generate beneficial local economic impacts. While maquiladoras have been the basis of the industrial activity in numerous cities on the Mexican border, this model has been shown to have limited scope in terms of economic linkages and social development (Trejo 2017). The development strategies in this region have been strongly oriented towards competitiveness as an archetype of local and regional economic success. Alternative schemes should be deployed to expand their productive possibilities according to specific local realities, to result in both economic and social strengthening given the limitations of the competitiveness paradigm. The economic reality at the border, which is highly vulnerable to international readjustment, exacerbates this pending national need.

6.2 Restructuring and Predominance of the Central Region

The Central Region was consolidated in the twentieth century as the demographic and political heart of the country, the engine of national growth, and the place of highest economic concentration, especially within the framework of the import substitution industrialization model. As a result of the implementation of the export-oriented model, both Mexico City and the region experienced several adjustments, including significant deterioration in their economic growth and a declining concentration of economic activity compared to previous decades. During the 1980s and early 1990s, the region saw little economic growth, although this varied significantly across states. In particular, the manufacturing sector saw significant relocation to the north of the country. The region has maintained a much stronger economic influence than its demographic weight, indicative of its position in the national economy, the product of the persistent geographic centralization of multiple economic and political functions in Mexico City, which is responsible for more than half of the regional GDP, followed by the State of Mexico (Trejo 2017).

Despite some reduction in Mexico City's contribution to the regional and national economy, the significance of these two states is still substantial due to the powerful agglomeration forces exerted by the national capital and its metropolitan area. In recent decades various medium-sized cities in the region have acquired greater weight and important changes to their local productive structures (ibid). The dynamics of cities such as Toluca, Puebla, and Pachuca and municipalities in the metropolitan area of Mexico City have contributed to supporting the regional economy. Yet the region shows significant internal heterogeneity and polarization in per capita GDP levels and growth. On the other hand, economic liberalization has fostered a sectoral change. In recent decades the Central region has specialized in commerce and services such as financial services, business services, and government activities; however, the more advanced service industries are concentrated in the largest urban centers, and there is significant heterogeneity in service activities in the rest of the region. Thus three major trends can be observed internally: Mexico City and to a lesser extent the region's service specialization; the geographic de-concentration of manufacturing from Mexico City, some of which have benefited a group of cities and metropolises near Mexico City; and slow economic growth and a general deterioration in labor productivity. This political and economic transition has created a regional scenario in which polarization and variation in local development processes are preventing regional integration. The central region remains the national node of high centrality and power. To maintain its status the region needs to encourage more balanced and integrated development and growth among states and cities, for example, by strengthening productive chains and diversifying its economic flows (Trejo Nieto and Negrete 2019).

6.3 The Rise of the Industrial Bajío

Since the 1980s states such as Guanajuato, Aguascalientes, and San Luis Potosí have increased their contribution to national production and employment, especially in the manufacturing sector, and their attraction of foreign investment. Important centers of industrial activity have emerged in the machinery and equipment sector in various towns and cities. In 1982 Nissan established an assembly plant in Guanajuato and in 1994 General Motors, one of the three major automotive companies in the USA, established a plant in Aguascalientes. In the last two decades, there has been a boom in investment in both established and new automotive industry plants. Volkswagen has invested in a plant that manufactures car engines in Silao, BMW in a plant in San Luis Potosí, Mazda in a plant in Salamanca, Honda in Celaya, and Nissan in new premises in Aguascalientes. This group of states (Aguascalientes, Guanajuato, and San Luis Potosí) has become a car production, foreign investment, and export activity hub (Trejo 2017).

Queretaro is considered one of the most important aerospace industry locations in the country, mainly in the field of design engineering. The industry has had a presence in the state since the 1990s (Villareal et al. 2016) and sustained economic growth even in 2008 and 2010 when the international crisis affected the Mexican economy and several states intensely.

The region has recently become known as the new automotive giant and in general the new industrial pole of Mexico. In one of the relatively few references to the industrial boom in the Bajío, Peniche and Mireles (2015) emphasize that the region is expected to become one of the largest manufacturing centers in the whole of North America. According to Stratfor (2013), the factors behind Bajío's emergence as a powerful industrial region are its educated and trained workforce, relatively low violence and insecurity, good transport and logistics infrastructure, strategic geographical position, and good climate. These define it as an ideal area for business, suitable for international trade and investment, with even better conditions than the northern border region.

Well-known as a historical mining and agricultural hub and once called the granary of Mexico, with a manufacturing tradition oriented towards textile and footwear production the Bajío region is a strategic territory for the immediate future of the country's economy. The industrial boom in the region is creating pressure on local governments with its demand for the adequate provision of services and public goods to meet its demographic and economic growth. Creating an appropriate social environment with a desirable overspill of economic benefits to the local population is a challenge for governments at different levels.

According to Peniche and Mireles (2015), the Bajío corridor does not have a guiding management plan to attract and locate industrial activity in an orderly and efficient way throughout the entire region. Despite the formulation of state and local development programs and plans, there has been no attempt to formulate a regional strategy for the required integration between cities and economic centers. The region undoubtedly benefits from productive international restructuring, trade agreements (especially NAFTA), and its proximity to the country's capital. Based on this it has forged an advantageous productive restructuring resulting in a demographic and economic dynamism that is above the national average. The continuity and integrality of development projects that involve adequate regional and local governance and public action will provide not only stability for local development but also a sustainable path in the light of future challenges.

6.4 Failed Regional Policy in the South and Southeast

One of the most important initiatives in the renewed interest in regional policy in Mexico in the 2012–2018 presidential period was the creation of Special Economic Zones (SEZs) in regions of the country with greater economic backwardness and significant social gaps. The SEZs were announced as a novel and ambitious project that symbolized a strategy for industrialization that would attract foreign and national investment with a package of incentives consisting mainly of tax and customs cuts and physical infrastructure. SEZs were envisaged as a powerful strategy for boosting economic growth, reducing poverty, providing public services, and expanding economic opportunities in poor regions. The project engendered high social and economic expectations, which were reflected in the formal name of the project: Special Economic Zones, the Great National Project (Ministry of Finance and Public Credit 2017).

The proposal for the development of the SEZs was part of a series of corrective measures across security, justice, and economic development announced by the President two months after the disappearance, in September of 2014, of 43 students from Ayotzinapa, Guerrero (Expansión 2014). It was this specific event, rather than a recognition that the South has historically been excluded from development processes with severe repercussions for the integration and cohesion of the country, that originated the proposal. After the required legal approval, in June 2016 the Federal Law on the creation of SEZs in Mexico stated that the first zones would be established in the port of Lazaro Cárdenas on the border between the states of Michoacán and Guerrero; on the Isthmus of Tehuantepec (Veracruz and Oaxaca); in Puerto Chiapas (Chiapas); and in the Coatzacoalcos/Ciudad del Carmen (Campeche) corridor. However, the project was canceled in March 2019 under a new presidency (DOF 2019b).

The SEZ model has been used generically worldwide to designate a variety of phenomena: free zones, free trade zones, export zones, etc. In general, these are limited portions of the national territory that adopt a special regulatory and fiscal regime to attract FDI, generate employment and international trade, and support the national reform and development strategy. Around the world, many SEZs have been populated by private companies taking advantage of tax cuts without producing substantial gains in either employment or exports. Others have been successful in attracting FDI and creating jobs in the short term but are unsustainable when faced with increases in labor costs or when they lose their preferential treatment in trade (Farole and Akinci 2011). The most paradigmatic cases are found in China, where they were implemented among the first steps towards trade and foreign investment liberalization and have supported industrial development and technological progress (Terán 2013).

In Mexico, the proposal to implement the SEZ program emerged within the framework of the Regional Economic Productivity Program in the middle of a third reformist wave. The general design of Mexico's SEZs followed international best practices. However, from the beginning, the proposal was subject to strong criticism as a project driven by a political agenda that entailed not only high economic expectations but also significant risk and public policy challenges, as well as considerable negative social and environmental impact (Gómez Zaldívar and Molina 2018). If the south of the country has been left out of development, it has been due to various structural barriers: low connectivity and poor infrastructure, low levels of human capital, lack of a critical mass of companies, poor innovation and technological development, limited access to credit, weak institutions, lack of security and legal certainty, and fragmented land use, among many other factors

(Trejo 2017). As with other major development projects for the South, the SEZs faced strong restrictions and contradictions due to their weak and short-term institutional design.

The amount of financial, human, and institutional resources required for the implementation of the SEZs would hardly outweigh the benefits. Due to productive, social, and cultural preconditions and the historical trajectory of southern Mexico, parallel policies in education, public safety, technology, communications, finance, support services and integration of national production chains would be necessary. Finally, the SEZs have never been an automatic catalyst for the reduction of inequality, and their impact on regional development has depended on the successful involvement of local actors.

References

Alba F (1999) La cuestión regional y la integración internacional de México: una introducción. Estudios Sociológicos XVII(51):611–631

Aokić I, Fröhlich Z, Rašić Bakarić I (2016) The impact of the economic crisis on regional disparities in Croatia. Camb J Reg Econ Soc 9(1):179–195. https://doi.org/10.1093/cjres/rsv030

Aroca P et al (2005) Spatial dimensions of trade liberalization and economic convergence: Mexico 1985–2002. World Bank Econ Rev 19(3):345–378

Barkin D (1972) Los beneficiarios del desarrollo regional. Secretaría de Educación Pública, México

Bassols A (1993) Geografía económica de México. Teoría, fenómenos generales, análisis regional. Trillas, México

Bataillon C (1967) Les regiones géographiques au Mexique. Institut des hautes études de l'Amérique Latine, Paris

BBVA Bancomer (2001) Desarrollo económico regional. Serie de propuestas (17). https://www.bbvaresearch.com/KETD/fbin/mult/0110_SPropuestasMexico_17_tcm346-188207.pdf (15 de agosto de 2018)

Borraz F, López-Córdova E (2004) Has globalization deepened income inequality in Mexico? Inter-American Development Bank, Washington

Calderon C, Tykhonenko A (2006) La liberalización económica y la convergencia regional en México. Comercio Exterior 56(5):374–381

Cárdenas E (2015) El largo curso de la economía mexicana. De 1780 a nuestros días. Fondo de Cultura Económica, Ciudad de Mexico

Chamboux-Leroux JI (2001) Efectos de la Apertura Comercial en las Regiones y la Localización Industrial en México. Comercio Exterior 7:600–609

Corona Jímenez MA (2003) Efectos de la Globalización en la Distribución Espacial de las Actividades Económicas. Comercio Exterior 53:48–56

Decuir-Viruez L (2003) Institutional Factors in the Economic Growth of Mexico. In: 43rd ERSA Congress 2003 on Peripheries, Centres, and Spatial Development in the New Europe, University of Jyvaskyla, Finland

Delgadillo J, Torres F, Gasca J (2001) El desarrollo regional de México en el vértice de dos milenios. Universidad Nacional Autónoma de México, Instituto de Investigaciones Económicas, México

Díaz Bautista A (2003) Apertura comercial y convergencia regional en México. Comercio Exterior 53(11):995–1000

Diaz Bautista A (2005) Agglomeration economies, economic growth and the new economic geography in Mexico. Econoquantum 1(2):57–79. Urban/Regional (0508001)

Díaz Bautista A, Mendoza E (2004) Regional convergence of income and labor productivity in Mexico. J Econ Financ 3(1):3–20

Díaz Dapena A, Fernández Vázquez E, Garduño Rivera R, Rubiera Morollón F (2017) ¿El comercio lleva a la convergencia? Un análisis del efecto del TLCAN sobre la convergencia local en México. El Trimestre Económico 84(333):103–120. https://doi.org/10.20430/ete.v84i333.263

DOF (2019a) Plan Nacional de Desarrollo 2019-2024. Diario Oficial de la Federación. Accessed 12 July 2019. https://www.dof.gob.mx/nota_detalle.php?codigo=5565599&fecha=12/07/2019

DOF (2019b) Decreto por el que se abrogan los diversos de Declaratorias de las Zonas Económicas Especiales. Diario Oficial de la Federación. Accessed 19 Nov 2019. https://www.dof.gob.mx/nota_detalle.php?codigo=5579365&fecha=19/11/2019

Dussel E (2018) La renegociación del TLCAN. Efectos arancelarios y el caso de la cadena del calzado. Investigación Económica LXXVII(303):3–78

Dussel Peters E (2003) Industrial policy, regional trends, and structuring change in Mexico's manufacturing sector. In: Kevin EZ, Middlebrock J (eds) Confronting development. Assessing Mexico's economic and social policy challenges. Stanford University Press, Stanford, pp 241–274

Esquivel G (1999) Convergencia regional en México, 1940–1995. El Trimestre Económico 66(264 (4)):725–761

Esquivel G et al (2002) ¿Por qué el TLCAN no llegó hasta el sur de México? World Bank, Washington

Expansión (2014) Tras el caso Ayotzinapa, Peña anuncia medidas de seguridad y justicia. Retrieved https://expansion.mx/nacional/2014/11/27/anuncio-pena-seguridad-caso-ayotzinapa. 16 de agosto de 2018

Farole T, Akinci G (2011) Special economic zones: Progress, emerging challenges, and future directions. The World Bank, New York

Gamboa R, Messmacher M (2002) Desigualdad Regional y Gasto Publico en Mexico. Inter-American Development Bank, Washington, D.C.

Garduño R (2014) La apertura comercial y su efecto en la distribución regional de México. El Trimestre Económico LXXXI(322):413–439

Garza G (2003) The dialectics of urban and regional disparities in Mexico. In: Kevin EZ, Middlebrock J (eds) Confronting development. Assessing Mexico's Economic and social policy challenges. Stanford University Press, pp 487–521

German-Soto V (2005) Generación del Producto Interno Bruto por Entidad Federativa, 1940–1992. El Trimestre Económico LXXII(287):617–653

Gómez Zaldívar F, Molina E (2018) Zonas Económicas Especiales y su impacto sobre el desarrollo económico regional. Problemas del desarrollo 49(193):11–32. https://doi.org/10.22201/iiec.20078951e.2018.193.61285

Hanson GH (1997) Increasing returns, trade and the regional structure of wages. Econ J 107 (440):113–133

Hanson GH (1998) Regional adjustment to trade liberalization. Reg Sci Urban Econ 28:419–444

Janetti ME (1988) El desarrollo regional en México. Evolución reciente de la política. Comercio Exterior 38(9):851–857

Jordaan J, Sanchez-Reaza J (2004) Industrial diversity and specialisation in Mexican regions under free trade. Centro de Investigación y Docencia Económica CIDE:1–15

Kemper RV, Royce AP (1979) Mexican urbanization since 1821: a macro-historical approach. Urban Anthropology 8(3/4):267–289

Krugman P, Livas R (1996) Trade policy and the third world metropolis. J Dev Econ 49:137–150

López H (2016) Diagnóstico y propuesta para el desarrollo regional en México. Centro de Estudios Sociales y de Opinión Pública, CESOP, México

Meixueiro G, Moreno S and Martínez C (coords) (2012) Desarrollo regional y competitividad en México. México: Centro de Estudios Sociales y de Opinión Pública, CESOP

Mendoza-Velázquez A, German-Soto V, Monfort M, Ordóñez J (2020) Club convergence and inter-regional inequality in Mexico, 1940-2015. Appl Econ 52(6):598–608. https://doi.org/10.1080/00036846.2019.1659491

Ministry of Finance and Public Credit (2017) Zonas Económicas Especiales. In: El gran proyecto de nación. SHCP, México. https://www.gob.mx/cms/uploads/attachment/file/287342/Libro_ZEE_2017_web.pdf

Ordóñez JA (2015) Desigualdades regionales en México: La importancia de considerar las capacidades regionales para el diseño de la política de desarrollo regional. Circunstancia XIII 36:1–17

Peniche S, Mireles JC (2015) El diamante mexicano: El Bajío bajo los ojos de los gobiernos del BID y del BM. Trayectorias 17(41):29–51

Petrakos G, Rodríguez-Pose A, Rovolis A (2005) Growth, integration, and regional disparities in the European Union. Environ Plan A Econ Space 37(10):1837–1855. https://doi.org/10.1068/a37348

Petrakos G, Saratsis Y (2000) Regional inequalities in Greece. Pap Reg Sci 79(1):57–74. https://doi.org/10.1007/s101100050003

Poder Ejecutivo (1983) Plan Nacional de Desarrollo 1983–1988. México: DOF. http://www.diputados.gob.mx/LeyesBiblio/compila/pnd/PND_1983–1988_31may83.pdf (16 de agosto de 2018)

Rodriguez-Oreggia E (2002) Polarization of income under structural changes: winners and losers of regional growth in Mexico. Papers in Environmental and Spatial Analysis LSE(71)

Rodrıguez-Oreggia E (2005) Regional disparities and determinants of growth in Mexico. Ann Reg Sci 39(2):207–220

Rodríguez-Pose A and Sánchez-Reaza J (2003) Economic Polarization through Trade, Trade Liberalization and Regional Growth in Mexico. Discussion Paper, 2003/60, Finland: Wider-United Nations University

Sanchez-Reaza J, Jordaan J (2002) Resource endowments, Externalities and Transport Costs: An Exploration of Alternative Explanations of Regional Production Structures in Mexico. Workshop on Agglomeration and Regional Labour Markets, Berlin, Germany, German Institute for Economic Research

Sanchez-Reaza J, Rodriguez-Pose A (2002) The impact of trade liberalization on regional disparities in Mexico. Growth Chang 33:72–90

Smętkowski M (2014) Regional Disparities and Development Dynamics of CEE Regions in the Period of Prosperity and Austerity. Growth– Innovation – Competitiveness: Fostering Cohesion in Central and Eastern Europe (GRINCOH) Working Paper Series No. 6.02.01. http://www.grincoh.eu/media/serie_6_spaces__territories_and_regions/grincoh_wp6.02.01_smetkowski.pdf

Stratfor (2013) Developing Mexico's Bajio Region. https://worldview.stratfor.com/article/developing-mexicos-bajio-region

Terán J (2013) Las zonas económicas especiales y la expansión urbano-regional: algunas acotaciones a partir de las experiencias chinas. Questiones urbano regionales 2(1):83–118

Tovar Landa R (2016) 30 años de apertura comercial en México: del GATT al Acuerdo Comercial Transpacífico. El Cotidiano 200:76–88

Trejo A (2013) Desafíos de la competitividad en la frontera norte de México en el marco del reajuste global. Frontera Norte 25(50):213–221. http://www.scielo.org.mx/scielo.php?script=sci_arttext&pid=S0187-73722013000200009&lng=es&tlng=es

Trejo A (2017) Localización manufacturera, apertura comercial y disparidades regionales en México: organización económico-espacial bajo un nuevo modelo de desarrollo. El Colegio de México, Centro de Estudios Demográficos, Urbanos y Ambientales, México

Trejo Nieto A (2020) Regional disparities in Mexico and the spatially cumulative effects of national development and economic cycles, 1940–2013. Reg Sci Policy Pract:1–14. https://doi.org/10.1111/rsp3.12311

Trejo Nieto A, Negrete MA (2019) Evidencia macroeconómica de la configuración territorial en el centro de México. In: Sobrino J, Ugalde V (eds) Desarrollo urbano y metropolitano en México. El Colegio de México, México City
Unikel L (1975) Políticas de desarrollo regional en México. El Colegio de México, México
Unikel L, Ruiz C, Garza G (1976) El desarrollo urbano de México. In: Diagnóstico e implicaciones futuras. El Colegio de México, México
Viesti G (2015) Diagnóstico de desarrollo regional: México. EUROSOCIAL, Madrid
Villanueva Ulfgard R, Villanueva C (2020) The power to transform? Mexico's 'fourth transformation' under president Andrés Manuel López Obrador. Globalizations 17(6):1027–1042. https://doi.org/10.1080/14747731.2020.1718846
Villareal A, Flores SM, Flores MA (2016) Patrones de Co-localización espacial de la industria Aeroespacial en México. Estudios Económicos 31(1):169–211
Villarreal MA, Fergusson IF (2019) NAFTA Renegotiation and the Proposed United States–Mexico–Canada Agreement (USMCA). Congressional Research Service, 26.

Regional Advantages: Why U.S.–Mexico Trade Is Robust and Permanent

James Gerber

Abstract Mexico and the USA have the second largest bilateral trade relationship in the world, after only U.S.–Canadian trade. The free trade agreement facilitates the flow of goods and services, but other factors are important enough that an abrogation of the agreement would not likely alter the volume of trade in a significant way. Mexico–U.S. trade is driven by five factors in addition to the effects of the trade agreement. First, the proximity of the USA and Mexico reduces transportation costs. Second, the size of both the U.S. and Mexican economies creates a large demand for each other's goods and services. Third, economic policy reforms in Mexico and the USA encouraged closer trade ties, particularly in the border region where Mexico's export processing zone was deeply integrated with the American economy. Fourth, new information and communication technologies led to the development of cross-border value chains that further integrated manufacturing systems. And fifth, state and local efforts along the border have strengthened cross-border economic ties.

Keywords Free trade · Border states · Gravity model · Paradiplomacy · Economic reform · Value chains

1 Introduction: U.S.–Mexico Trade Is Robust and Permanent

On July 1, 2020, Canada, Mexico, and the USA replaced the North American Free Trade Agreement (NAFTA) with an updated version of the trade accord. The NAFTA had been in effect since January 1, 1994 and was in need of changes to cover new issues such as digital commerce, electronic payment systems, and data storage and security. The new agreement, called the United States–Mexico–Canada

J. Gerber (✉)
San Diego State University, San Diego, CA, USA
e-mail: jgerber@sdsu.edu

A. de León-Arias, P. Aroca (eds.), *NAFTA's Impact on Mexico's Regional Development*, New Frontiers in Regional Science: Asian Perspectives 51,
https://doi.org/10.1007/978-981-16-3168-9_2

Agreement (USMCA),[1] is similar to NAFTA in most respects although it has additional clauses covering some of the aforementioned issues, as well as new rules governing trade in automotive products and intellectual property protections. In the end, however, the net benefits are expected to be limited. The United States International Trade Commission (USITC) estimated that U.S. GDP would increase by 0.35% once the agreement was fully implemented and as long as it was adequately enforced. Even so, as modest as the estimated benefits are, they stemmed almost entirely from the USITC's assumption that uncertainty would be reduced and that the agreement would be fully enforced (United States International Trade Commission 2019). While there is little in the agreement itself that will generate significant new benefits, the new rules of origin and wage requirements in the automobile sector will add administrative and record keeping burdens that may be a step backward in terms of trade facilitation.

In the short run, there is no doubt that the successful negotiation and legislative passage of the agreement reduced most of the uncertainty that had been introduced by the rhetoric and actions of the ex-U.S. President who had campaigned in 2016 on a platform that was hostile to trade agreements in general and NAFTA in particular. After he assumed office on January 20, 2017, the ex-President moved quickly to demonstrate that his administration would treat international trade differently than his predecessors. On Monday, January 23, 2017, he pulled the USA out of the Trans-Pacific Partnership, a 12-country negotiation that his predecessor had viewed as an expansion and update of the NAFTA.[2] Approximately 3 months later, on April 28, the new administration formally agreed to begin negotiations for a replacement of NAFTA but continued to create uncertainty with threats to terminate both the negotiations and NAFTA whenever a roadblock was encountered. Further, in March of 2018, the administration announced that it would impose tariffs of 25% on steel and 10% on aluminum as necessary national security measures. These tariffs fell most heavily on the U.S.' main trading partners, Canada and Mexico, and close allies such as the European Union and caused many economists and observers to question the legitimacy of the national security rationale.

In spite of these obstacles, the three NAFTA nations successfully concluded modifications to the agreement and gave it a new name in order to disassociate it from the old NAFTA. In effect, there is less that is new than supposed. New rules of origin and wage standards were applied to the car industry, intellectual property rights were extended in some cases, particularly pharmaceuticals, and Mexico was required to make it easier for workers to unionize. Most other changes were minor. Furthermore, the new agreement does not eliminate uncertainty since threats of new and increased tariffs continued and the text of the new agreement included a sunset

---

[1]The name and acronym of the treaty vary by country. English speaking Canadians call the agreement the Canada–United States–Mexico Agreement (CUSMA), while Mexico refers to it as the Tratado entre México, Estados Unidos, y Canadá (T-MEC).

[2]The TPP was eventually signed without the USA and is now called the Comprehensive and Progressive Agreement for Trans-Pacific Partnership (CPTPP) and includes Australia, Brunei, Canada, Chile, Japan, Malaysia, Mexico, New Zealand, Peru, Singapore, and Vietnam.

clause and a periodic mandatory review of the agreement. The sunset clause stated that the terms of the agreement expire after 16 years and the review process required all three countries to affirm a continued commitment to the agreement every 6 years. Nevertheless, in spite of the new uncertainties and the relatively modest changes, many business executives, farmers, and other interested parties breathed a sigh of relief that at least there was an agreement.

In what follows, I will argue that the direct effects of any free trade agreement between the USA and Mexico are overestimated and that there are several more fundamental reasons why the two countries are important trade partners to each other.[3] Consequently, a revised NAFTA in the form of the USMCA, or a continuation of the status quo, or even the absence of any formal agreement, would not radically alter the volume of trade between the two countries (or between the USA and Canada). To be sure, uncertainty reduces trade flows and an abrogation of the free trade agreement would be a shock that would require adjustments that might prove costly. Nevertheless, disruption and the forced adjustments would not lead to significant declines in the volume of trade.

In the sections that follow, the reasons for a robust and ever-present trade relationship between the USA and Mexico are explored. Section 3.2 focuses on the gravity model of trade as the primary force behind the long-run trade relationship. The gravity model is consistent with the main theoretical approach of international trade theory, known as the Heckscher–Ohlin model (Deardorff 1998) and is probably the most robust explanation for bilateral trade flows in general. The model is discussed within the context of the long history of U.S.–Mexico trade. Section 3.3 explores some of the policy changes that caused manufacturing in the border region to take off before there was an FTA. The four U.S. and six Mexican border states account for more than half of their respective country's exports to each other. Section 3.4 follows with a brief discussion of the ways that new developments in information and communication technologies have enabled the growth of cross-border value chains and further integrated Mexican and U.S. manufacturing. Section 3.5 delves into some of the efforts by state and local governments in the border region to support trade and economic development through the encouragement of cross-border commerce and investment. A final section offers a few concluding remarks.

[3]By extension and with a few changes, the same arguments could be made for Canada–U.S. trade. However, this chapter is focused on Mexico–U.S. trade.

Fig. 1 Share of Total Mexican Exports and Imports with the USA. Source: International Monetary Fund 2020; Instituto Nacional de Estadística y Geografía (INEGI) 2020

2 The Gravity Model and U.S.–Mexico Trade in Historical Perspective

The U.S. and Mexico bilateral trade relationship is the second largest in the world and is only slightly smaller than the world's largest flow of trade between Canada and the USA. The importance to both Mexico and the USA of trade between the two has persisted for many decades through different trade regimes, profound political changes, and turbulent economic conditions. In the 1880s, the USA began to purchase more than half of Mexico's exports and has continued to do so for 140 years, without exception. By the first years of the twentieth century, the USA was supplying more than half of Mexico's imports. That trend continued until 2007, when the U.S. share of Mexican imports dropped below 50% for the first time since 1913 (Kuntz Ficker 2007, pp. 467–474; INEGI 2020). Figure 1 shows the U.S. share of Mexican imports and exports, 1950–2020. The decline in the import share that began around 2001 aligns with the entrance of China into the WTO although it is uncertain if that is the main causal factor.[4] Even so, Mexico entered the top group of traders with the USA as early as the late 1800s, moved into the top three in 1989, and

[4]China's share of Mexican imports rose from 1.6% in 2000 to 19.1% in the first months of 2020 (INEGI 2020). China's growing share is nearly two-thirds of the decline in the U.S. share which fell from 73.1% in 2000 to 43.3% in early 2020. China's entrance into the WTO was probably an important factor but not the only one.

Table 1 Average annual growth in real U.S. imports and exports

	World	Canada	Mexico
Imports			
1961–1990	6.90	6.09	8.63
1990–2019	4.53	3.28	7.74
Exports			
1961–1990	6.38	6.90	8.61
1990–2019	4.06	3.45	6.86

Source: Bureau of Economic Analysis 2020a, 2020b; International Monetary Fund 2020; author's calculations

U.S. trade with Mexico has grown faster than trade with Canada and with the world. Trade with Mexico grew faster in the decades before the free trade agreement.

continues to be the second most important trade relationship, after Canada (Irwin 2006, Tables Ee533-Ee568).

The Mexico-U.S. trade relationship persisted through the first wave of globalization in the late 1800s and early 1900s, the Mexican Revolution (1910–1917), highly protectionist U.S. policies during the late nineteenth century and the first half of the twentieth century, through two world wars, the worldwide Great Depression of the 1930s, Mexico's adoption of protectionist trade policies during its import substitution industrialization period from the 1940s through the 1970s, Mexico's switch to neoliberal market-oriented reforms in the 1980s, and various presidential administrations in both countries. It would be incorrect to say that trade policies and trade agreements do not matter, but the size, longevity, and persistence of U.S.-Mexico trade through a wide range of political and economic conditions imply a deeper set of factors than trade policies alone.

The gravity model explains this trade pattern. The model is based on Newton's description of the forces that determine the gravitational attraction of bodies in space. In Newton's model, gravitational strength is a function of the size of the celestial bodies and their distance from each other. The gravity model of trade uses the same idea to explain the flow of goods between two countries with size represented by GDP and distance by the actual physical distance between main commercial centers. The gravity model illustrates a fundamental trade law: Countries trade more with bigger economies and with closer neighbors, all else equal. With or without the NAFTA or the USMCA, the USA and Mexico would be major trade partners by virtue of location and size. This was true before there was a free trade agreement and would continue to be true if it were to disappear. Major policy changes such as an abrogation of the trade treaty or major world events such as China's reclaiming of a prominent position in the world economy, undoubtedly cause significant disruptions and adjustments, but the USA and Mexico continue as main trading partners for each other.

Another perspective that supports a gravity model interpretation of Mexico-U.S. trade can be viewed through the lens of comparative rates of growth of imports and exports before and after the free trade agreement. Table 1 shows real, price adjusted average annual growth rates of U.S. trade with Mexico. For purposes of comparison, total U.S. merchandise trade with the world and with Canada is also included. The data are for 1961–1990 and 1990–2019. The year 1990 is selected instead of 1994, when the agreement was implemented, because it is the year that NAFTA was proposed, after which firms began adjusting their future plans. As shown, total U.S. merchandise trade with Mexico has grown faster than trade with either the world or Canada. Further, and perhaps surprisingly, trade grew faster in the 29 years before the beginning of NAFTA negotiations than in the subsequent 29 years.[5] Clearly, the lack of a trade agreement was not a hindrance to trade growth. There are many possible explanations for the patterns shown in Table 1 but one of the key explanations is illustrated by the contemporary geography of Mexico–U.S. trade.

Table 2 shows the percentage of Mexican exports that originate in its six northern border states and the percentages of U.S. exports to Mexico originating in the four U.S. southern border states. The Mexican and U.S. panels of Table 2 are not symmetric since the U.S. panel shows exports to Mexico, while the data for Mexican states is all exports, including those to the USA and other countries. Mexican trade data does not identify the destination country for state exports but given border states' proximity to the U.S. market and the dominance of trade with the USA in overall Mexican exports, the data give a good idea of border state exports to the USA. Table 2 assumes that their share of exports to the USA is the same as their share of overall exports, but if gravity effects are present, this is probably an underestimate of their share.

Three elements stand out in Table 2. The first is that both Mexican and U.S. border states dominate their nation's exports to their USMCA partner.[6] Exports to the U.S. from Mexican border states range from 13.7% of total national exports originating in Chihuahua to 4.6% in Sonora. U.S. border states are heavily dominated by Texas which is on the direct infrastructure route to the main Mexican industrial and commercial centers, has over 60% (1254 miles) of the Mexico-U.S. border running through it, and a preponderance of border crossings. Texas' role appears lopsided, but its percentage matches the estimate of Mexico's exports to the USA that originate in the four Mexican states on the Texas border (Tamaulipas, Nuevo Leon, Coahuila, and Chihuahua).

A second element shown in Table 2 is the dominance of two categories: Computers and Electronic Products (NAICS 334) and Transportation Equipment (NAICS 336).[7] These two industries are also the main categories of overall Mexico-U.S. trade, a fact that points to the importance of the composition of border states' exports

[5]One hypothesis for faster trade growth pre-NAFTA is the occurrence of financial crises (1994–1995 and 2007–2009) in the later period. This does not explain why trade with the world and with Canada was consistently slower.

[6]This assumes that Mexican border states and all other states match the national figure of 80 percent of exports going to the USA. Given proximity of border states to the U.S. market, it is likely that the percentage is higher, and, in that case, their share would be greater than 80 percent.

[7]NAICS is the North American Industrial Classification System. It is used by Canada, Mexico, and the USA to classify industries. The codes range from 2 to 6 digits and trade data show the industrial origin of products.

Table 2 Share of border states in Mexico-U.S. trade, 2019

Country/State	Percent of national exports to:	Top 2 items (percent of state exports to U.S. or Mexico)
Mexico	USA[a]	
Baja California	10.1	Computers and electronics (34.6) Transportation equipment (20.7)
Chihuahua	13.7	Computers and electronics (49.7) Transportation equipment (23.7)
Coahuila	11.5	Transportation equipment (68) Basic metals (7.9)
Nuevo Leon	9.6	Transportation equipment (45.0) Electrical apparatus (16.1)
Sonora	4.6	Transportation equipment (31.8) Minerals and ores (11.5)
Tamaulipas	7.0	Transportation equipment (68%) Basic metals (7.9)
Total for six border states	56.5	
USA	Mexico	
Arizona	3.2	Computers and electronics (20.1) Mineral and ores (19.7)
California	10.9	Computers and electronics (21.0) Transportation equipment (13.2)
New Mexico	0.9	Computers and electronics (61.0) Electrical apparatus (7.9)
Texas	42.3	Computers and electronics (24.5) Petroleum and coal products (18.1)
Total for four border states	57.3	

Source: Instituto Nacional de Estadística y Geografía, 2020; International Trade Administration 2020
aAssumes that all states export in the same proportion to the USA and other countries
Mexican and U.S. border states account for more than 50% of the exports from each country to the other

as well as their volume. As discussed below, the products exported by border states reflect the growth of extensive cross-border value chains in the manufacturing sectors of transportation equipment and computers and electronic products. These sectors have a relatively long history and have played key roles in the development of Mexico-U.S. trade, production off-shoring. and the rise of transborder value chains. As shown in the next section, their role antedates the growth of global value chains in international trade.

A third item of importance shown in Table 2 is lesser but yet important role of traditional natural resource based exports. Petroleum products exported by Texas through its many pipeline connections to Mexico are significant at the national as well as the state level, and while minerals and basic metals are less so, in Arizona, Sonora, and Coahuila these traditional exports continue to be important.

3 How Border Manufacturing Grew to Prominence

Although geography and GDP are probably the two most important factors in the determination of Mexico–U.S. trade, they are not the only ones. Another influential factor that shaped bilateral trade flows was the change in Mexican economic policies that began in the 1960s. Policy changes were initially small and regional in scope, but they gained momentum and depth in the 1980s. This section briefly describes the changes and then illustrates how Mexico moved from traditional resource based exports towards mostly manufactured goods. In the process of its transformation, it created much closer economic ties to U.S. businesses and the U.S. economy.

An important impetus for the growth of non-traditional manufactured exports was the beginning of the Border Industrialization Program (BIP) in 1965. As the name implies this program was focused on the industrialization of Mexico's northern border and was probably a central reason for the concentration of manufactured export industries in border states. In short, the BIP created a different set of incentives for Mexican manufactured exports, particularly in the northern border region. Responding to the incentives, manufacturing in the border region started to grow noticeably in the 1960s, continued to build slowly in the 1970s, and took off in the 1980s, particularly after a more comprehensive set of policy changes was enacted. The BIP, or maquila program, was Mexico's version of an export processing zone (EPZ).[8] It was a small but important shift away from the existing import substitution industrialization (ISI) policies that had focused on the twin goals of production for the domestic market and greater autonomy from the U.S. economy. With the BIP, Mexican authorities created tax incentives for export industries, whether Mexican or foreign. As with other EPZs, raw materials and intermediate goods were allowed duty free entrance for processing in Mexico so long as the output, whether a final product or not, was exported. Initially the program was limited to Mexico's northern border region in an area that is close to the USA. Its original purpose was to absorb the large number of unemployed Mexican workers who had been seasonal migrants in the USA until that country's guest worker program was terminated on December 31, 1964. The idea for the BIP came from Mexico's Secretary of Industry and Commerce, Campos Salas, after a tour of U.S. owned manufacturing plants in the export processing zones of several Asian countries, including Hong Kong, Singapore, Malaysia, and others (Taylor Hansen 2003). Campos Salas saw the BIP as a solution to northern unemployment, but in creating the program, he subtlety shifted Mexican economic policy towards greater economic ties with the USA.

The USA cooperated by agreeing to allow Mexican intermediate goods imports to move through its ports without being subjected to U.S. tariffs. This enabled firms in Mexico to import intermediate goods through ports in Los Angeles, Houston, and other nearby U.S. ports and to avoid the higher transportation costs for goods

[8]According to the U.S. International Trade Administration (2019), there are over 600 EPZs in the world (2016). See: https://www.export.gov/article?id=Export-Processing-Zones.

entering through Mexican ports. After processing in Mexico, goods shipped back to the USA were only tariffed on the Mexican value added. The policy was designed to encourage collaboration between U.S. and Mexican firms and to encourage investment in border manufacturing. The ability of manufacturers to cut their value chain into discreet steps and locate the unskilled or semi-skilled processes in Mexico was still in its infancy and awaited revolutions in communication and information technologies to take off, but the potential for collaboration embodied by the maquila industry was significant and the industry flourished through the 1970s and 1980s. As the EPZ grew, limits were removed on the location of firms and the volume of manufacturing and manufactured exports began a long-run increase.

Between 1964, the year before the BIP began, and 1984, real manufacturing output increased 3.2 times, or nearly 6% per year (INEGI 2009, 11.1). The growth of manufacturing in Mexico was particularly notable along its northern border with the USA where proximity to the wealthy U.S. market attracted foreign direct investment from the north and job seekers from the south. Gravity model effects led to the development of large manufacturing sectors in Mexico's northern border states and in cities directly adjacent to the USA. As shown in Table 3.3, the composition of exports changed as traditional resource based exports declined, and manufactured exports increased. In 1964, Mexico's top-10 2-digit SITC export categories comprised 77% of total exports and were nearly entirely resource based (see Table 3) They included tropical fruits and coffee, sugar, fish products, petroleum, lead, zinc and other minerals, yarns and fabric, and live animals. Twenty years later, in 1984, the composition of exports was fundamentally different. Natural resource based products were still present (petroleum, coffee, fish) but so were several new categories of more sophisticated manufactured goods, including electrical machinery, power generation equipment, telecommunications equipment, and automobiles. In 1964, all of the top products are resource based; 20 years later, at least four of the top ten exports are manufactured, non-resource based products. The BIP played an important role in the transformation of Mexican exports through its ability to attract foreign investment, particularly but not only from the USA, and its incentives for closer economic ties with U.S. manufacturing interests.

Mexican goods exports to the USA shifted from agricultural and mineral commodities to manufactured goods between 1964 and 1984; petroleum and its products also increased in importance.

Closer ties with the USA were also supported by pre-NAFTA changes in Mexico's commercial policies. Throughout the post-World War II period, Mexico pursued an industrial development strategy known as import substitution industrialization (ISI). As the name implies, ISI promotes industrialization by concentrating on production of goods that substitute for imports. Mexico abandoned this policy framework in the 1980s, but until then, one key component was a relatively high level of trade barriers. Over time, these increasingly took the form of quantitative restrictions and were less dependent on tariffs (King 1970; Wallace 1980). Beginning in the 1980s, tariffs began to fall unilaterally, and quotas were removed so that they were nearly gone by the early 1990s. For example, in 1987, Mexico's average unweighted tariff rate was cut from 23 to 11%; by the time NAFTA was

Table 3 Top 10 Mexican Goods Exports to the USA, 1964 and 1984

1964: SITC rev. 1--Description	Value, U.S.$	Cum. percent
7-coffee, tea, cocoa, spices, and manufactures thereof	89,874,211	0.1480
6-sugar, sugar preparations and honey	79,160,963	0.2783
5-fruit and vegetables	66,275,460	0.3875
3-fish and fish preparations	60,505,816	0.4871
27-crude fertilizers and crude minerals, not elsewhere specified	36,934,035	0.5479
33-petroleum and petroleum products	33,640,887	0.6033
68-non-ferrous metals	29,872,059	0.6525
93-special transactions, not classified, according to kind	25,728,187	0.6949
65-textile yarn, fabrics, made up articles, etc.	25,437,295	0.7368
0-live animals	21,011,438	0.7714
TOTAL exports of goods to U.S.	607,279,665	1.0000
1984: SITC rev. 2--description		
33-petroleum, petroleum products, and related materials	7,779,121,152	0.4259
77-electric machinery, apparatus and appliances, and parts, not elsewhere specified	1,695,139,968	0.5187
76-telecommunications, sound recording, and reproducing equipment	1,193,933,056	0.5840
71-power generating machinery and equipment	744,282,304	0.6248
5-vegetables and fruit	665,953,600	0.6612
78-road vehicles	520,033,152	0.6897
93-special transactions, commodity not classified according to class	472,960,576	0.7156
68-non-ferrous metals	436,541,792	0.7395
3-fish, crustacean and mollusks, and preparations thereof	400,231,136	0.7614
7-coffee, tea, cocoa, spices, and manufactures thereof	349,016,256	0.7805
Total exports of goods to USA	18,266,857,472	1.0000

Source: United Nations 2019

implemented, its applied average tariffs varied from 0 to 25% with an average of 10%. U.S. tariffs before NAFTA averaged 4%, but on a trade weighted basis were 3.1% (Agama and McDaniel 2002). The NAFTA agreement began a phased elimination of all tariffs so that by 2003, trade between the U.S. and Mexico was mostly tariff free, with the exception of some sensitive products with long phase-out periods, such as corn in Mexico and tomatoes in the USA.

4 Post-NAFTA: The Rise of Global Value Chains

The ability of multi-plant firms to send information back and forth between their different sites is a relatively new phenomenon. Looking back to the moment in 1994 when the NAFTA was implemented, or even further to the late 1980s before the announcement of the NAFTA negotiations, the differences in technology between then and now are striking. For example, the Internet was just beginning to come into widespread usage in the 1990s. Google Ngram Viewer tracks the frequency of words and concepts over time, based on the digitalization of millions of books dating back to 1500. The term "World Wide Web" is never used before the 1960s and only rarely appears in print books up until the mid-1980s. Around the end of the 1980s the usage of the term hits an inflection point and comes into wide usage by 1995. The pattern for the term "Internet" is similar and is approximately the same for the term "global value chain" (Google Books 2019).

The advent of the Internet is an example of the types of radical breakthroughs that occurred in information and communication technologies and also illustrates how young these technologies are. As new technologies led to radical improvements in the quality and quantity of information that could cheaply and easily move across large geographical distances, manufacturing firms began to shift production stages to different locations where they could exploit the comparative advantages of different regions and countries. In the earlier age of fax machines and expensive telephone landlines, cross-border coordination of production activities was expensive, risky, and complicated. However, with the new ability to communicate and move information across national boundaries, the transaction costs of using off-site production facilities in another country were much less.[9]

Within the NAFTA region, the development of new information and communication technologies promoted the growth of trade in intermediate goods such as car parts, electronic assemblies, parts for medical devices, and others. In 2015, 40% of Mexico's goods exports and 63% of its goods imports were intermediate goods (WTO 2019).[10] And Mexico's share of intermediates trade between the three NAFTA partners has increased continuously between 1995 and 2015 (World Bank 2017, p. 62). Overall, 36.1% of the value of Mexican exports is value added that was created outside Mexico, mostly in the USA and with the percentage varying by industry. For example, 48% of the value of Mexico's motor vehicle exports and 58.4% of computer and electronic parts exports are created outside the country. Most other Mexican manufacturing sectors have a smaller percentage of foreign value added in exports, but these two are notable for three reasons: (1) they are at the core of exports from border states (see Table 3.2), (2) they are among the largest export sectors, and (3) they have high percentages of intra-industry trade. The implication is that many goods exported to Mexico from the USA are likely to return to the USA

[9]Baldwin (2016) offers an eye-opening exploration of the potential consequences of the revolutions in information and communication. In this essay I am focused on the ways those technologies have integrated US and Mexican (and by extension, Canadian) production.

[10]Measurement of global value chains is in its infancy. Standard concepts and methods for collecting trade data focus on exports and imports without regard for the production location of value added. In order to measure value added trade, national data collection agencies need to adopt new methods and, to date, few governments are doing this. Hence, most of the estimates of value added trade are from multilateral agencies such as the OECD or the WTO which collaborate on periodic estimates. There are no annual updates.

after having been transformed in some way and that a large share of U.S. imports from Mexico contain significant amounts of U.S. value added. For example, in 2019 the USA exported to Mexico $20.7 billion in Motor Vehicle Parts (NAICS 3363) and $3.6 billion in Motor Vehicle Bodies (NAICS 3362). At the same time, it imported $70.7 billion in motor vehicles, many of which had U.S. made parts in them. Similarly, in the same year the USA imported over $50 billion in motor vehicle parts from Mexico, which it used in its production of $787 billion in gross motor vehicle output. Transportation Equipment (NAICS 336) was the largest ($128 billion) U.S. import from Mexico in 2019 and earlier and was nearly double the size of the second category, Computers and Electronic Components (NAICS 334, $65 billion). Transportation equipment was also the most important category of exports from four of the six Mexican border states and the second most important after Computers and Electronic Components in the other two border states.

The movement of auto parts between plants in Mexico and the USA played an important role in the construction of the three-country North American auto industry, not only in the border region but in all of the places where production occurs. U.S. imports of $50 billion in auto parts went to Texas ($12 billion) and California ($2.6 billion) but also to traditional auto manufacturing states such as Michigan ($16 billion) and Ohio ($3.3 billion) and relatively newer auto manufacturing states such as Tennessee ($2.5 billion), Kentucky ($2.3 billion), and South Carolina ($2.2 billion). These value chains played an important role in the NAFTA/USMCA renegotiations because they were responsible for the creation of a broad base of political support for maintaining existing value chains and opposition to a new agreement that would weaken them (Althaus and Rogers 2016). It is conceivable that an upheaval in U.S.–Mexico relations or a radical nationalist agenda could break these ties, but under normal circumstances, it seems unlikely. Multinational automobile manufacturers, auto parts companies, and their affiliates have taken advantage of the opportunities to locate production stages on both sides of the U.S.–Mexico border and their business models and their future competitiveness in the global economy depend on those efficiency enhancing efforts.

5 State and Local Governments Support Mexico–U.S. Trade

The auto, electronics, and other industries have a set of allies in the border region that help keep trade flowing. These are state and local officials concerned about the economic development and prosperity of their communities and engage in paradiplomacy when it is in their interests.[11] In most countries, paradiplomacy is extremely limited or even completely forbidden given the reasonable fears of national governments that local diplomatic efforts might undermine national

[11]Paradiplomacy is diplomacy conducted by sub-national governments.

agendas. There is evidence, however, Mexico is somewhat more receptive to sub-national interinstitutional agreements and that sub-national governments in both the USA and Mexico engage in paradiplomacy to attract foreign investment and promote exports. In addition, state and local governments on the border are more likely to engage in paradiplomacy (Kincaid 1984; Schiavon 2010, 2018).

U.S.–Mexico border states and communities have a wide range of interinstitutional agreements and cross-border private agreements, both formal and informal. Even small scale entrepreneurs use the asymmetric conditions found across the borderline to gain competitive advantages through multi-site operations that often do not include formal cooperation agreements (Pisani and Richardson 2012). While some state and local agreements deal with issues of public health and law enforcement, many are focused on the facilitation of trade and regional economic development. The degree of closeness between cross-border communities is not well perceived by outsiders but should be unsurprising when one considers that all four U.S. border states were Spanish colonies and part of the territory of Mexico after its independence in 1821. Texas' formal ties to Mexico lasted until 1836 when it achieved its own independence, and the other U.S. border states were ceded to the USA in 1848 after the war between the two countries (1846–1848). Although the border region was sparsely populated in the mid-1800s, the drawing of the contemporary borderline divided families, businesses, and urban centers and created the system of twin cities that dominates the region today. To be sure, before modern communication and transportation technologies, the border region was a long way from the centers of political and economic power in both countries, but that only served to allow for the development of a more hybrid society with shared U.S. and Mexican characteristics of language, culture, economy, and politics.

Texas may be the best example of paradiplomacy with Mexico given its long border, its numerous border cities that form single metropolitan conurbations with Mexican cities, its many ports of entry, and the seaport, rail, highway, and pipeline infrastructure that connect central Mexico to Texas and U.S. industrial and commercial centers. Paradiplomacy began in the 1970s with the opening of the state's first and only foreign trade office in Mexico City. By the 1980s the state was signing state-to-state agreements with Mexican states. The 1984 Texas-Tamaulipas Bilateral Exchange Committee was followed by agreements with border states Nuevo Leon and Coahuila and, in 1985, an agreement with the federal government of Mexico called the Mexico-Texas Exchange Commission, or M-TEC (Blase 2003). Most of these agreements had a heavy trade promotion focus and were largely superseded by the NAFTA. Before that, however, a decade-long economic crisis in the 1980s in Texas convinced state officials of the opportunities presented by its geographical location on the Mexican border and of the need to strengthen ties beyond what occurred at the national level. Today, the state has more foreign trade zones than any other U.S. state where in-bond storage facilities help to attract investment from many countries and facilitate cooperation with Mexican manufacturing on the Texas border. The state has a Border Trade Advisory Group, overseen by the state-level Secretary of State, that engages in various forms of trade promotion and national lobbying. The Advisory Group recommends trade facilitation policies such as the creation of the Texas–Mexico Border Transportation Master Plan (BMTP) which is a collaboration with several bordering Mexican states and the Mexican and U.S. federal governments. Texas also has a multi-agency Texas–Mexico Strategic Investment Commission to facilitate trade and to lobby the federal government.

The private sector also engages in cross-border trade facilitation. One of the most significant efforts is the Borderplex Alliance collaboration between three cities in three states and two countries: El Paso, Texas; Las Cruces, New Mexico, and Ciudad Juarez, Chihuahua. The goal is trade facilitation, but also lobbying at the federal level to encourage favorable policies, the attraction of new investment to the region, and economic development. Las Cruces is in New Mexico which is the state with the smallest border with Mexico and the smallest border economy and population. Hence, it is the border state with the least amount of trade and other relations with Mexico although its state agency, the New Mexico Border Authority has successfully attracted one of the largest U.S. railroads to build an intermodal rail facility to connect El Paso to Los Angeles and industrial centers in the Midwest.

Arizona began to strengthen commercial ties with Mexico long before the free trade agreement was considered. In 1959, the governors of Arizona and Sonora founded what was to become the Arizona–Mexico Commission (AMC). The goals of the AMC are to promote trade, commerce, tourism, and infrastructure development, and to collaborate in education and research (Arizona-Mexico Commission 2019). While Arizona lagged Texas and California in its creation of a trade office in Mexico, the AMC was an active promoter of closer ties to Mexico. The strength of Arizona's state policy varied with different state leaders but was often in favor of much closer commercial ties even when contentious issues such as trade in illegal drugs and unauthorized migration flows were obstacles.[12]

California is an outlier compared to the other border states and is the only state with a smaller share of U.S. exports to Mexico (10.9) than its share of U.S. income (14.5). This is probably a result of its relatively small border with Mexico (140 miles, approximately) and its location further away from central Mexico and the primary transportation infrastructure linking the two countries. In addition, California's location on the Pacific Ocean and the fact that its most vibrant centers of economic activity are the non-border regions of the Los Angeles basin and the San Francisco-Bay Area gives the state a trans-Pacific economic orientation that is absent in other border states. Mexico is an important commercial partner for California, but so are China, Japan, Korea, Taiwan, and other Asian economies. Nevertheless, the state has long held important commercial ties to Mexico which have been supported and developed further by local initiatives. The CaliBaja Mega Region supports industrial clusters and cross-border value chain development in Baja California and Southern California, particularly in the border cities. And private interests have developed an

[12]For example, in the lead up to the passing of the NAFTA, the AMC proposed that businesses in Arizona accept the Mexican peso (Mitchell 1993).

innovative self-financing port of entry that directly connects the city of San Diego to the Abelardo Rodriguez Airport in Tijuana.[13]

Given the differences in geography, history, and proximity to industrial heartlands, commercial centers, and population concentrations, each U.S. and Mexican border state has responded differently to the opportunities offered by trade. Mexican cities and states are more constrained by limited budgets and Mexico's more centralized federal, but local private initiatives in collaboration with cross-border counterparts have been significant factors in lobbying both federal governments for policies that support international commercial ties and trade facilitation. The cumulative effect of these efforts is to reduce trade frictions and transaction costs, increase awareness on each side of the possibilities and opportunities on the other, and to support the growth of cross-border value chains.

6 Conclusion

The main argument of this essay is that U.S.–Mexico trade is less a result of the free trade agreement than often assumed. Consequently, fears surrounding the recent renegotiations were mostly unwarranted. To be sure, a revocation of the free trade agreement would create major disruptions and a period of transition as firms adjusted to a new reality. The necessary changes would be difficult and expensive and would take some time. Nevertheless, there are strong reasons and historical precedents for believing that the absence of a formal agreement would create smaller changes than many people feared.

Two consequences follow directly from this analysis. First, proponents of a formal free trade agreement who argue that its termination would create significant harm to the USA and Mexico economies are not correct. Regardless of the asymmetry between the two economies, Mexico probably has more room to maneuver and less need to accede to unreasonable or undesirable U.S. demands. Second, opponents of the agreement who argue that it has imposed painful and lasting costs on the U.S. economy and workers are not correct either. Setting aside the issue of trade impacts on wages and economic growth, the factors discussed in this chapter show that the U.S.–Mexico trade relationship is not dependent on a free trade agreement. Even if it had never been implemented, we would likely have something very close to present conditions.

Geographical proximity and the size of the NAFTA economies all but guarantee that Canada, Mexico, and the USA will continue to be each other's main trading partners. Furthermore, the last 35 to 40 years of economic policy in all three

[13]This was possible because the airport is a wide boulevard from the USA. For a small fee, one walks approximately two blocks from a parking area in San Diego, California, through a covered hallway and directly into the center of the airport in Tijuana, Baja California. Or, going the other way, from the airport to one's car or other transportation in the USA.

countries at national, state, and local levels have reinforced this pattern and have been further supported by recent developments in information and communication technologies. None of those facts will change, and while a determined and radical nationalist might try to undo some of the policies and the effects of technological changes, they would encounter a series of very strong opposing currents in both the private and public sectors.

References

Agama L, McDaniel CA (2002) The NAFTA Preference and U.S.-Mexico Trade. Office of Economics Working Paper, U.S. International Trade Commission. No. 2002-10-A

Althaus D, Rogers C (2016) Donald Trump's Nafta Plan Would Confront Globalized Auto Industry. Wall Street J. November 10

Arizona-Mexico Commission (2019 About Us: Our History. https://www.azmc.org. Accessed 13 April 2020

Baldwin R (2016) The great convergence: information technology and the new globalization. Harvard University Press, Cambridge

Blase JM (2003) Has globalization changed U.S. federalism? The increasing role of U.S. states in foreign affairs: Texas-Mexico relations. Dissertation. University of Texas

Bureau of Economic Analysis (2020a) Exports of goods (implicit price deflator) [A253RD3A086NBEA], retrieved from FRED, Federal Reserve Bank of St. Louis; https://fred.stlouisfed.org/series/A253RD3A086NBEA. Accessed 10 Oct 2020

Bureau of Economic Analysis (2020b) Imports of goods (implicit price deflator) [A255RD3Q086SBEA], retrieved from FRED, Federal Reserve Bank of St. Louis; https://fred.stlouisfed.org/series/A255RD3Q086SBEA. Accessed 10 Oct 2020

Deardorff A (1998) Determinants of bilateral trade: does gravity work in a neoclassic world? In: Frankel JA (ed) The regionalization of the world economy. University of Chicago Press, Chicago, pp 7–32

Google Books (2019) Ngram viewer. https://books.google.com/ngrams. Accessed 1 Nov 2019

Instituto Nacional de Estadística y Geografía (INEGI) (2009) Estadísticas históricas de México 2009. INEGI, Aguascalientes

Instituto Nacional de Estadística y Geografía (INEGI) (2020) Sector externo. Banco de información económica. https://inegi.org.mx/app/indicadores/bie.html. Accessed 2 Oct 2020

International Monetary Fund (2020) Direction of trade statistics. https://data.imf.org. Accessed 2 Oct 2020

International Trade Administration (2019) Export processing zones. https://www.export.gov/article?id=Export-Processing-Zones. Accessed 6 Nov 2019

International Trade Administration (2020) National Trade Data: TradeStats Express. http://tse.export.gov/tse/TSEHome.aspx. Accessed 9 Oct 2020

Irwin D (2006) International trade in goods and services. In: Carter et al (eds) Historical statistics of the United States. Earliest times to the present. Millennial edition. Volume 5, part E. Governance and international relations. Cambridge University Press, New York

Kincaid J (1984) The American governors in international affairs. Publius 14(4):95–114

King T (1970) Mexico: Industrialization and Trade Policies since 1940. OECD and Oxford University Press, London

Kuntz Ficker S (2007) El comercio exterior de México en la era del capitalismo liberal, 1870–1929. El Colegio de México, Ciudad de México

Mitchell LA (July 12, 1993) Economic planners call for peso acceptance in Arizona. Arizona Daily Star
Pisani MJ, Richardson C (2012) Cross-border informal entrepreneurs across the South Texas–Northern Mexico boundary. Entrepreneurship & Regional Development 24(3–4):105–121
Schiavon J (2010) Sub-state diplomacy in Mexico. Hague J Diplomacy V(1–2):65–97
Schiavon J (2018) Comparative Paradiplomacy. Routledge, New York
Taylor Hansen L (2003) The origins of the maquila industry in Mexico. Comercio Exterior 53 (11):1–16
United Nations (2019) Comtrade Database. https://comtrade.un.org/data. Accessed 10 Oct 2019
United States International Trade Commission (2019) U.S.-Mexico-Canada Trade Agreement: Likely Impact on the U.S. Economy and on Specific Industry Sectors. Investigation number TPA 105–003, USITC Publication 4889
Wallace, R B (1980) Policies of protection in Mexico. In: Kate, A, and Wallace, R, with Waarts, A and Ramirez de Wallace, M D (eds) Protection and economic development in Mexico. New York: St. Martin's Press
World Bank (2017) Global value chain development report 2017: measuring and analyzing the impact of GVCs on economic development. The World Bank, Washington DC
World Trade Organization (WTO) (2019) Mexico: Trade in value added and global value chains. https://www.wto.org/english/res_e/statis_e/miwi_e/countryprofiles_e.htm. Accessed 4 Nov 2019

Regional Economic Development in Mexico: Past, Present, and Future

Rafael Garduño-Rivera

Abstract To talk about Regional Economic Development in Mexico, we first need to understand Regional Economic Development (RED). RED is the search for a better standard of living for all people. However, RED explores a better standard of living for all the people in all regions and sectors of a nation. To reach this goal, there are several factors involved. Some of the factors that have been studied and proved to affect (positively or negatively) are Climate, Security, Production, Specialization, Trade, Infrastructure, and Investment. In addition, these factors influence topics such as the concentration of economic activity, production efficiency, economic growth, the mobility of factors such as labor and foreign direct investment (FDI), economic integration, regional convergence, and gender participation in the formal economy. This chapter will analyze these factors and their effect on the Regional Economic Development in Mexico in the last years and what would happen in the future.

Keywords Regional history · Regional economic development · Regional economic activity · Regional migration · Wage differentials · Trade and labor market interactions · Size and spatial distributions of regional economic activity · Firm location

JEL Codes N96 · O18 · R11 · R23 · J31 · F16 · R12 · R30

1 Regional Economic Development (RED)

RED is an economic area specializing in (among other things) economic growth, socio-economic development, and the standard of living of all the different regions (Dziembała 2018). Therefore, it is of extreme interest to analyze how Mexico has behaved in this aspect during the last three decades.

R. Garduño-Rivera (✉)
Universidad Panamericana, School of Business and Economics, Ciudad de México, Mexico
e-mail: rgardunor@up.edu.mx

A. de León-Arias, P. Aroca (eds.), *NAFTA's Impact on Mexico's Regional Development*, New Frontiers in Regional Science: Asian Perspectives 51,
https://doi.org/10.1007/978-981-16-3168-9_3

Lomelí Vanegas (2012) does an extraordinary work analyzing what has happened in Mexico, in terms of economic development, during the twentieth century. This analysis shows the vicissitudes of the economic development in Mexico and how, after all these decades, Mexico still lacks sustainable economic development. Another study that discusses RED in Mexico is by Ascani et al. (2012), where they mentioned the emergence of spatial inequality caused by development processes and innovative activities. They conclude that Mexico's trade liberalization has benefited Mexico City and cities near the US border, causing more regional, sectorial, and individual disparities. However, both studies focus on the big picture, mainly in the macroeconomic frame, leaving behind the analysis at the regional level. They had also been done almost a decade ago, and there have been many changes in that period. Therefore, this chapter will focus on analyzing the RED in Mexico has had in the last years, at the regional level, and pay particular attention to the studies done in the last decade. Nevertheless, instead of presenting an analysis divided by subsectors, this chapter will focus on dividing this chapter into the different factors and their effect on different regions. Thus, considering the studies done during the last decades and what lays ahead.

Results suggest that many factors influence Regional Economic Development in Mexico. But the most important to consider is trade openness. We observed that trade openness increased regional disparities, internal migration (mainly from the rural south to the urban North), and migration to the U.S., reducing wage inequality. In this way, we are creating an uneven RED across Mexico. In addition, we observed that Mexico benefited from specialization/concentration since it promotes innovation and competitiveness (among firms in the same sector). Finally, we also notice that road infrastructure investment boosts Mexico's economic growth through increased trade, structural transformation, and agglomeration. The policy implications of these results are that Mexico should focus on a unique sector (mainly manufacturing) to increase its economic activity and regional economic development.

In the next section, we look at trade openness and the changes it has caused in the world, particularly in Mexico. Next, we analyzed how Trade openness has affected wage inequality in Mexico. Section 4 explores how trade openness influences internal migration in Mexico and the US. Section 5 explores how specialization has impacted RED across Mexico and sectors and benefited more from that. Section 6 explores the regional convergence across Mexico. Section 7 studies how road infrastructure influences RED through Mexico. Section 8 studies the RED challenges that the current Mexican government face. And finally, Sect. 9 concludes.

2 Trade Openness (Globalization)

Globalization has opened markets to products and services, often through international agreements that facilitate trade. While economists generally agree that trade can deliver benefits to an economy, the distribution of those benefits has been questioned (Anderson and Van Wincoop 2004). One of the criticisms of globalization is that by benefiting some regions and workers, globalization may accentuate economic inequality and induce greater mobility of people (Anzaldo Gómez et al. 2008).

Developing countries, such as Brazil, China, India, and Mexico, have experienced rapid economic growth. As a result, they have made significant policy adjustments to foster globalization, including lowering tariffs and other trade barriers, reducing foreign direct investment (FDI) barriers, and entering into complex trade agreements. The main motivation for these changes was the promise of growth, higher wages, and lower income inequality (Robertson 2007; Harrison 2007). While increased trade may have benefited the Mexican economy, some initial evidence shows that North American Free Trade Agreement (NAFTA)[1] may have worsened inequality in Mexico (Baylis et al. 2012; Nicita 2004). Not only income inequality but also regional and sectoral inequality too.

New Economic Geography also generates predictions about which regions might reap the gains from trade. For example, the economic effects of trade may increase the concentration of economic activity in certain regions more than others (Krugman 1991). This concentration generates increased labor demand in these regions and their sectors, which results in increased wages in these markets. As a result, labor migrates to these regions to take advantage of these higher wages. Other effects of the trade such as skill-biased technological change, modifications in industry-specific wage premiums, foreign investment, quality upgrading, skill scarcity, exchange rate, and demographic changes have all been suggested as being more accurate explanations for the increase in wage inequality (Robertson 2007; Ranjan 2008).

Mexico's trade liberalization, via NAFTA, created important changes in regional economic growth, exacerbating the disparities between the North and South of Mexico which have existed since industrialization began in the 1930s (Walton and López 2005; Hanson 2007; Baylis et al. 2012; Alvarez et al. 2017). Geography may also play a role in determining the distributions of trade benefits (Esquivel 2000). In the case of Mexico, one might anticipate that, due to lower transportation costs, regions closest to the U.S. border, which also tend to be wealthier, might stand to gain from trade (Blankespoor et al. 2017; Baylis et al. 2012). Similarly, those regions with pre-existing export industries, such as the Northern manufacturing centers, would likely benefit the most from trade (Rostow 1990). Further, the urban labor market will benefit more (than workers in rural regions) because of their higher reliance on skilled wages, whereas rural labor tends to work more in agriculture and often consumes most of what they produce (Nicita 2009). Thus, we may expect increasing inter-regional wage disparities, inducing migration (Robertson 2000, 2004). I will analyze these effects in the next sections.

[1] Since July 1, 2020, it has become the US–Mexico–Canada Agreement (USMCA) and entered into force. https://ustr.gov/trade-agreements/free-trade-agreements/united-states-mexico-canada-agreement accessed on October 18, 2020.

3 Trade Liberalization and Wage Inequality

One of the main topics of trade liberalization is induced wage inequality since a trade agreement benefits only certain regions, sectors, and individuals (Beaulieu et al. 2004; Mercenier and Schmitt 2002; Hanson and Harrison 1999). This brings an uneven regional economic development in the country. The Heckscher-Ohlin trade model states that countries should benefit overall from trade, particularly low-skilled labor should reap higher wages in developing countries where such labor is abundant. If inputs were not completely mobile across sectors and regions, we would expect factors employed in the export-oriented sectors to benefit more than those in import-competing industries. Further, we expect those regions with lower transport costs to benefit more, which may improve or exacerbate wage inequality if labor is not freely mobile, depending on whether those same regions were relatively high or low income before the trade.

Several studies shed light on the impact of trade liberalization on wage inequality in Mexico[2]. For example, Nicita (2004) shows that trade benefits have not spread to all households and have primarily gone to more skilled workers, especially in Mexican states close to the US border[3]. Similarly, Hanson (2007) and Baylis et al. (2012) find that Northern states, which have greater access to the US market than the Southern states, benefit more from trade by obtaining higher prices because lower transportation costs translate into higher labor income. However, one disadvantage of these papers is that they do not consider that households may respond to variations in labor demand by changing the type of labor they offer or relocating[4].

The distribution of benefits from NAFTA will presumably not only accrue to those already working in export industries and/or living in regions close to the US border but also to those who can more easily migrate into those regions and sectors. There is a growing literature on the effect of trade liberalization and migration on wages in Mexico, primarily focused on the effect of the international labor movement, but not many on internal migration. Mishra (2007) finds that "emigration has a strong and positive effect on Mexican wages due to changes in local labor supply" (p. 180). Unger (2005) also finds a positive link between migration and local development, working through remittances, boosting average wages. On the other hand, Aroca and Maloney (2005) find that trade and FDI slow migration. Increased linkages to global markets decrease the incentive to emigrate due to helps the

[2]Some of them are Esquivel and Rodriguez-López (2003); Airola (2008); Cragg and Epelbaum (1996); Feenstra and Hanson (1996); Feliciano (2001); Hanson (2003); Hanson and Harrison (1999); Revenga (1997); Robertson (2007); Chiquiar (2005).

[3]Robertson (2007) finds that the expansion of assembly activities in Mexico has increased the demand for less-skilled workers, and Chiquiar (2005) finds that physical capital and infrastructure are the main reasons why Northern Mexican states reaped the benefits from trade liberalization more than the Southern states. While insightful, these papers do not explicitly analyze the distribution of gains across income levels and geographical regions.

[4]For example, Hanson (2007) assumes that "labor is sufficiently immobile across regions of Mexico for region-specific labor demand to affect regional differentials in labor income" (p. 419).

average wage in the origin region. However, if trade affects different regions within a country differently, it might induce internal migration, making benefits from trade available primarily to those households who can move (Arends-Kuenning et al. 2019). I will discuss the effect of trade on migration in the next section.

While workers close to the US market have a higher wage, workers far away from the United States receive a lower income. This spread reduces over time as the tariff decreases. However, north-south disparities are only one part of the story. Also, large manufacturing sectors seem to be associated with a smaller wage. This implies that because trade benefits manufacturing, it decreases income disparity.

The studies cited show that trade liberalization has reduced wage inequalities, leading to a smaller regional polarization. However, large traded sectors also induced migration, particularly for the poor, and offered a higher wage overall, increasing wage inequality because it has only benefited workers in traded sectors but not in non-traded sectors.

Potential policy implications are that investment in manufacturing can be used as means to ease regional wage inequality. The evidence shown in previous studies also suggests that policies that facilitate internal migration will be good for economic growth and reduce income inequality. However, it is important to mention, that those policies should have broad access to ensure it reaches all the households and regions. In this way, it will avoid increasing inequality among households and regions.

4 Trade Openness and Internal Migration

Another effect of Trade Openness is migration, as mentioned before: Since labor is one of the main factors of production, its reallocation is vital for the boost of economic activity in a region and for the improved standard of leaving of those labor that manages to migrate in search of a better-paid job (Todaro and Smith 2011). However, only a limited number of papers study how internal migration responds to international trade in a developing country like Mexico (Arends-Kuenning et al. 2019; Aroca and Maloney 2005; Aguayo Tellez 2005; Flores et al. 2013), and much of the internal migration literature has failed to find a significant impact of international trade on internal migration. Baylis et al. (2012) showed that NAFTA increased regional disparities in Mexico, which might be mitigated through internal migration. Conversely, the structural shift in the economy brought about by trade penalized those who face higher migration barriers most of the time. Failure to account for labor migration may result in an over-estimation of the growing income in the region receiving migrants since 3.98 million Mexicans (4% of the total population in 2000) and 5% of working-age men migrated from one state to another between 1995 and 2000 (Vega 2005; INEGI 2008)[5]. Most of these migrants are workers from the Southern states of Guerrero, Oaxaca, Veracruz, Puebla, and Hidalgo (SEDESOL

[5] Between 1985 and 1990, the interstate migration was 6% and for 2005 to 2010 was 4%.

2004). The recipient states are in the North—mainly Sinaloa, Sonora, Baja California, and Baja California Sur. By exclusively looking at growth within a region, one will overestimate the benefits of pre-existing residents and estimate a higher increase in income disparity in Mexico because of NAFTA.

Arends-Kuenning et al. (2020) find that the effects of trade liberalization, such as regional transportation benefits, have slightly increased migration towards the US–Mexico border. This evidence agrees with Krugman and Livas-Elizondo's (1996) finding that trade leads to more migration because the US market appears to be increasing in importance. One of the latest researches (Arends-Kuenning et al. 2019) studies whether migration has increased in response to increased U.S.-Mexico trade and explores factors that facilitate and hinder labor mobility within Mexico.

Unlike earlier work, to identify the effect of NAFTA on internal migration, Arends-Kuenning et al. (2019) estimate the effect of trade openness on the economic activity of different sectors in different locations; then, they estimate the effect of this activity on migration. In this way, they explicitly measure the effect of NAFTA on migration through its effect on regional economic output. Second, they use migration flows at the state-to-district level (instead of the state-to-state level that used previous studies) to identify the relationship between trade and internal migration more clearly. Using spatial state-district level regressions increases the number of observations and the ability to observe geographic patterns. Finally, they explicitly control the spatial nature of the data by using a spatial econometric gravity model of origin-destination flows (LeSage and Pace 2008).

As a result, from previous studies and especially from the latest study (Arends-Kuenning et al. 2019), we conclude that trade openness has increased internal migration in Mexico. But the trade openness effect has diminished across time since Mexico has followed a trade openness policy ever since it joined the GATT in 1986. They also found that the Mexican labor migration to the USA instead of reducing (due to the increase in migration costs and border security), has increased, especially due to the stable US economic growth, especially years after NAFTA, that attracted more Mexican migration (Luckstead et al. 2012). This agrees with Audley et al. (2004), which expected to see a "hump" on Mexican migration to the USA after a trade agreement. This finding contradicts what Aroca and Maloney (2005) discovered: FDI and trade deter Mexico's out-migration.

Arends-Kuenning et al. (2019) also find other discoveries like increased rural-to-urban migration after NAFTA[6] and how other factors influence migration, such as income disparities in origin and destination regions decreased migration. In addition, investment in infrastructure attracts labor, while the lack of it generates out-migration.

[6]Like Aguayo Tellez (2005).

5 Specialization

Economic inequality has been a challenge throughout Mexico's history (Lomelí Vanegas 2012). It represents a problem with social, political, and economic implications. According to the World Bank, the Gini index in Mexico reached its highest point (since 1990) in 1996 (54.8) and has been declining until then, reaching 45.4 in 2018.[7] Also, Esquivel (2015) mentions that Mexico belongs to the 25% of countries with the highest rate of inequality in the world. In the face of this background of inequality in Mexico, it is necessary to promote public policies that reduce the gap between rich and poor. Specialization could reduce the asymmetry between regions by promoting economic growth and development and increasing the productivity of the less developed regions.

Specialization can foster competitiveness among firms of the same sector, considering that they have a common market. However, this can be challenging for new firms with competitive disadvantages, making them vulnerable against large firms with an established market, suppliers, and customers. In this context, small firms face high entry barriers. In contrast, clustering may cause a market saturation and thus a price reduction. If a region specializes in a certain product, a market saturation can originate competition between producers in terms of prices. The increase of competition (and thus the price reduction) would cause those companies that exceed the market price to leave the market, leading to an oligopolistic market. Consequently, over-saturation of the market would lead to price competition between companies without focusing on achieving innovation or improving the product (Pacheco-Vega 2007).

Also, there is the risk of over-specialization. That means that if most regional production is concentrated in a sector and that industry collapses, the risk of the region's economy being heavily affected increases (Palazuelos 2005). Finally, a large proportion of the economic policy of clusters implies long-term processes that evaluate these policies highly difficult (Navarro 2003). However, despite the risks that exist for markets, the government is an actor that regulates and monitors the markets.

Several case studies in Mexico analyze the effects of different factors in specialized regions. Some of them are Unger (2003), Unger and Chico (2004), Dávila Flores (2008), Pérez and Palacio (2009), and Monge (2012). However, none of them analyzes the impact of specialization on regional economic growth. Only some works analyzed this impact. Díaz-Dapena et al. (2019) find that specialization plays an important role in Mexico's regional economic growth. Conclusion: Better policies fostering specialization, especially through tradable sectors (i.e., manufacturing), will help avoid regional disparities and create more even regional economic growth. In a regional efficiency study, Alvarez et al. (2017) find that states

---

[7] See https://data.worldbank.org/indicator/SI.POV.GINI?locations=MX accessed on May 16, 2020.

with more specialized economic activity increase output. This also enhances regional economic growth.

As a result, specialization has positively impacted on the region for the Mexican case since it promotes product innovation and competitiveness among firms in the same sector, improves concentration, lowers transaction costs, and impels foreign trade. However, it is worth mentioning that specialization does not imply market concentration or relies on a single regional economic activity. The role of the state, as discussed above, must consider that specialization leads to greater economic growth. Therefore, it must encourage specialization in different productive sectors. In this sense, specialization can be achieved in different economic sectors in the same region. This would transform a municipality or region into a diversified and specialized area.

The conclusions of these studies have far-reaching implications for public policies. Mainly, the results suggest that a region should focus on a unique sector. It must look for the specialization of sectors to increase its economic activity and regional economic development. Therefore, as mentioned before, regional economic policymakers must seek to specialize. And that they should do a rigorous analysis of the municipality's conditions before promoting a strategy of clusters as a trigger for regional economic development.

6 Economic Integration and Regional Convergence

Economic integration has a positive impact on the gains of international economics (Paelinck and Polèse 1999). For this reason, it has taken a very important role in the regional economic development literature in the last years. One method to make sure all different regions benefit from economic integration, and there is no evolution of disparities among regions, is using spatial conditional β-convergence.

Among the many papers on convergence applied to the case of Mexico, the following stand out for being the most recent and for their use of more advanced estimation techniques: Díaz-Dapena et al. (2017, 2019), López-González (2016), Rodríguez-Benavides et al. (2016a, b, c), Mendoza and Valdivia (2016), Asuad and Quintana (2010), Carrion-i-Silvestre and Germán-Soto (2009), Gómez and Ventosa-Santaularia (2009), Pedroza et al. (2009), Villarreal and Tykhonenko (2007), Aroca et al. (2005), Chiquiar (2005), Rodríguez-Pose and Sánchez-Reaza (2005), Esquivel and Messmacher (2002), Esquivel et al. (2002) and Sánchez-Reaza and Rodríguez-Pose (2002). Particularly, Sánchez-Reaza and Rodríguez-Pose (2002), Rodríguez-Pose and Sánchez-Reaza (2005), Villarreal and Tykhonenko (2007), and Gómez and Ventosa-Santaulària (2009), found that Mexican States doing more trade with the USA grew faster than others, but that there was no significant change in this pattern after NAFTA was signed. However, they do find evidence that the economic pull of Mexico City lessened after entering NAFTA, lending support to the hypothesis that trade has decreased agglomeration in Mexico. Gómez and Ventosa-Santaulària (2009) underline that trade reforms negatively affected Mexico City and the poorest states in Mexico, while López-González (2016), Rodríguez-Benavides et al. (2016c), Pedroza et al. (2009), Chiquiar (2005) and Carrion-i-Silvestre and German-Soto (2009) find convergence, but mainly during the 1980s, which is to say that while a convergence process continued after NAFTA, it was less intense. They also find that (richer) Northern States converged faster than the rest of the country, widening the disparity between the Northern States and the rest of the country. This divergence among North and South of Mexico is particularly explored by Esquivel et al. (2002). Rodríguez-Benavides et al. (2016b) find evidence of relative convergence, forming six convergence clubs, when analyzing the period 1970–2012. These results agreed with Rodríguez-Benavides et al. (2016c) where, using a period of 70 years (1940 to 2010), find signs of convergence for the period 1940–1985, but no-evidence of convergence for 1986–2010. Rodríguez-Benavides et al. (2016a) also find divergence across time on all the Mexican states: Only the richer 11 states present convergence during the 1980s period. In contrast, Aroca et al. (2005) do not find that NAFTA substantially changed growth patterns in Mexico, and instead argue that agglomeration has emerged in the form of several income clusters. Similar conclusions were reached by Valdez (2019), Díaz-Dapena et al. (2017) and Baylis et al. (2012), although, different from previous work, they use a spatial growth model and municipal level data.

Apart from Baylis et al. (2012), Díaz-Dapena et al. (2017), and Valdez (2019), the rest of the previously mentioned empirical studies use state-level data, which masks the spatial distribution of economic activity and severely restricts the number of observations. Only Díaz-Dapena et al. (2019), applies this approach to municipal data to observe the intra-state differences that may be occurring. The main sources of agglomeration externalities arise from improved opportunities for labor market pooling, knowledge interactions, specialization, the sharing of inputs and outputs, and the existence of public goods. As the scale and density of urban and industrial agglomerations grow, the external benefits available to companies are also expected to increase (Graham 2006).

Studies done until now agree with each other and show that the integration process has significantly changed the economic activity in Mexico. The results found so far also agree with Paelinck and Polèse (1999) that economic integration has increased regional disparities for the case of Mexico. In addition, there is evidence of a lack of convergence after the signing of NAFTA, increasing regional disparities. There are also proofs that proximity to the USA-Mexico border affects convergence: those places closer to the US border have a higher convergence speed than their counterparts in all the other regions.

As in the other sections, these results highlight the need for a regional development policy; otherwise, regional disparities will continue increasing over time. This policy should foster infrastructure, education, and specialization, especially in those regions that have not converged, such as the south. In addition, however, it would be interesting to analyze how the new political and economic changes in the USA and Mexico since 2017 have affected the regional economic development in Mexico. For this reason, it will be necessary to study how the regional economic development (and the regional divergence) behave under these new scenarios once the data at the municipal level is available.

7 Road Infrastructure and RED

One of the main factors that influence RED is infrastructure, especially road infrastructure. In previous studies, we have seen how market proximity obtained through investment in road infrastructure fosters economic activity in the presence of trade openness (Baylis et al. 2012). Moreover, this investment generates agglomeration and increases productivity: those locations that get better market access (through investment in infrastructure) become more attractive to firms and FDI, which become more productive, concentrate economic growth, generate regional economic development, and, as a result, increased the living standards of the people on the region (Blankespoor et al. 2017).

Mexico experienced large roads in the last decades, mainly from the Federal government (Bess 2014, 2016a, b, 2017). For this reason, Mexico is an excellent place to study how this investment triggered regional economic development and to what sectors and individuals benefited. It is also important to observe how trade openness combine with road investment helped the economic growth in certain areas. Therefore, this section discusses some of the studies done analyzing this factor. One of the latest studies is Blankespoor et al. (2017), which studies how roads influence economic activity in Mexico. Blankespoor et al. (2017) find that road infrastructure has a positive and significant effect on specialization, which, as discussed previously, boost economic activity. These results also agree with Duran-Fernandez and Santos (2014a, b), who find that road infrastructure enhances productivity in Mexico's manufacturing sector. This also fosters regional economic activity. These results agree with previous studies like Calderón et al. (2015), who find that a 10% investment in infrastructure increases GDP per capita between 0.7 and 1%. Due to the lack of infrastructure in Latin-America, the impact is higher (Blankespoor et al. 2017).

Consequently, investing in road infrastructure fosters economic activity, especially in those regions that are left behind. Also, developing nations, such as China and Mexico, are experiencing an increase in transportation demand that must be taken advantage of (Kaack et al. 2018). Thus, Mexico could take this opportunity to boost the economic activity in those regions that are lagging.

There have been other studies on Mexico's road infrastructure. However, there is still a lack of researches that analyzes issues like how railroads[8] and maritime and airports influence economic activity in Mexico. In addition, most of the studies focus on the USA, Canada, and Europe, but not on developing countries.

[8] Also, due to environmental concerns, we should explore shifting as much freight as possible, from road to rail transportation (Kaack et al. 2018).

As a conclusion of this section, we observed that investments in road infrastructure boost Mexico's economic growth through increased trade, structural transformation, and agglomeration. Moreover, this investment helps creating better trade networks and facilitates the mobility of goods and labor at a lower cost and time. Thus, these studies confirm that investment in infrastructure can help less favored municipalities achieve regional economic development.

8 RED Challenges for the New Government

The new president of Mexico, Andres Manuel Lopez Obrador (AMLO), took office on December 1, 2018, and in his inauguration speech, he asked to leave the neoliberalism that had caused so many problems and so much corruption (Mares 2018). Indeed, the model that we have followed has not helped reduce poverty and regional, sectoral, and income disparities in recent years. On the contrary, it has increased them. But we were not told what role model the government would follow. And apparently, the recipe that the president has continued after two years continues to be purely neoliberal (Flórez-Ramírez 2018).

Nevertheless, can we assume that leaving neoliberalism means that Mexico will enter Marxism? Is that what the new government is trying to pursue? In the next paragraphs, we will confront the new government's plan with the effect on RED across Mexico and Mexico's challenges in the next years.

Marxism plays a fundamental role in local and regional development as it studies the correct allocation of production factors (land, labor, capital, and entrepreneurial skills). Capitalism also studies the correct allocation of the factors of production. But for Marxism, the allocation and valorization of labor play a fundamental part. Marxism sought the most efficient allocation of each labor unit to the process where it provides the best profit (utility). Logically, the payment is given to the worker to attract him and make sure he does not go with the competition, also comes into play. It is always seeking to improve the economic well-being of all people and, in this way, society.

Another fundamental factor that comes into play is the factor's mobility (Pike et al. 2016). Especially (again) the workforce. Not only national but also international. Since the early 1900s, people began to migrate to places where there was work, better pay, security, infrastructure, and possibilities for development. The world wars did not help much either in that respect, as people left unsafe places for places where they could grow professionally. This made for an attraction towards growth poles such as the USA or Argentina. Mexico and the US governments created the "Brasero program" (from 1942 to 1964), where many Mexicans migrated to the USA to help Americans produce whatever was necessary to win the war. Most Mexican worked in agriculture. The Mexicans were expected to return to Mexico at the end of the program. But most stayed there, causing the first wave of illegal migrants from Mexico to the USA (Hanson 2006).

In the same way, growth poles were also created, such as rural areas in Mexico where there was no possibility of obtaining work or having growth and where most of the young people migrated to the big cities. This generated economic, social, gender, and even ethnic disparities. Thus, the marxist economic policy focuses on external forces transforming the economy and social change in localities and regions (Pike et al. 2016).

In Mexico, this created a "black hole:" Mexico City grew insatiably at the expense of the surrounding regions. But it created a lack of growth on the periphery. Everything that was produced in the province was to satisfy the growth of Mexico City. Even the human factor from any part of the provinces decided to migrate to Mexico City because it was the only place that offered a stable and secure job. Without knowing that even within Mexico City, an income disparity was brewing between the various social classes, which would lead to the Tlatelolco massacre (which we will explain later). This caused decades of regional disparities that only came to a minority with the North American Free Trade Agreement (NAFTA). Although it created a new regional disparity: the border states began to grow rapidly, leaving the rest of the country behind (Sánchez-Reaza and Rodríguez-Pose 2002).

During the late 1960s through the 1980s, the structural changes caused by capitalism created a renewed interest in Marxism. The growth disparity that caused countries in the Northern Hemisphere to grow while countries in the Southern Hemisphere lagged was believed to be due to colonialism and the capital system that came with it (Pike et al. 2016). The force of Marxist perspectives then fell on the study of classes and their problems. Mainly in its economic problems and how they can be solved through political institutions addressing these problems. That is why the role of the state is so important in Marxism. This was what caused various social groups to take up arms in 1967 in France and Chile. This was reflected in the student uprising (better known as the 1968-movement), which ended in the "Plaza de las 3 Culturas" massacre on October 2, 1968. Hence, the Marxist movements began to fade to the point that, by the end of 1969, there was no longer the same force.

The neo-Marxist ideas began in the 1970s, where political reductionism and a movement towards the social bases of power are sought, without an armed struggle, but rather, a social analysis of adaptation. It is of interest the concern for issues as important (and essential) as housing for society. Since it was thought that housing was an emphasis towards "tenure policy." The state's political power over private capital stands out to provide housing to all social groups (Kemeny 2013).

In the 1980s, the Marxist theory of the state came to life, particularly in ideological terms where the return to the state is sought again. But unfortunately, for the Mexican case, this never happened. On the contrary, they only sought to solve the problems in the short term, which was detonated in the armed uprising of the EZLN in Chiapas on January 1, 1994.

It is through examples such as Mexico that Marxism interpreted economic growth as episodes of convergence and divergence. Thus, criticizing neoliberalism creates these geographic disparities and fragmentation in different social classes (Pike et al. 2016). For example, this is what caused the uprising in arms of the Zapatista Army in Chiapas in 1994: Seeing so much disparity, so much class struggle, and the ignorance of the federal government headed by President Carlos Salinas de Gortari towards the problems of Chiapas, an armed group decided to rise in arms and take several municipalities. For these same reasons that Neo-Marxism became so important in the late 1960s in Mexico.

We can conclude, for this section, that both Marxism and Neo-Marxism of the twenty-first century seek a large State that influences, as a political instrument and mediator, in the search and satisfaction of the interests of society. But it is no longer a Marxism like that of Marx and Engel, which sought to liberate the workers from the yoke of the capitalists (bourgeoisie) through the revolution. Rather, it is a Marxism that measures its forces to seek, from the state's economic policy, to intervene, as an arbitrator, in which the minimum standards for the workers are met. Thus, ensuring that societies are cared for. Especially the low-income groups. It is what is now known as a paternalistic state or social capitalism.

As I have tried to explain, neoliberalism is concerned with economic growth, income, regional disparities, and convergence. We colloquially call "free markets," where international trade and comparative advantages are key to success. In a way, Marxism is also concerned with economic growth. But it focuses on the division of labor and on monitoring the equity of benefits to workers. Thus, both ideologies are not opposites or substitutes for each other. Rather, they are complementary: one needs the other because while neoliberalism is concerned with economic growth, it neglects its inequalities in its wake. Marxism worries that the lower social classes do not lack anything. It is like capitalism with a paternalistic state or social Neoliberalism.

History has shown us that either of these two ideologies alone does not guarantee a good result. That is why Mexico will have to get the best of each one and adapt it to our case, "Tropicalize it to our environment," because each of them has shown us failures. Flaws that the other ideology has tried to correct. And that, as a conclusion, we have to look for the resources and capacities that we have so that (under a neoliberal social model) we look for our comparative advantages and thus achieve sustainable economic growth. And that, with strong institutions, we achieve a paternalistic State that implements social programs that manage to correct the market failures that cause these disparities (regional, income, and sectoral). But that we cannot only focus on creating social programs since we would have a fiscal deficit, and the new administration has been hectic to increase taxes to have a balanced budget. It has taken decisions to reduce government expenditure instead. Therefore, we have to grow the economy first to collect more taxes and then create social programs and monitor effectiveness. As Antonio Solá, political strategist, said, "govern the business community with the right hand [using a neoliberal model] and the sectors and social programs with the left [using a Marxist model]." That is why the best model that AMLO could follow, but has not followed, is a Social Democratic government, which considers the private property of capitalism and the private initiative of neoliberalism. But continues to care about society, especially the most vulnerable.

During the last 2 years, Mexico has experienced a recession that has been worsened by the COVID pandemic in most of 2020, creating a severe economic crisis. Unfortunately, the second wave of infections in October 2020 forecast that the economic recovery will take many years to recover the GDP Mexico reached in 2018. OECD (2020) forecast that Mexico will have a GDP growth in 2020 of −9% and unemployment will reach 8.5%. These will create a heavy burden on RED in Mexico. There will be more regional disparities. Regions that have had stable growth in the last years (i.e., the US–Mexico border region, the Bajio) will continue growing at a lower phase. But regions with low (or no) economic growth in the last decade will lag further. These will create a larger diversion among regions. These effects will also be noticed among sectors: tradable sectors will reactivate faster than non-tradable sectors, leaving a large disparity. This will also create a larger internal migration than the one seen before. People will leave south/rural areas for north/urban areas, close to the border, search for better and more secure income. Unfortunately, AMLO's administration has not presented a regional policy to foster economic growth in those regions lagging. Neither have they presented a regional policy to counteract this pandemic. This lack of a real regional policy will create an even lengthier recuperation and heavier regional disparities. Therefore, the challenge facing the new future is to have a regional policy focused on regions, sectors, and individuals more vulnerable to the crisis. As Ascani et al. (2012) mention, Mexico should focus on a devolution: to transfer the central power to a more local/regional administration to reach regional economic growth and avoid regional disparities. No better entity knows the needs of the region than their local government. Without a regional policy, at a local level, Mexico will only increase its spatial inequalities. Therefore, It is impossible to reach RED in the future without a devolution. To analyze the challenge each region and sector faces in the next decade to tackle it and reach RED.

9 Conclusions

As discussed in this chapter, many factors influence Regional Economic Development in Mexico. Here I focused only on a few of them. First, we discussed how trade openness increased regional disparities, increased internal migration and migration to the USA, and reduced wage inequalities, evading an even regional economic development. Second, regions closer to the US border, which tend to be wealthier, benefited more from trade to grow faster than other regions. Similarly, those regions with pre-existing export industries, such as the Northern manufacturing centers, benefited the most from trade. Third, the urban labor market benefited more (than labor in rural regions) because of their higher reliance on skilled wages, whereas rural labor tends to work more in agriculture and often consumes most of what they produce. Finally, we observed an increasing inter-regional wage disparity, which induced more internal migration and migration to the USA.

We observe that trade liberalization reduced wage inequalities, leading to a smaller regional polarization. However, large traded sectors also induced migration, particularly for the poor, and offered a higher wage overall, increasing wage inequality because it has only benefited workers in traded sectors but not in non-traded sectors. Potential policy implications are that investment in manufacturing can be used as means to ease regional wage inequality. The evidence also suggests that policies that facilitate internal migration will benefit economic growth and reduce income inequality. However, those policies should have broad access to make sure it reaches all household and regions. In this way, it will avoid increasing inequality among households and regions.

Trade openness has increased internal migration in Mexico. But the effect of trade openness has diminished across time since Mexico has followed a trade openness policy ever since it joined the GATT in 1986. We also learned that Mexican labor migration to the USA instead of reducing (due to the increase in migration costs and border security) has increased, especially due to the stable US economic growth, especially years after NAFTA, attracting more migrants. Also, we learned about an increase in rural-to-urban migration after NAFTA and how other factors influence migration: income disparities in origin and destination regions decreased migration. The policy implication of this is that investing in infrastructure will attract labor.

We learn that Mexico benefited from specialization in the region since it promotes product innovation and competitiveness among firms in the same sector, improves concentration, lowers transaction costs, and impels foreign trade. The policy implications of these results are that Mexico's regions should focus on a unique sector to increase its economic activity and regional economic development. But, a rigorous analysis of the conditions of each municipality should be done before promoting a strategy of clusters as a trigger for regional economic development.

From the convergence studies, we learned that there is a lack of convergence after the signing of NAFTA, increasing regional disparities. And that proximity to the US–Mexico border affects convergence. Therefore, there is a need for a regional development policy since the regional disparities will continue increasing over time. This policy should foster infrastructure, education, and specialization, especially in those regions that have not converged, such as the south.

We observed that investments in road infrastructure boost Mexico's economic growth through increased trade, structural transformation, and agglomeration. Moreover, this investment helps create better trade networks and facilitates the mobility of goods and labor at a lower cost and time. Thus, these studies confirm that investment in infrastructure can help less favored municipalities achieve regional economic development.

Finally, we also notice that the current federal administration does not count with a regional policy. And that the lack of it during the recession and the pandemic Mexico has suffered in the last year will hinder the RED of most of the Mexican regions for the next years. The situation Mexico is having in the last two years will increase the spatial inequalities across the nation. To avoid that, Mexico should create a regional policy focus on devolution. This will let each region focus on their comparative advantages, create programs that will allow them to face their problems better, and reach sustainable economic growth faster.

This chapter has some limitations. For example, it does not study the impact climate has on regional economic development. This is because there are no studies yet analyzing this impact in Mexico. I have also left out the studies done about how security, or lack of it, has also influenced regional economic development. For this topic, I recommend Alvarez et al. (2017), Nuñez et al. (2017), Garduño-Rivera and Nuñez (2014), Nuñez and Garduño (2014), among others.

Bibliography

Aguayo-Tellez E (2005) Rural–Urban migration in the 1990s Mexico: switching the 'Ejido' for the 'Maquiladora'. In: Rice University, economics. Unpublished, Houston

Airola J (2008) A regional analysis of the impact of trade and foreign direct investment on wages in Mexico, 1984–2000. Rev Dev Econ 12(2):276–290

Alvarez A, Garduño-Rivera R, Nuñez HM (2017) Mexico's North-South divide: The regional distribution of state inefficiency 1988–2008. Papers in Regional Science 96(4):843–858

Anderson JE, Van Wincoop E (2004) Trade costs. J Econ Lit 42(3):691–751

Anzaldo C, Hernández J, Rivera A (2008) Migración interna, distribución territorial de la población y desarrollo sustentable. Consejo Nacional de Población, La situación demográfica de México:129–141

Arends-Kuenning M, Baylis K, Garduño-Rivera R (2019) The effect of NAFTA on internal migration in Mexico: a regional economic analysis. Appl Econ 51(10):1052–1068

Arends-Kuenning M, Baylis K, Garduño-Rivera R (2020) Effect of tariff liberalization on Mexico's income distribution in the presence of migration. Under review at Applied Geography

Aroca P, Maloney WF (2005) Migration, trade, and foreign direct investment in Mexico. World Bank Econ Rev 19(3):449–472

Aroca P, Bosch M, Maloney WF (2005) Spatial dimensions of trade liberalization and economic convergence: Mexico 1985–2002. World Bank Econ Rev 19(3):345–378

Ascani A, Crescenzi R, Iammarino S (2012) Regional economic development. A Review, SEARCH WP01/03, pp 2–26

Asuad Sanén N, Quintana Romero L (2010) Crecimiento económico, convergencia y concentración económica espacial en las entidades federativas de México 1970-2008

Audley JJ, Demetrios PG, Polaski S, Vaughan S (2004) NAFTA's promise and reality: lessons from Mexico for the hemisphere. Carnegie Endowment for International Peace, Washington, DC

Baylis K, Garduño-Rivera R, Piras G (2012) The distributional effects of NAFTA in Mexico: evidence from a panel of municipalities. Reg Sci Urb Econ 42(1–2):286–302

Beaulieu E, Benarroch M, Gaisford J (2004) Intra-industry trade liberalization, wage inequality, and trade policy preferences. University of Calgary Discussion Paper, 6

Bess M (2014) Routes of conflict: building roads and shaping the nation of Mexico, 1941-1952. J Transp Hist 35(1):78–96

Bess M (2016a) Revolutionary paths: motor roads, economic development, and national sovereignty in the 1920s and 1930s Mexico. Mexican Stud/Estudios Mexicanos 32(1):56–82

Bess M (2016b) 'Neither motorists nor pedestrians obey the rules': transit law, public safety, and the policing of Northern Mexico's roads, the 1920s-1950s. J Transp Hist 37(2):155–174

Bess M (2017) Routes of conflict: building roads and shaping the nation of Mexico, 1917-1952. University of Nebraska Press, 246 p

Blankespoor B, Bougna T, Garduno-Rivera R, Selod H (2017) Roads and the geography of economic activities in Mexico. The World Bank

Calderón C, Moral-Benito E, Servén L (2015) Is infrastructure capital productive? A dynamic heterogeneous approach. J Appl Econometr 30(2):177–198

Carrion-i-Silvestre JL, German-Soto V (2009) Panel data stochastic convergence analysis of the Mexican regions. Empir Econ 37(2):303–327

Chiquiar D (2005) Why Mexico's regional income convergence broke down. J Dev Econ 77 (1):257–275

Cragg MI, Epelbaum M (1996) Why has wage dispersion grown in Mexico? Is it the incidence of reforms or the growing demand for skills? J Dev Econ 51(1):99–116
Dávila Flores A (2008) Los clusters industriales del noreste de México (1993-2003): Perspectivas de desarrollo en el marco de una mayor integración económica con Texas. Región y sociedad 20(41):57–88
Díaz-Dapena A, Fernández-Vázquez E, Garduño-Rivera R, Rubiera-Morollón F (2017) Does trade imply convergence? Analyzing the effect of NAFTA on local convergence in Mexico. El Trimestre Económico 84(1):103–120
Díaz-Dapena A, Fernández-Vázquez E, Garduño-Rivera R, Rubiera-Morollon F (2019) Economic integration and regional convergence: effects of NAFTA on local convergence in Mexico, 1980–2008. Appl Econ 1-13
Duran-Fernandez R, Santos G (2014a) Road infrastructure spillovers on the manufacturing sector in Mexico. Res Transp Econ 46:17–29
Duran-Fernandez R, Santos G (2014b) Regional convergence, road infrastructure, and industrial diversity in Mexico. Res Transp Econ 46:103–110
Dziembała M (2018) The economic and social cohesion of the NAFTA countries–selected aspects and policy recommendations. Int Bus Global Econ 2018(Tom 37): 493–505
Esquivel G (2000) Geografía y desarrollo económico en México. Inter-American Development Bank
Esquivel G (2015) Desigualdad extrema en México: concentración del poder económico y político. Reporte de Oxfam México 23:1–43
Esquivel G, Messmacher M (2002) Sources of regional (non) convergence in Mexico. World Bank Report
Esquivel G, Lederman D, Messmacher M, Villoro R (2002) Why NAFTA did not reach the South. World Bank, Washington, DC
Esquivel G, Rodriguez-López JA (2003) Technology, trade, and wage inequality in Mexico before and after NAFTA. J Dev Econ 72(2):543–565
Feenstra RC, Hanson GH (1996). Globalization, outsourcing, and wage inequality (No. w5424). National Bureau of Economic Research
Feliciano ZM (2001) Workers and trade liberalization: the impact of trade reforms in Mexico on wages and employment. ILR Rev 55(1):95–115
Flores M, Zey M, Hoque N (2013) Economic liberalization and contemporary determinants of Mexico's internal migration: an application of spatial gravity models. Spat Econ Anal 8 (2):195–214
Flórez-Ramírez G (2018, December 11) Ímpetu Económico. Obtained from El Economista. https:// www.eleconomista.com.mx/opinion/AMLO-y-el-neoliberalismo-20181211-0018.html
Garduño-Rivera R, Nuñez H (2014) Evaluación Económica Del Efecto Regional de Las Drogas Ilícitas En México. Colección de Cuadernos de Trabajo Del Programa de Política de Drogas, México
Gómez M, Ventosa-Santaulària D (2009) Liberación comercial y convergencia regional del ingreso en México. El Trimestre Económico:215–235
Graham DJ (2006) Wider economic benefits of transport improvements-link between agglomeration and productivity-stage 2 report
Hanson GH (2003) What has happened to wages in Mexico since NAFTA? (No. w9563). National Bureau of Economic Research
Hanson GH (2006) Illegal migration from Mexico to the United States. J Econ Lit 44(4):869–924
Hanson, G. H. (2007). Globalization, labor income, and poverty in Mexico. In: Globalization and poverty. University of Chicago Press, pp 417–456
Hanson GH, Harrison A (1999) Trade liberalization and wage inequality in Mexico. ILR Rev 52 (2):271–288
Harrison, A. (2007). Globalization and poverty: an introduction. In: Globalization and poverty. University of Chicago Press, pp 1–32.
INEGI (2008) Catálogo de entidades, municipios y localidades

Kaack LH et al (2018) Decarbonizing intraregional freight systems with a focus on modal shift. Environ Res Lett 13(8): 083001
Kemeny J (2013) Housing and social theory. Routledge
Krugman P (1991) Increasing returns and economic geography. J Polit Econ 99(3):483–499
Krugman P, Elizondo RL (1996) Trade policy and the third world metropolis. J Dev Econ 49 (1):137–150
LeSage JP, Pace RK (2008) Spatial econometric modeling of origin-destination flows. J Reg Sci 48 (5):941–967
Lomelí Vanegas L (2012) Interpretaciones sobre el desarrollo económico de México en el siglo XX. Economía UNAM 9(27):91–108
López-González JÁ (2016) El proceso de convergencia regional en México: un análisis de la dinámica de transición bajo heterogeneidad estatal y temporal (No. TESG 002). CIDE, División de Economía
Luckstead J, Devadoss S, Rodriguez A (2012) The effects of North American Free Trade Agreement and United States farm policies on illegal immigration and agricultural trade. J Agric Appl Econ 44(1):1–19
Mares MA (2018, December 3) El Economista. Obtained from El Economista: https://www.eleconomista.com.mx/opinion/AMLO-fin-del-modelo-neoliberal-20181203-0016.html
Mendoza González MÁ, Valdivia López M (2016) Remesas, crecimiento y convergencia regional en México: aproximación con un modelo panel-espacial. Estudios Económicos (México, DF) 31 (1):125–167
Mercenier J, Schmitt N (2002, November) A simple general equilibrium model with international labour market linkages. In: HRDC-IC workshop on Social and Labour Market Aspects of North American Linkages, Montreal
Mishra P (2007) Emigration and wages in source countries: evidence from Mexico. J Dev Econ 82 (1):180–199
Monge MF (2012) Análisis de la cadena productiva de Tequila: El caso de Jalisco, Bachelor's degree thesis. Economics Department. UAM-Azcapotzalco, pp 1–69
Navarro M (2003) Análisis y políticas de clústeres: teoría y realidad. Ekonomiaz: Revista vasca de economía, No. 53(2003):14–49
Nicita A (2004) Who benefited from trade liberalization in Mexico? Measuring the effects on household welfare. The World Bank
Nicita A (2009) The price effect of tariff liberalization: measuring the impact on household welfare. J Dev Econ 89(1):19–27
Nuñez H, Garduño R (2014) Un análisis económico de la oferta de drogas ilícitas y de la política contra el narcotráfico en México en el periodo 2004-2009. Cuadernos de Trabajo del Seminario de Política de Drogas 2
Nuñez H, Paredes D, Garduño-Rivera R (2017) Is crime in Mexico a disamenity? Evidence from a hedonic valuation approach. Ann Reg Sci 59(1):171–187
OECD (2020) Mexico economic snapshot: economic snapshot of Mexico. Accessed October 20, 2020, from http://www.oecd.org/economy/mexico-economic-snapshot/
Pacheco-Vega R (2007) Una crítica del paradigma de desarrollo industrial mediante clústeres forzados. Estudios Sociológicos XXV 3:683–707
Paelinck JH, Polèse M (1999) Modelling the regional impact of continental economic integration: lessons from the European Union for NAFTA. Reg Stud 33(8):727–738
Palazuelos M (2005) Clusters: myth or realistic ambition for policy-makers? Local Econ 20 (2):131–140
Pedroza JD, Vargas AS, González MÁM (2009) Convergencia hacia la economía regional líder en México: un análisis de cointegración en panel. El Trimestre Económico:407–431
Pérez S, Palacio M (2009) Desarrollo regional y concentración industrial: Impacto en el empleo (1994-2004). In: Observatorio de la Economía Latinoamericana, no. 117
Pike A, Rodríguez-Pose A, Tomaney J (2016) Local and regional development. Routledge

Ranjan P (2008) Growth and inequality in closed and open economies: the role of the product cycle. BE J Econ Anal Policy 8(1)
Revenga A (1997) Employment and wage effects of trade liberalization: the case of Mexican manufacturing. J Labor Econ 15(S3):S20–S43
Robertson R (2000) Wage shocks and North American labor-market integration. Am Econ Rev 90 (4):742–764
Robertson R (2004) Relative prices and wage inequality: evidence from Mexico. J Int Econ 64 (2):387–409
Robertson R (2007) Trade and wages: two puzzles from Mexico. World Econ 30(9):1378–1398
Rodríguez-Benavides D, Mendoza-González MÁ, Venegas-Martínez F (2016a) ¿Realmente existe convergencia regional en México? Un modelo de datos-panel TAR no lineal. Economía, Sociedad y Territorio 16(50):197–227
Rodríguez-Benavides D, López-Herrera F, Mendoza-González M (2016b) Clubs de convergencia regional en México: un análisis a través de un modelo no lineal de un solo factor. Investigaciones Regionales-J Reg Res 34:7–22
Rodríguez-Benavides D, García JCT, González MÁM (2016c) Pair-wise approach to test the regional convergence hypothesis in Mexico. J Rev Global Econ 5:59–68
Rodríguez-Pose A, Sánchez-Reaza J (2005) Economic polarization through trade: trade liberalization and regional growth in Mexico. In: Kanbur R, Venables JA (eds) Spatial inequality and development. Oxford University Press
Rostow WW (1990) The stages of economic growth: a non-communist manifesto. Cambridge University Press
Sánchez-Reaza J, Rodríguez-Pose A (2002) The impact of trade liberalization on regional disparities in Mexico. Growth Change 33(1):72–90
SEDESOL (2004) Programa de Atención a Jornaleros Agrícolas. Secretaria de Desarrollo Social, Mexico City
Todaro MP, Smith SC (2011) Economic development 11. Pearson, Addison-Wesley. ISBN, 10, 0-13
Unger K (2003) Los clusters industriales en México: especializaciones regionales y la política industrial. Centro de Investigación y Docencia Económicas
Unger K (2005) Regional economic development and Mexican out-migration (No. w11432). National Bureau of Economic Research
Unger K, Chico R (2004) La industria automotriz en tres regiones de México. Un análisis de clusters El Trimestre Económico:909–941
Valdez RI (2019) Spatial diffusion of economic growth and externalities in Mexico. Investigaciones Regionales-J Reg Res 45
Vega D (2005) Migración interna: Dimensión, alcances y desafíos. Dirección General de Estudios Sociodemográficos y Prospectiva. Guanajuato, Gto.: Consejo Nacional de Población (CONAPO)
Villarreal CC, Tykhonenko A (2007) Convergencia regional e inversión extranjera directa en México en el contexto del TLCAN, 1994-2002. Investigación Económica:15–41
Walton M, López AG (2005) Pobreza en México una evaluación de las condiciones, tendencias y la estrategia de gobierno. En Breve 61:4–10

Identification and Spatial Hierarchy of Industrial Conglomerates with Census Data. A Suggested Procedure and Application to the Mexican Case of Study

Jesús A. Treviño C.

Abstract This study suggests a new methodological combination and sequence of existing techniques of spatial analysis to identify industrial conglomerates and set up their spatial hierarchy. The word "conglomerate" refers to the fusion of concentration and agglomeration processes of magnitude or intensity. In this research, concentration is the occurrence of high global values, regardless of their location. On the other hand, agglomeration is the concentration of adjacent high local values. Both agglomeration and concentration create conglomerates of magnitude or intensity when they are merged through a geographical overlay procedure. While magnitude refers to size, intensity refers to importance of the studied variable. For the first time in the study of the spatial pattern of manufactures, the spatial hierarchy is obtained by overlaying conglomerated and non-conglomerated high values of magnitude and intensity.

Potential benefits of the suggested procedure for an area-based public policy are illustrated by assessing industrial employment in 2352 and 2457 Mexican municipalities in 1998 and 2013, respectively. The suggested procedure in this study may easily be extended to identify spatial patterns of diseases, crime, poverty, aging population, pollution or environmental justice in different areas or countries.

Keywords Spatial analysis · Concentration · Agglomeration · Conglomerates · Spatial hierarchy of manufactures

---

J. A. Treviño C. (✉)
Universidad Autonoma de Nuevo Leon, Graduate Program of Urban Studies, School of Architecture, San Nicolás de los Garza, Nuevo León, Mexico
e-mail: jesus.trevinocn@uanl.edu.mx

A. de León-Arias, P. Aroca (eds.), *NAFTA's Impact on Mexico's Regional Development*, New Frontiers in Regional Science: Asian Perspectives 51,
https://doi.org/10.1007/978-981-16-3168-9_4

1 Introduction

1.1 Relevance and Preliminary Definitions

What is the spatial distribution of manufactures within a country or state? The answer to this question refers to the spatial pattern of industries. The interest for studying the spatial pattern of industries has recently been increasing because of its importance in focalizing decisions on local economic development (Kaygalak and Reid 2016; Jing and Cai 2010; Carroll et al. 2008).

Studying the spatial distribution of industries is important in identifying places to set up or stimulate activities; provide alternative locations for public infrastructure; design mechanisms of regulation and a portfolio of incentives; or support existing activities or encourage the creation of new industries. This knowledge is particularly relevant for big countries such as Mexico. The provision of transport infrastructure to the Mexican state of Chihuahua (247,460 km^2), for example, must cover an area similar to that of the United Kingdom (242,900 km^2). The same may be said for the state of Sonora (179,355 km^2) in relation to the Republic of Uruguay (176,215 km^2).

The expression "spatial pattern" in this study indicates the geographic distribution of a variable (e.g., industrial employment) in a specific moment (situation in t_0) and its locational change in a period of time (process from t_0 to t_1). This change is the geographic expression of the observed variable that expands, contracts, or keeps this distribution over time.

Three basic geometric elements represent the territorial distribution of the economic activity or any social or natural variable: lines or arches (e.g., winds, rivers, roads, migration flows or transport networks), dots (e.g., cities in the country), or polygons (e, g., state areas, counties, municipalities, census tracts). Individual or aggregated points or polygons, depending on the scale of resolution, generally represent social or economic variables (Wong and Lee 2005).

The spatial pattern of points or polygons representing an industrial variable may refer to its magnitude or intensity. Magnitude refers to "critical mass," quantity, number, size or volume of industry (spatially extended). Intensity gives the idea of grade, relevance, or importance of the activity (spatially intensive) (Goodchild and Lam 1980). Both magnitude and intensity may be expressed in absolute or relative terms.

The spatial pattern of magnitude or intensity of a variable, in relative or absolute terms, may be concentrated and/or agglomerated, dispersed or random. The present study clearly highlights that in spatial analysis: (a) concentration and agglomeration, because both refer to geographic space, may easily be confused or mixed up. In this research, concentration is not agglomeration, although both of them may simultaneously occur in space (Arbia 2001). And (b) concentration and agglomeration processes may overlap in space creating conglomerates of the variable. In this research, conglomerates are agglomerations of high local values extended by high global values located in their periphery. This spatial connotation of industrial conglomerates in this research is a term that has nothing in common with industrial conglomerates of multi-industry companies studied in the theory of industrial organization or industrial economy. The name refers to the merging of concentration and agglomeration processes.

Territorial concentration is the location of a variable in few areas, regardless their contiguity and it is measured by high *global* values (HGV). Agglomeration, on the other side, is the co-location process of high *local* values in adjacent areas (HLV).

Values are global when they consider the whole array of observations in the area of study and they are high because they are above a threshold value valid for all cases in the sample. On the other hand, values are local because they only refer to the surrounding areas and they are high in relation to the average of neighboring values.

1.2 The Present Study

This study overlays concentration (HGV) and agglomeration (HLV) to answer specific research questions on the spatial pattern of industrial location in a case study, such as where do industries locate within a given time period? This exploration does not look for descriptive answers but it seeks to gather elements to accomplish the following specific objective: to identify industrial conglomerates and set up their spatial hierarchy with a new approach and new methodological sequence.

The six sections in this research are specially organized to present and illustrate the suggested procedure. This first section presents the relevance, specific objective and general structure of the study. The second section concentrates on eight problems in spatial analysis which demand a methodology to simultaneously address them in spatial studies. They are the two traditional problems: MAUP and checkerboard problems. Besides these traditional problems, *form, location, and size* of the spatial units also complicate spatial analysis. Two seldom addressed issues are included: mismatch of the concentration and agglomeration processes, and intensity and magnitude effects. In this context, outliers and zero value cases are also reviewed. So far, there is no research recognizing them in the way they are articulated in this study. The third section presents the suggested methodology to deal with the eight problems previously presented in section two. The fourth section points out benefits and limitations of the suggested methodology applied to the Mexican case of study. The fifth section interprets and discuses results and presents main lessons from the case study. Finally, the sixth section concludes with a summary of the study, adds some final notes, and suggests future research directions.

Briefly, the study proposes a new procedure to identify and analyze spatial patterns of social or economic variables. This procedure is illustrated with industries in a case study.

2 Eight Problems in Spatial Analysis

In spatial analysis (spatial statistics) eight operative problems may affect the measures of the agglomeration and concentration processes. The operative problems may be grouped under two distinct topics: (a) Geometric attributes of polygons and (b) Value of the analyzed variable.

2.1 Geometric Attributes of Polygons

2.1.1 Modifiable Areal Unit Problem (MAUP)

MAUP refers to problems derived from scale and zoning. The scale problem refers to the inconsistency of results from a zone tabulated for units at a distinct level of aggregation, such as census tracts or blocks. The zoning problem, on the other side, relates to inconsistencies of values from different size units, arbitrarily delimited, with no social meaning. Census tracts in USA and AGEBs in Mexico are examples of arbitrary subdivisions because their boundaries are set up for census surveying. Zoning is problematic when it wrongly leads us to think that two industries in the same Census tract are more similar than those located in other areas. The use of techniques explicitly considering space, such as spatial autocorrelation, partially solves this problem.

2.1.2 The Checkerboard Problem

It occurs when the value of a specific spatial unit (e.g., persons occupied in manufactures, E_i, in a specific county) is analyzed neglecting the values of the same variable in its surrounding areas. As an example, let us assume that all counties in a country are black and white squares, as in a checkerboard, and they represent different levels or strata for the E_i variable. If all black squares were grouped on one side of the checkerboard and white squares on the opposite side, it would be reasonable to think that the territorial concentration of industry increases because the E_i in every county (square) is similar to that of its neighbor counties. Aspatial indices, such as the Coefficient of Variation, do not distinguish one pattern from the other one. Their values would be the same for the checkerboard or agglomerated distribution. If all spatial units were mixed up as in dominoes or a card deck, the index value obtained from any aspatial procedure would be the same. As in MAUP, spatial statistics techniques partially solve this problem.

2.1.3 Form, Location, and Size

At the strictly physical level, form, location, and size of polygons should be added to the classical Modifiable Areal Unit Problem (MAUP) and checkerboard problems in spatial analysis. Literature on these two issues is abundant but it is significantly reduced when the interest centers on the influence of the physical characteristics of polygons on spatial autocorrelation.

Geometric attributes may affect the contiguity matrix and, therefore, the spatial autocorrelation value. In general, mixing large and small polygons, more compact (less elongated) polygons have fewer neighbors (less links in the contiguity matrix). On the contrary, the number of neighbors in the contiguity matrix increases if the index of location (near to the center of the study area) is larger, the area (size or scale) of the polygon is bigger, and the roughness of the perimeter is larger (Zhang 2008). However, there may be groups of large polygons and groups of small polygons inside a case study, as in the west and east of the USA, respectively. The group of larger areas may have greater impact on the contiguity matrix because they have fewer neighbors and, therefore, accentuate any effect (Frizado et al. 2009).

The number of links is an important input datum to measure spatial autocorrelation but is not the only one. The final impact of the number of neighbors depends on the value of the variable in the surrounding areas. If the value of the variable in the neighboring areas is high and the number of links is low, the average will be high. If, on the other hand, the number of links is high, the probability of including a low value neighbor increases and, thereby, the average of the surrounding values decreases. The influence of the physical characteristics of polygons on the matrix of contiguities and, therefore, on the measurement of spatial autocorrelation is a topic still open to debate.

2.1.4 Suggested Solutions for Geometric Attributes

MAUP and *checkerboard* problems demand the aggregation of similar units and the explicit consideration of space. Local spatial autocorrelation measurements partially address these two requirements. Additionally, standardized matrices in spatial autocorrelation (Rogerson and Yamada 2009; Moro and Villa 2016) or transferring the information to a regular grid may prevent distortions caused by physical characteristics of polygons (Li and Monzur 2017).

2.2 *Value of the Variable*

When variable values are considered, the following elements affect measurements of agglomeration and concentration processes: (1) Presence of atypical and extreme values, including zeros in the database; (2) Simultaneous occurrence of the concentration and agglomeration processes; and (3) Effects of intensity and magnitude.

2.2.1 Atypical and Extreme Values, Including Zeros

The presence of atypical and/or extreme values generates instability in the variation of the information. Rates or ratios to measure intensity or absolute values to measure magnitude may lead to instability in the variations of the indicator. This instability stems from the overvaluation of intensity in small economies and its undervaluation or omission in large and diversified economies. Magnitude, measured in absolute terms (e.g., number of employees), generates instability in the variance when the weight exerted by the most industrialized areas minimizes or causes the small economies to disappear from the map. In small economies, not necessarily small areas, usually only one or a few activities dominate the local economic structure. These instabilities may produce misguided taxonomies based on spatial association and generate spurious values of local spatial autocorrelation (Anselin et al. 2007; Kaygalak and Reid 2016).

In spatial autocorrelation, it is important to point out the effect of absent variable values (spatial units with zero value). A zero value may create the illusion that low local values are high local values. The "jump" from zero may cause a low local value to appear as a high local value when in fact it is low in the context of its neighboring values.[1]

2.2.2 Simultaneous Occurrence and Spatial Mismatch of Concentration and Agglomeration Processes

High Global Values (HGV) and High Local Values (HLV) also are called first-order and second-order effects, respectively. HGV follow a large-scale trend, the process of industrial concentration, for example. HLV are the result of spatial autocorrelation or deviations of local values from the large-scale trend, such as industrial agglomerations. When the concentration and agglomeration processes overlap each other, *some high global values detected by the concentration analysis* (by resampling or descriptive statistics) *may go unnoticed in agglomeration analysis that identifies high local values* (by spatial autocorrelation), and vice versa. High local values are not necessarily high values from the national or global perspective.[2] This mismatch

[1]Treviño (2016) presents a graphical explanation of these and other problems mentioned in this section.

[2]It is important to mention that the possibility of having high local values (HH hot spots and HL spatial outliers) increases when the original database is smoothed or standardized in a way that reduces the influence of atypical global cases (Zhang et al. 2008).

between HLV and HGV tells us that concentration and agglomeration processes are complementary.

2.2.3 Intensity and Magnitude Effects

While magnitude refers to the "critical mass" or quantity of the variable (i.e., number of employees in manufactures), intensity has to do with its superiority or dominance in reference to a norm or parameter. The variable that provides the measurable operational definition of the magnitude or intensity can be expressed in relative or absolute terms. What differentiates "absolute" from "relative" is the presence or absence of a benchmark (further details in Fracasso and Vittucci Marzetti 2018).

In Exploratory Spatial Data Analysis, besides measuring intensity, it is also advisable to consider magnitude to "control the intensity effect" (overvaluation of small economies and undervaluation or omission of large and diversified economies). On the other hand, the dominance of magnitude in spatial analysis demands the inclusion of intensity to "control the magnitude effect" (omission of high concentration of industries in small economies, especially those located in the vicinity of potential regional conglomerates, PRC).

2.2.4 Suggested Solutions for Value of the Variable

Atypical and Extreme Values If intensity is measured with the Location Quotient (Excess Risk), percentages (Raw Rate) or individual components of the Hoover index, the Empirical Bayes Smoothing is the most common option. On the magnitude side, one way of reducing the influence of extreme values is the data transformation.[3] However, as Anselin et al. (2007) warn, excessive smoothing or data transformation may hide atypical or extreme cases that might be interesting. It should be clarified that the smoothing of rates or ratios does not guarantee control of the overvaluation of small economies or the undervaluation or omission of diversified economies in the case of intensity. Data transformation of magnitude variables does not necessarily increase the relevance of small economies.

On the other hand, observations with zero value may be eliminated (e.g., Shiode et al. 2014). The final decision always depends on the researcher and the nature of the case study.

---

[3]In this research, standardization is not transformation. Data *standardization* (z-values) re-scales the information without changing the shape of the original distribution: asymmetry is the same and extreme cases, if they exist, also remain. The median-based z-MAD standardization is recommended for asymmetric distributions because it is less affected by extreme values than the z-values, based on the mean. In asymmetric distributions, z-MAD detects more extreme cases than z-values. On the other hand, the *transformation* of values, such as logarithms, square root, Box-Cox transformation, *changes the shape of the distribution and causes some or all extreme cases to disappear.*

Concentration and Agglomeration The existence and coexistence of the concentration (measured with HGV) and agglomeration (measured with HLV) processes have been detected in current literature (Arbia 2001; De Dominicis et al. 2013) but so far, they have not been articulated in space. There is not a satisfactory procedure to integrate or articulate HGV and HLV. Recently, authors have tried to combine these two processes by using dynamic links in Windows environment to connect fragmentary results from non-spatial tools (box maps, box plots, and maps of quartiles) with spatial autocorrelation products, such as Ii or Gi* (Kaygalak and Reid 2016; Jing and Cai 2010). This data exploration is very laborious, the description of the procedure imprecise and results obtained are difficult to explain or communicate. The present study suggests an alternative procedure to systematically amalgamate concentration and agglomeration of intensity and magnitude.

Intensity and Magnitude The inclusion of magnitude as a compensatory variable to previous drawbacks of intensity, and vice versa, demands the simultaneous articulation of these two dimensions of the concentration and agglomeration processes. Recent studies partially address this methodological challenge or they do it in an intuitive way. For example, Van den Heuvel et al. (2012) and Atkins and Tonts (2015) combine intensity and magnitude but they neglect the agglomeration process. On the other hand, Riguelle et al. (2007) address the agglomeration process but the identification of conglomerates is incomplete because LISA only identifies cores and HGV (concentration) in their peripheries are omitted or not integrated to the results of spatial autocorrelation. With the exception of the studies by Kaygalak and Reid (2016) and Jing and Cai (2010) already cited, to my knowledge, there are no other authors simultaneously analyzing concentration and agglomeration of intensity and magnitude of social or economic variables. The procedure suggested in the present study methodically combines concentration and agglomeration of intensity and magnitude.

It is evident that it is not enough to include intensity and magnitude simultaneously, but also to control or compensate their undesirable effects (over/sub-valuation or omission of important areas). The neutralization of these effects is not an easy task. This research considers several control mechanisms: articulation of the conglomerates of intensity and magnitude using Venn diagrams; comparative analysis of spatial data in the period of study; detailed review of the matrix of neighbors and values of the variable in all surrounding areas in a period of time; and assessment of magnitude in areas of high intensity and of the latter in areas of high magnitude. The need to apply all these options shows that there are no statistical techniques that replace the analytical scrutiny of results. The support of ancillary or complementary information and thematic knowledge is also needed.

2.3 Additional Observations to Common Problems

The list of problems mentioned in spatial analysis so far are: scale (size), zoning, checkerboard, shape, location, perimeter roughness, outliers and presence of zeros, mismatch of global and local values (representing concentration and agglomeration process, respectively), and magnitude and intensity effects. A relatively recent critique to spatial statistics states that its exclusive focus on local values neglects the global perspective (Jiang 2014). However, it also is undeniable that global values conceal local problems. Both perspectives are illustrated in the classic example of trees in the forest: it is true that the attention to the trees prevents the forest from being seen, but it is also true that the observation of the forest sacrifices the vision of the trees. These observations demonstrate the methodological limitations of procedures that only use spatial statistics or non-spatial statistics to identify conglomerates or define the spatial hierarchy of a variable. Some examples are the unique use of spatial statistics in the identification of urban centers or subcentres (Baumont et al. 2004; Arribas-Bel and Sanz-Gracia 2014) or only descriptive statistics for the location of industrial clusters (Ketels and Sölvell 2005).

3 A Procedure to Identify Industrial Conglomerates and Set Up Their Internal Spatial Hierarchy

The suggested solutions to the previous eight problems in spatial analysis demand the integration of non-spatial and spatial statistics. This integration is necessary to measure and articulate magnitude and intensity of the concentration and agglomeration processes. This section presents a three-step procedure to identify conglomerates of intensity and magnitude and set up their internal spatial hierarchy. The first step identifies High Global Values (HGV) and High Local Values (HLV). The starting point in this first step is that there are high global values that do not match high local values, and vice versa, as described below. The second step identifies conglomerates. It suggests overlapping HGV and HLV to identify, on one side, industrial conglomerates of intensity and, on the other, of magnitude. A full conglomerate includes both HLV (agglomerated areas) and HGV (the periphery). Conglomerates are HLV (cores) expanded by HGV located in their periphery. As a result, conglomerated areas may be more extensive than those agglomerations identified by spatial statistics. Finally, the third step overlaps previously identified conglomerates of intensity and magnitude to set up their internal spatial hierarchy.

3.1 *Step 1. Identification of High Global Values (HGV) and High Local Values (HLV)*

In general, HGV are obtained with aspatial statistics; they are values above the mean in normal distributions or above the median in positively skewed distributions. They are "high" in terms of the overall set of data. On the other hand, HLV are qualified only by considering values located within a certain distance, spatial range or neighborhood. HLV are identified with spatial statistics and their significance is estimated by permutations. Based on preliminary empirical evidence, it should be noted that *some contiguous areas in space that are high from the local point of view may be low in the overall data set*. This situation demands a procedure dealing with this discrepancy, as detailed in step 2.

3.1.1 Identification of HGV of the Concentration Process by Resampling

HGV can be identified in many ways, depending on the purpose of the study. This work suggests bootstrapping (resampling with replacement) to identify HGV in the data set and see what areas concentrate the variable of interest (e.g., employment in manufactures) regardless of their location. The decision to use resampling to identify HGV lies in its general character and statistical rigor. There are two robust resampling procedures to deal with the usual problem of asymmetry in spatial distributions: resampling for interval of *Bias-corrected and accelerated-BCa* and *Tilting* resampling (Chihara and Hesterberg 2011; Hesterberg et al. 2010). Both procedures generate similar results and improve the accuracy of confidence intervals by adjusting percentiles to correct bias and asymmetry (Hesterberg et al. 2010). If these robust resampling procedures are used, global values are "high" if they are above upper limit of the bootstrapped mean interval, with 95% of probability with one tail.

3.1.2 Identification of HLV of the Spatial Agglomeration Process by Local Spatial Autocorrelation

Spatial autocorrelation is a statistical technique that measures the presence and strength of the interdependence between values of a specific variable in a focal area to values of the same variable in neighboring areas. It is the autocorrelation of a variable with itself in space, generally measured by the Moran's global or local index (Burt et al. 2009). A variable is autocorrelated if it presents a systematic spatial pattern. In the global or local Moran's Index (*I* or *Ii*, respectively), this pattern can be identified with zero, positive, or negative values. The null hypothesis (H_0) assumes zero spatial autocorrelation and suggests that the spatial pattern is random or the spatial variation of the data has no relation to its spatial distribution. A positive spatial autocorrelation indicates that similar values (high or low) tend to co-localize

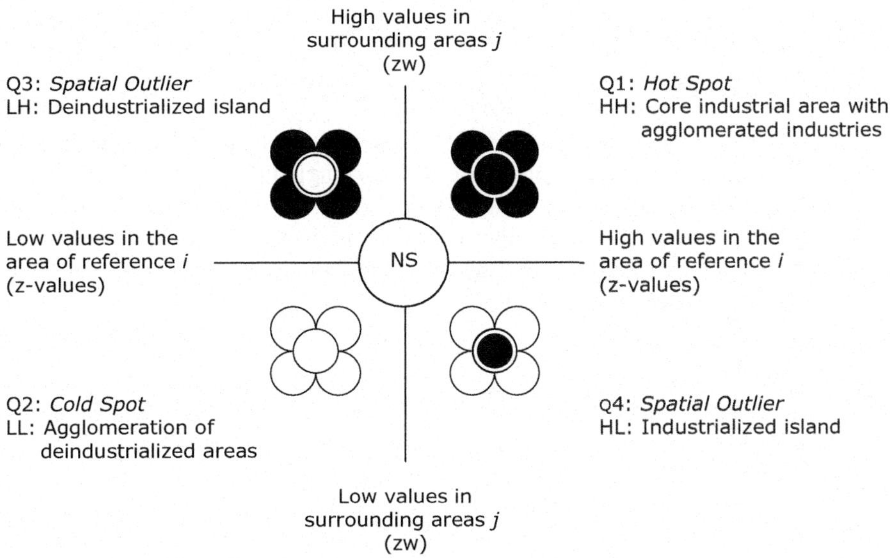

Fig. 1 Moran's Scatter Plot. Taxonomy of High Local Values (HLV) for an Industrial Agglomeration Process. *Source:* Elaborated by the author after Anselin (1995). *Note*: In these "flowers" representing Local Indices of Spatial Autocorrelation (LISA), the core is the focal area and petals are its neighbors. LISA values may be the Local Moran's Index (Ii) or the Getis-Ord statistic G_i^*. All cases (centers and petals) in Q1 (HH) and Q2 (LL) are statistically significant. In LH and HL only the core is significant. Petals in Q3 (LH) and Q4 (HL) are not significant. The unusual numbering of the Cartesian quadrants corresponds to the identification of HLV in the *GeoDa* software.

or to be more similar than the more distant ones (Tobler's first law of geography). There is positive spatial autocorrelation if similar data in intensity or magnitude are close to each other. Negative spatial autocorrelation, on the other hand, indicates that dissimilar characteristics or values, as in a checkerboard, tend to be close to each other: high values tend to be surrounded by low values, and vice versa. These relationships are the basis of the Moran's I Scatter Plot (Anselin 1995, 1996; Anselin et al. 2004). In the Moran's Scatter Plot, values on the X-abscissa are in units of standard deviation, with mean zero and variance one. On the axis of Y-ordinates are the spatial lag values (values in contiguous areas) of the standardized variable in the X-abscissa.

The Moran's Scatter Plot classifies spatial autocorrelation into two categories: spatial agglomerations and *spatial* outliers (not to be confused with *global* outliers superior to the two standard deviations in descriptive statistics). Each quadrant in the diagram corresponds to a different type of spatial autocorrelation (Fig. 1). The lower left (LL) and the upper right (HH) quadrants indicate positive autocorrelation, but of a different type. While LL contains areas with low values surrounded by areas with low values (Low-Low), HH includes areas with high values surrounded by areas with high values (High-High). These differences between HH and LL show that agglomerations identified by positive spatial autocorrelation may be a core or agglomeration of industries (HH) or agglomeration of deindustrialized areas (LL). In contrast, the upper left (LH) and lower right (HL) quadrants suggest negative spatial autocorrelation. Cases in LH and HL are spatial outliers. While LH contains low values surrounded by high values (deindustrialized islands), HL contains high values surrounded by low local values (industrialized islands). Note that all cases in HH and LL are significant; all agglomerated cases form a single nucleus, core or center. In LH and HL only the core is significant. In these LISA abbreviations, the first term always refers to the focal area and the second to the average value of its neighbors. NS indicates "not significant" cases; the core area value is not significantly different from the average of its neighbors.[4]

Summing up Previous lines suggest that not all high global values (HGV) are high local values (HLV) and vice versa. HGV, identified by resampling, have a statistically defined limit (the bootstrapped mean). On the other hand, HLV, identified by spatial autocorrelation, might exist if the value in the focal area is greater than the average of the values in the surrounding areas, even though they are below the HGV threshold. Spatial autocorrelation might also omit HGV if the focal area is surrounded by global values that are on average even higher (Treviño 2016, provides a graphical description of these statements). This discrepancy between HGV and HLV demands a procedure to simultaneously consider the agglomeration and concentration processes in magnitude and intensity. Current literature already registers this demand but it has only been addressed partially (Arbia 2001; Feser et al. 2005).

3.2 *Step 2. Identification of Conglomerates of Intensity or Magnitude. Thinking Outside-the-Box: Overlapping HGV and HLV*

Once HGV and HLV are identified, the next step is to identify spatial conglomerates by layer overlapping. Layer analysis is a basic routine in geographical analysis and has already been used to integrate different variables of intensity (e.g., education and

[4]Spatial data hardly fit the assumptions of normality or randomness (as it is assumed in the ArcGis software). Therefore, this study uses a statistical pseudo-significance obtained by 9999 permutations with the *GeoDa* software. Anselin et al. (2013) and North et al. (2002) provide a clear description of this procedure. The statistical significance of the Moran's global (I) and local (Ii) indices confronts the null hypothesis (H_0) of absence of spatial autocorrelation (the variable has a random spatial autocorrelation). H_0 may be rejected under the NOT-NOT principle: NOT significant, NOT rejected. If I or Ii are significant for a probability less than 5% ($p < 0.05$), H_0 is rejected and it is concluded that the spatial pattern of the variable is agglomerated. It is recommended to test hypotheses for more than 60 spatial units. Because of the unequal size of these units, the law of big numbers requires a sample size relatively big (Griffith 1996, p. 80). This rule is not always followed: Aroca et al. (2005) calculate the Ii for the 32 Mexican states and Parajuli and Haynes (2012) do the same thing for the 48 conterminous US states.

poverty in Choudhury and Räder 2014). To our knowledge, this procedure has not been used to identify conglomerates of magnitude or intensity of the same variable. In this procedure, the layer of agglomeration contains the HLV that are the core of the conglomerate. The layer of concentration provides the HGV adjacent to cores. Both HLV and their adjacent HGV create a conglomerate. In layer overlapping in this method, the three main practical criteria are:

- HGV overlapped with HH or HL are core values, as in cases (a), (b), or (d) in Fig. 2. If there are no HGV adjacent to these core values, the conglomerate is only formed by HLV that simultaneously may be HGV. It is also possible to have conglomerates only formed by HLV when overlapped or adjacent HGV are absent. It should be clear that HGV alone do not form conglomerates if they are not overlapped with or adjacent to HLV.
- The addition of HGV adjacent to HLV extends the core area, either a hot spot (HH) or an island of industrialization (HL), as in cases (c) and (e) in the resulting layer of Fig. 2.
- HGV far away from, in the second crown, or not contiguous to core values (HH or HL) are not part of the conglomerate, as in case (f) in Fig. 2. This restriction can be conveniently relaxed to include in the conglomerate HGV in the second crown of HLV.

From the point of view of industrial conglomerates, locally important areas matter for economic policies, even if they are not globally significant. However, *it would be absurd if such policies only include important areas from the local point of view while excluding neighboring areas globally relevant but locally insignificant.* It is against common sense to exclude HGV in the periphery of HLV. The suggested procedure deals with this illogical situation by fusing adjacent HGV with hot spots (HH) and industrialized islands (HL) to create industrial conglomerates.

In sum, the identification of conglomerates of intensity, on one hand, and magnitude, on the other one, is possible by layer overlapping of HGV and HLV (HH and HL). Overlay analysis in Geographic Analysis Systems mathematically integrates (e.g., by joining, clipping or intersecting) layers of concentration and agglomeration to create a new layer containing resulting conglomerates. The overlapping process adds contiguous HGV to the *periphery* of HH and HL values (cores) creating conglomerates. HGV overlapped with core values merge with those same values. This procedure is first applied to intensity. Then, as an independent and separate task, the same procedure is repeated for magnitude. Figure 2 graphically synthesizes the main methodological steps described in this section.

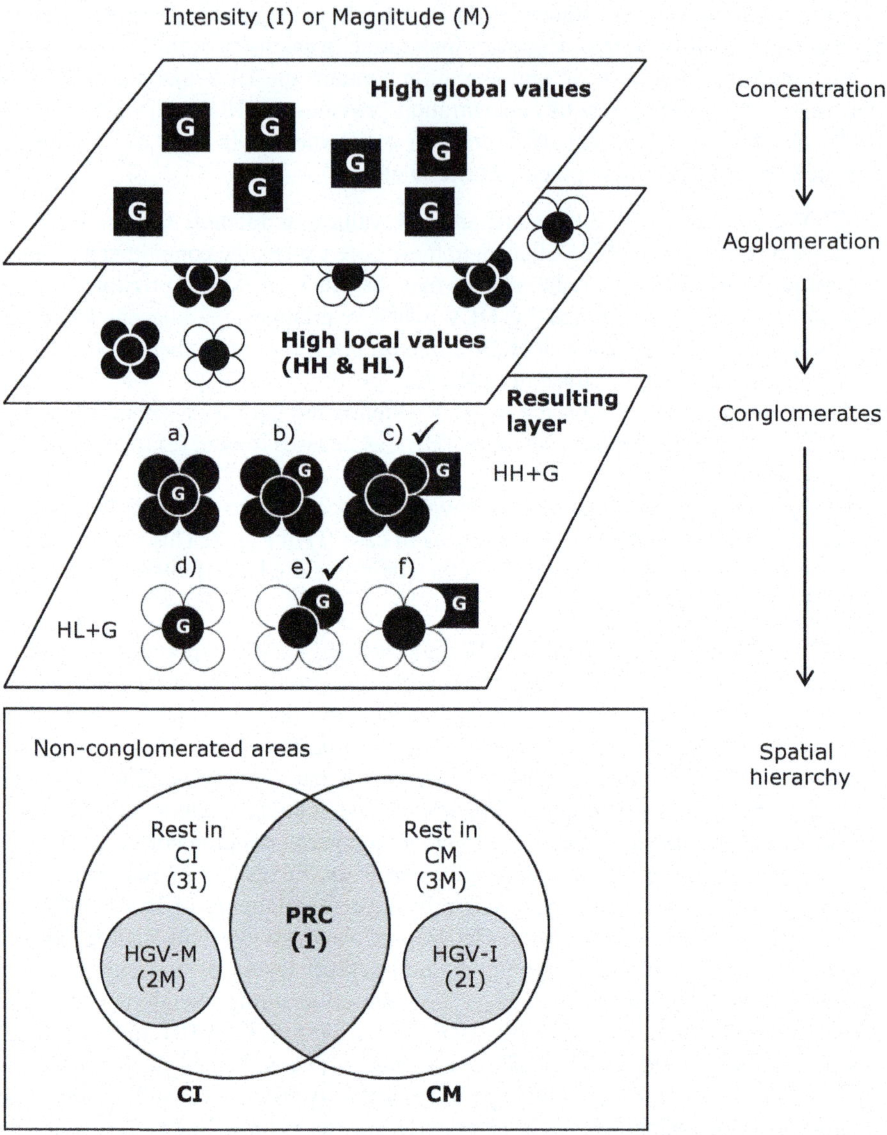

Fig. 2 Methodological procedure to identify industrial conglomerates and their spatial hierarchy. *Source*: Own elaboration. Notes: In overlaid layers: G = High global values (HGV). In Venn diagrams: CI = Conglomerates of intensity; CM = Conglomerates of magnitude; HGV-I = High global values of intensity; HGV-M = High global values of magnitude. PRC = Potential regional conglomerates. Numbers represent: 1 = PRC; 2 M = HGV of magnitude within the conglomerate of intensity (CI); 2I = HGV of intensity within the conglomerate of magnitude (CM); 3I = Rest of values in the conglomerate of intensity (CI); 3 M = Rest of values in the conglomerate of magnitude (CM). Checkmarks in c) and e) indicate HGV contiguous to HH or HL, respectively, creating conglomerates. Further explanation provided in the text

3.3 Step 3. Setting up the Industrial Spatial Hierarchy by Overlaying Conglomerates of Magnitude and Intensity

In this step, Venn diagrams are used to represent conglomerates of intensity or magnitude. The overlay of these two conglomerates creates a five-level spatial hierarchy: Potential Regional Conglomerates (PRC); High Global Values of Magnitude in the Conglomerate of Intensity (2I); High Global Values of Intensity in the Conglomerate of Magnitude (2 M); and Remaining Values in the Conglomerate of Intensity (3I) and Magnitude (3 M).

3.3.1 Intersection of the Conglomerates of Intensity and Magnitude

Cases of the highest hierarchy are located at the intersection of these two sets. This intersection contains conglomerated cases with values that simultaneously are high in magnitude and intensity. For this reason, cases at the intersection receive the highest spatial hierarchy (Level 1) and are referred as Potential Regional Conglomerates (CRP).

There is a variety of terms that, regardless of its theoretical origin and operational definition, has as a reference the agglomeration of industries: clusters (Porter 1990), complexes (Feser et al. 2005), districts (Becattini 2002), *innovative milieux* (Brenner 2004), and local production systems (Paunero Amigo et al. 2007). *The European Cluster Observatory*, for example, uses the term "cluster" to refer to the agglomeration of activities without necessarily having a cluster type organization. Other authors refer to the simple agglomeration of firms as "horizontal cluster" without implying any kind of relationship or interconnection between them or institutions or the existence of pecuniary or technological externalities (Fingleton et al. 2007). Sharing a similar idea, some studies use the term "potential cluster" or "potential cluster regions" to indicate the geographic concentration (agglomeration) of industries that is a precondition for clusters, with the potential to be a cluster, regardless of whether it becomes a cluster (Szanyi et al. 2010; Carroll et al. 2008). This research uses the term *Potential Regional Conglomerates* (CRP) in the following sense:

- *Potential* (P) because they offer the greatest possibility of success to industrial development strategies based on the co-location of industries. The existence of conglomerates does not ensure the presence of inter-sector relations or de facto intra-industrial relations, but makes them more likely to occur. Concentration or geographical proximity of a critical mass of employees in manufactures and a relative spatial industrial concentration provide the combined industrial potential of these areas.
- *Regional* (R) because their influence goes beyond the municipal boundaries as they are identified, on one hand, by a threshold for concentration based on the whole national set of values and, on the other hand, by a process of delimitation of high local values that includes contiguous areas.

- *Conglomerates* (C) because they are the result of the superposition of two processes, one of spatial concentration in the national framework (first-order effects) and spatial agglomeration of a local nature (second-order effects). Conglomerate = Concentration + Agglomeration.

3.3.2 Spatial Relevance of Areas Located outside the Intersection, but within Conglomerates

When conglomerates of intensity (CI) and magnitude (CM) overlap, some high global values of magnitude outside the intersection area remain within conglomerates of intensity (HGV-M in CI), with 2 M-hierarchy. Similarly, some high global values of intensity remain within conglomerates of magnitude (HGV-I in CM), with 2I-hierarchy.

In this approach, high global values and high local values are complementary and not necessarily different. On the contrary, each value *simultaneously* has several characteristics (Table 1). A specific value at the intersection (PRC) has four characteristics at once: It is a: (1) high global value of intensity (HGV-I); (2) high local value of intensity (HLV-I); (3) high global value of magnitude ((HGV-M); and (4) high local value of magnitude (HLV-M). In PRC converge two spatial processes (concentration and agglomeration) and two dimensions (intensity and magnitude).

A specific 2I-value, located in the conglomerate of magnitude, *simultaneously* has three characteristics: (1) high global value of intensity (HGV-I); (2) high local value of magnitude (HLV-M); and (3) HGV of magnitude (HGV-M). Located in the conglomerate of magnitude, 2I-values express the two spatial processes of magnitude (concentration and agglomeration) and the concentration process of intensity.

Similarly, 2 M-values, located in the conglomerate of intensity, *simultaneously* have three characteristics: (1) high global value of magnitude (HGV-M); (2) high

Table 1 Spatial hierarchy of conglomerated values of intensity and/or magnitude

	Conglomerate of				Belongs to the conglomerate of	
	Intensity		Magnitude			
Spatial hierarchy	HGV-I	HLV-I	HGV-M	HLV-M	Intensity	Magnitude
PRC	✓	✓	✓	✓	✓	✓
2I	✓	X	✓	✓	X	✓
2 M	✓	✓	✓	X	✓	X
3I	✓	✓	X	X	✓	X
3 M	X	X	✓	✓	X	✓

Source: Own elaboration
Notes: HGV: High global values; HLV: High local values; I: Intensity; M: Magnitude
PRC: Potential regional clusters are at the intersection of both conglomerates of magnitude and intensity; 2I: High global values of intensity (HGV-I) overlap conglomerate values (HGV and HLV) of magnitude; and 2 M: High global values of magnitude (HGV-M) overlap conglomerate values (HGV and HLV) of intensity. Please note that while 2I is a value of intensity belonging to the conglomerate of magnitude, 2 M is a value of magnitude in the conglomerate of intensity

global value of intensity (HGV-I); and (3) high local value of intensity (HLV-I). 2 M- values express the two spatial processes of intensity (concentration and agglomeration) and the concentration process of magnitude.

Finally, 3I-values *simultaneously* have two characteristics: (1) high global value of intensity (HGV-I); and (2) high local value of intensity (HLV-I). They only express the two spatial processes of intensity. On the other hand, 3 M-values *simultaneously* have (1) high global and local values of magnitude (HGV-M and HLV-M). They only express the concentration and agglomeration processes of magnitude.

Most empirical research in spatial analysis focuses on intensity, either considering HGV-I (classical aspatial statistics) or HLV-I values (spatial statistics), partial classificatory categories of 3I-values. The remaining four values in this spatial hierarchy (PRC, 2I, 2 M, and 3 M) usually are neglected in current literature.

This research considers that 2I and 2 M space units have the same hierarchy. The same principle applies to 3I and 3 M values. However, one may have greater emphasis than the other depending on the orientation of the public policy. If the objective of the public policy is to encourage spatial competitiveness, the emphasis is on intensity and the spatial order would be: PRC > 2 M > 2I > 3I > 3 M. If the objective of the public policy is to increase the number of employees, the emphasis is on magnitude (quantity) and the spatial hierarchy would be: PRC > 2I > 2M > 3M > 3I. All levels are important for a spatially focused industrial policy, especially those located in the vicinity of the PRC.[5]

3.3.3 Spatial Relevance of Areas Outside of Conglomerates

Areas outside conglomerates are spatially differentiated because they contain both high and low global values. The current methodology was originally designed to include areas outside the conglomerates, if necessary. This research does not apply the complete scheme because it unnecessarily increases the number of classifications in the spatial hierarchy.

3.4 Contribution to the Treatment of the Eight Selected Problems in Spatial Analysis

The advantages of the described procedure are: (1) It partially compensates for the problems of MAUP and checkerboard by combining two or more spatial units, as in Van Den Heuvel et al. (2012). (2) It solves the problem of the discrepancy between

[5]It is possible to extend the current spatial hierarchy by including areas within conglomerates that are close to or distant from PRC. In this research, this step is done analytically to preserve the methodology in as abbreviated way as possible.

HGV and HLV in spatial analysis by simultaneously articulating concentration and agglomeration processes. The agglomeration measurement uses standardized matrices to cushion the influence of physical characteristics of polygons (form, size and location), as recommended by the literature review in this section. (3) It compensates for the overvaluation of small economies, or undervaluation, or omission of diversified areas and the exclusion of small economies by simultaneously articulating magnitude and intensity. The methodology prevents the existence of extremely spurious cases by noting the effect of spatial units with zero value and testing various options to smooth input data, if necessary. Finally, the procedure recommends an analytical scrutiny of results from previous steps. There are no statistical techniques or geospatial procedures replacing the critical review and analytical thinking in the interpretation of results.

4 Case Study

The basic structure of this section is organized into two main parts to illustrate the methodology previously described. The first part presents the main results of the methodology suggested. The processes of concentration and agglomeration in intensity are analyzed to identify the respective conglomerate. Then, the same procedure is repeated for magnitude. Once the conglomerates of intensity and magnitude are identified, they are overlaid to obtain their internal spatial hierarchy. Industrialized areas located at the intersection of these two conglomerates are the Potential Regional Conglomerates (PRC) and have the highest spatial hierarchy (Level 1). Remaining areas within the conglomerates are in levels 2 and 3 according to the criteria established in the methodology. Finally, the spatial hierarchy obtained for the period is analyzed to detect cases of actual or apparent disappearances of PRC and identify promising industrial zones. The graphic representation of this hierarchy is based on maps of choropleths (municipalities) that visually exaggerate the presence of industries located in urban areas occupying a reduced space within municipal polygons.

The variable of interest is employees in manufactures (E_i) in 2352 and 2457 Mexican municipalities of the 32 states (Fig. 3), for 1998 and 2013, respectively.[6] This research, after several preliminary tests, uses the individual component H_{ij} of the Hoover global index (H) to measure intensity and the raw number of employees to assess magnitude.[7] These measurements of intensity and magnitude are similar to

[6]These municipalities register manufacturing activity in the respective economic censuses. This research eliminates municipalities that do not report employees in manufactures. This methodological decision prevents municipalities with very low levels of manufacturing employment from emerging as industrialized islands (high local values surrounded by low local values (zero industrial activity), as explained in the methodology.

[7]The disaggregation at the municipal level (H_{ij}) of the Hoover index (H) may be expressed in the following way:

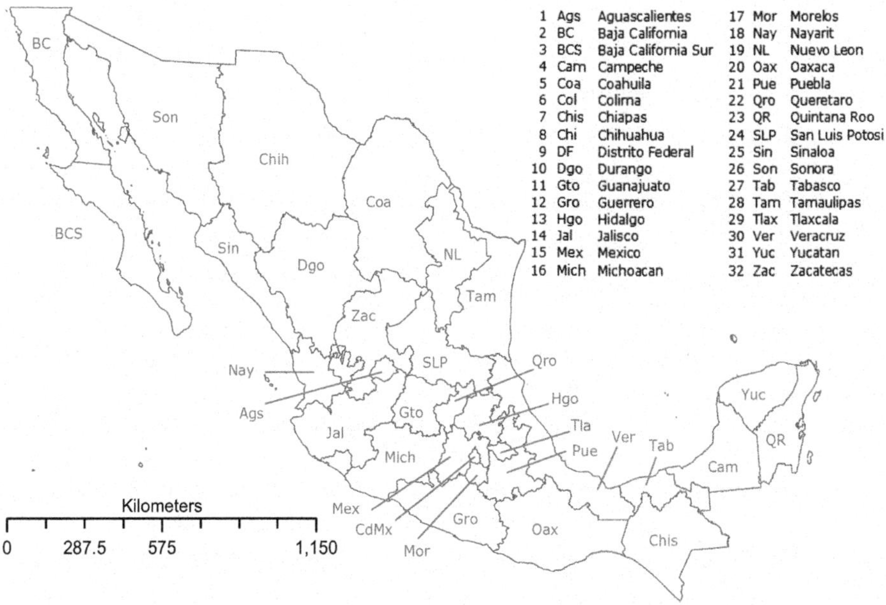

Fig. 3 Political division of Mexico

those used by Kaygalak and Reid (2016) and Carroll et al. (2008). The evidence in the case study, the overlapping of the Global High Values and High Local Values and the desire not to omit extreme cases support this decision. Like the county in Feser et al. (2005), the Mexican municipality is the smallest major space unit in which data can be reliably added at an important administrative level, without significant omissions due to the confidentiality of information. Some authors argue that in some specific industries the economic influence exceeds the municipal and state level, so the notion of contiguity must be defined in terms of the case study: e.g., 50 miles for any industry (May et al. 2001), 150 miles for greenhouses or 450 miles in the automotive industry (Frizado et al. 2009). The truth is that there is no single criterion for defining spatial contiguity (Paez and Scott 2004).

$H_{ij} = (E_{ij}/\Sigma E_{ij}) - (E_j/\Sigma E_j)$, where, E_{ij} and E_{ij} = Employees in manufactures in municipality j and total employees in manufactures in Mexico, respectively. E_j and E_j = Total employees in all activities in municipality j and total employees in all activities in Mexico, respectively. H_{ij} is positive (H_{ij}^+) or negative (H_{ij}^-), depending on whether the first term is greater than the second one, or vice versa. $H = \Sigma H_{ij}^+ = \left|\Sigma H_{ij}^-\right|$. Note that the location quotient (LQ_{ij}) uses the same variables in H_{ij}:$LQ_{ij} = (E_{ij}/\Sigma E_{ij})/(E_j/\Sigma E_j)$. Therefore, when H_{ij} is positive, LQ is >1. Based on this connection between H_{ij} and LQ_{ij}, it is possible to conclude that concentration of industries in certain areas makes them relatively specialized in this activity. This inference should be taken in the context of the "intensity effect" (omission of highly diversified areas) in the present research. The relationship between concentration and specialization is a topic of importance by itself beyond the objective of this study (Treviño 2017; Aiginger and Rossi-Hansberg 2006)

4.1 Intensity

Following the steps suggested in Fig. 2, intensity is addressed first.

Concentration Process The H_{ij} index is resampled to determine the overall intensity values that are statistically significant (HGV-I). This statistical procedure identifies high global values irrespective of their location as a result of the industrial concentration process. H_{ij} values are resampled for manufactures in 1998 and 2013, respectively.

The case study applies *Tilting*, the most refined robust resampling procedure, to find the upper limit of the confidence interval of the mean. In the case of intensity, the value obtained by Tilting with 95% in the right tail, for 10,000 replications of the initial average, is $H_{ij} = 0.482 \times 10^{-4}$ and 0.458×10^{-4} for 1998 and 2013, respectively. These very small values of H_{ij} are due to the difference in ratios calculated for almost all municipalities in Mexico. These values of H_{ij} are threshold values for high global values of the intensity (VGA-I). Some of these HGV-I will match the cores of intensity; others will be their periphery or will be merely non-agglomerated areas of high concentration located in the rest of the country.

Agglomeration Process The global Moran's index (I) for intensity (H_{ij}), using a queen type matrix of contiguity, rejects the null hypothesis of randomness. The global index I indicates that industry intensity is spatially concentrated in the country in 1998 ($I = 0.2044$, $p = 0.01\%$f) and in 2013 (0.2312, $p = 0.01\%$).

The local Moran's index (I_i), with a probability $p < 5\%$, identifies core areas (HH) and islands (HL) of industrial intensity. Although HH and HL municipalities are different, for practical reasons, this research considers that these two values are the core of potential regional conglomerates of intensity. These core areas are the seed to identify conglomerates of intensity. The periphery of these cores is created with high global values of the concentration process.

Overlaying Concentration and Agglomeration of H_{ij} Values The resulting layer contains several options of the overlay process. Cores (HH and HL values) merge with adjacent HGV to form conglomerates of intensity represented in Venn diagrams (CI) in Fig. 2. The case study reveals the notorious presence of conglomerates of intensity in Oaxaca, Chiapas, and Yucatan, in both years. These cases show that the existence of small and remote economies could erroneously be taken as relevant industrial conglomerates when intensity is the only dimension used in the research. When a variable of intensity is used, the undervaluation or omission of large and diversified economies adds to the overvaluation of small economies. The central municipalities of Monterrey, Guadalajara and 14 of the 16 Delegations of the DF (now CdMx) would go unnoticed for having a negative H_{ij} (or $LQ < 1$) in 2013. These highly diversified municipalities and delegations are not recognized in any conglomerate of intensity but, because of their high volume of industrial employment and proximity to municipalities of similar characteristics, they are registered in conglomerates of magnitude, as described below.

4.2 Magnitude

Steps applied to identify conglomerates of intensity are the same for magnitude.

Concentration Process The threshold value for magnitude, identified by resampling the number of industrial employees, is 2203 and 2466 people occupied in manufactures (E_i) in 1998 and 2013, respectively. The *Tilting* procedure is used considering 95% in the right tail, for 10,000 samples. Municipalities with an E_i greater than or equal to these figures are considered global high values of magnitude (VGA-M). As expected, VGA-M are located in the most populated areas. A similar pattern is confirmed for the agglomeration process of E_i.

On the other hand, if only magnitude is measured, municipalities with more industry would dominate the spatial analysis, ignoring the high concentration of E_i in small but important economies (magnitude effect). Magnitude overlooks, for example, municipalities with important industrial concentration (intensity) bordering the Metropolitan Area of Monterrey, such as Pesqueria, Cienega de Flores, and Montemorelos. South and Southeast regions of Mexico are completely "erased from the map," with the exception of the municipality of Izamal (Yuc) in 2013, if the identification of conglomerates is only addressed in terms of magnitude, in the period of study.

In Summary, regarding the concentration process, on one hand, intensity may include remote and irrelevant areas and exclude very important diversified municipalities. On the other hand, magnitude may partially correct this problem by including highly diversified areas, but neglecting important industrial areas surrounding them. Therefore, both intensity and magnitude should be included in the spatial pattern analysis of manufactures.

Agglomeration Process Although the methodological steps for magnitude and intensity are the same, results are different. The Moran's global index (I) for magnitude (number of E_i), using a queen type matrix of contiguity, rejects the null hypothesis of randomness. The global index I indicates that magnitude is spatially concentrated in the country in 1998 ($I = 0.2105$, $p = 0.01\%$) and 2013 (0.1905, $p = 0.01\%$).

As for intensity, magnitude centers are the HH and HL values identified by the local Moran's index (I_i). Most of these centers are located in densely populated areas, such as capital cities. High global values representing the concentration process are the periphery of these centers.

Overlaying Concentration and Agglomeration of E_i The superposition of layers merging HH and HL centers with high global values to identify conglomerates of magnitude is a two-step procedure:

(a) Intersection of HH and HL areas with areas containing 2203 or more of E_i in 1998 and 2466 or more in 2013. This step integrates in a single map overlapped local and global values, and

(b) Integration of core areas (HH and HL) with high global values in the neighboring areas.

Figures 4 and 5, for clarity of exposition, only show the location and evolution of the Potential Regional Conglomerates (CPR), enumerated from one to twelve in 1998 and 2013. The complete list of municipalities for the hierarchy of the three levels of magnitude and intensity in both years is available from the author by request.

In 2013, the dominance of manufacturing in small economies consolidated a continuous corridor of industrial intensity between the CdMx and ZM de Queretaro, which had already been detected in 1998. These spatially continuous municipalities disappear when conglomerates of magnitude are considered (Figs. 5 and 6).

4.3 Conglomerate Overlaying and Spatial Hierarchy inside Them

Layer overlay in previous paragraphs creates conglomerates. This section describes the relevance of conglomerates obtained and, in turn, overlays them to set up their internal spatial hierarchy. Once the conglomerates of intensity and magnitude are identified, this research generates a five-level classification of the municipalities inside them, as indicated in the methodology. Because of space reasons, results are only synthesized for year 2013.

Potential Regional Conglomerates (PRC) The intersection of the conglomerates of intensity and conglomerates of magnitude define the Potential Regional Conglomerates (PRC). At the end of the period of study, there were 85 municipalities that simultaneously were in both conglomerates. These PRC represented only 9% of the total municipalities with industrial activity in the country and concentrated three quarters of the national employment in manufactures (E_i).

Besides the PRC, conglomerates of intensity and conglomerates of magnitude include municipalities of lower spatial hierarchy. This hierarchy, however, revolves around the PRC because they are the most important spatial units in this research.

Level 2I There were 12 municipalities with high global values of intensity (HGV-I), located in the conglomerate of magnitude (CM); therefore, they belong to the CM.[8] The fact that 2I-areas belong to the CM is a guarantee that they have a critical mass and that their specialization is not the result of the "intensity effect." Examples of 2I-municipalities in 2013 are Cortazar and Salamanca (Gto), Cajeme and Empalme (Son), and Huejotzingo (Pue).

[8]It is important to remember that in this overlapping the *same* value *simultaneously* is conglomerated in magnitude but concentrated in intensity. The same idea applies to similar situations.

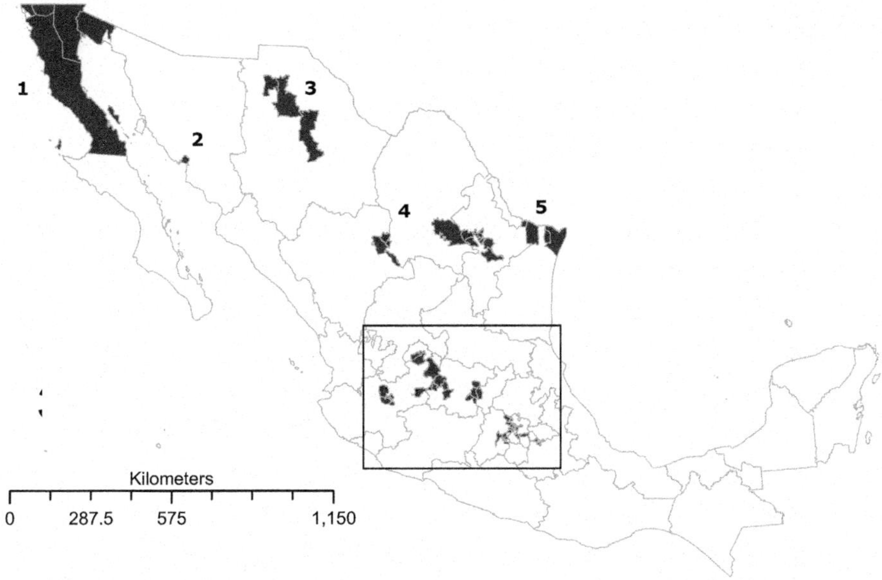

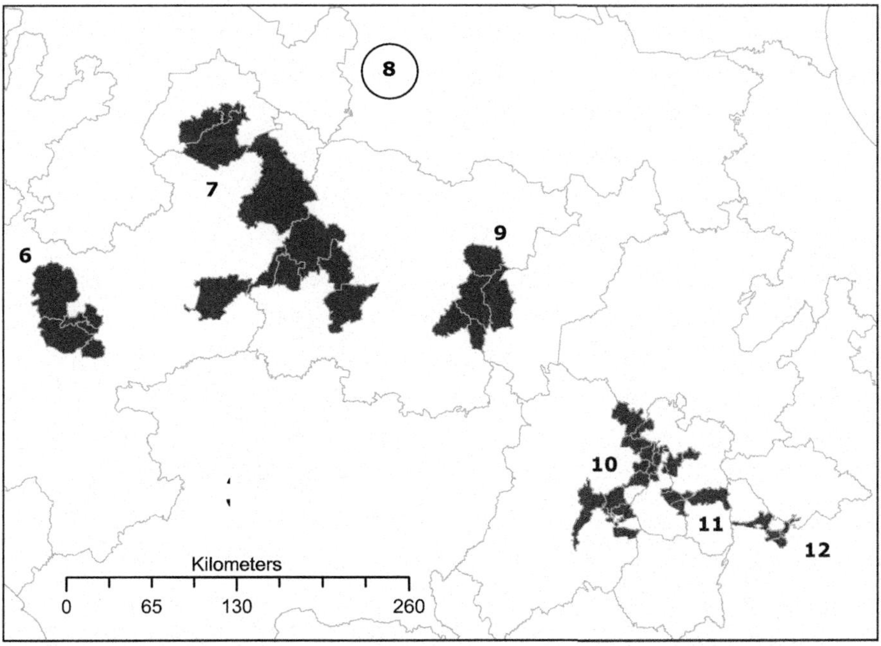

Fig. 4 Potential Regional Conglomerates (PRC), 1998. *Source*: Elaboration by the author based on the methodology in this study. Note: PRC result of the intersection of conglomerates of magnitude and intensity, as described in the methodology. Local spatial autocorrelation Moran's indices were obtained with *GeoDa* using a row-standardized matrix of the queen contiguity type. Threshold values for concentration of intensity is $H_{ij} = 0.482 \times 10^{-4}$ and for magnitude is 2203 employees. The circled number eight indicates a non-existing PRC in 1998 that came into existence in 2013 (SLP-Villa de Reyes), as it is explained in the text

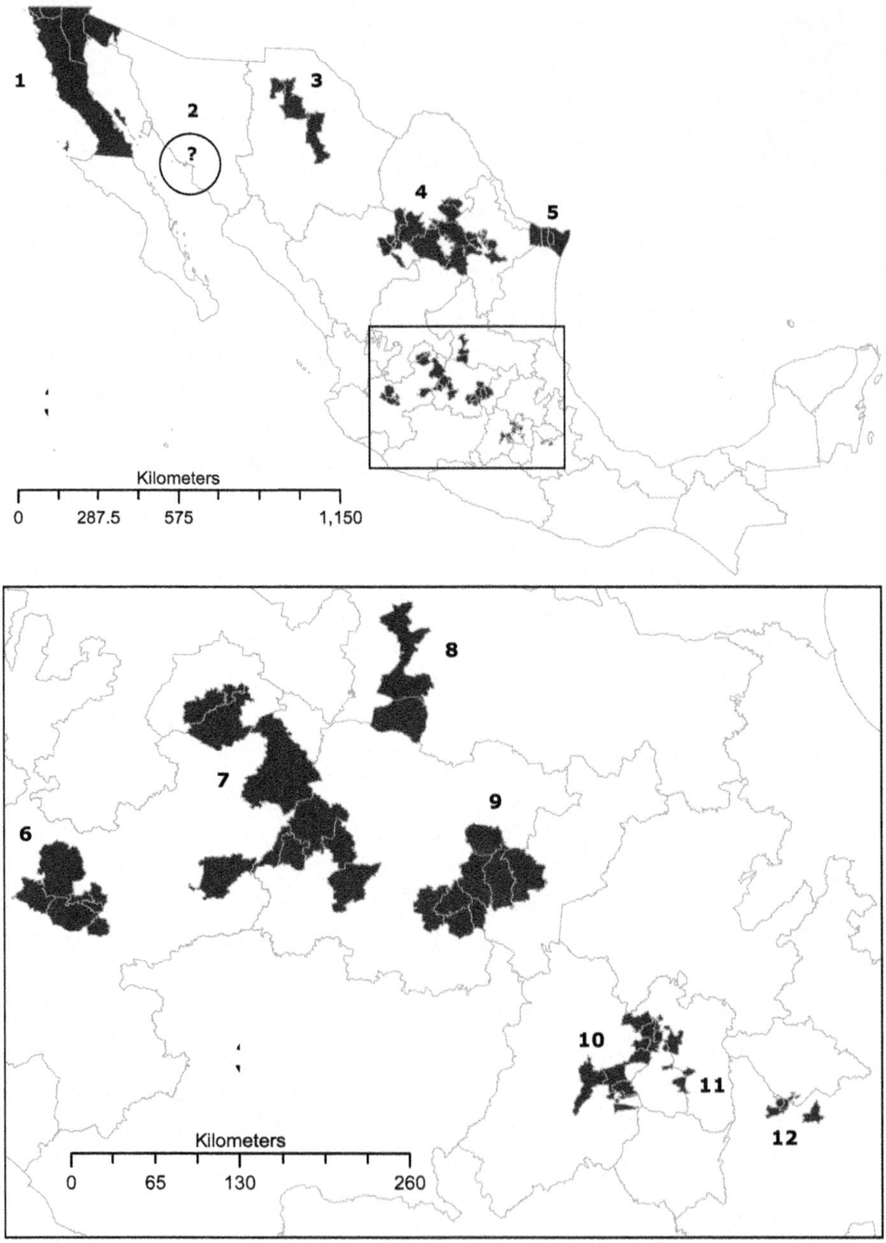

Fig. 5 Potential Regional Conglomerates (PRC), 2013. *Source*: Elaboration of the author as for map in Fig. 3. Threshold values for the concentration of intensity is $H_{ij} = 0.458\text{x}10^{-4}$ and for magnitude is 2466 employees. The circle indicates the deceiving disappearance of the PRC-2, as it is explained in the text

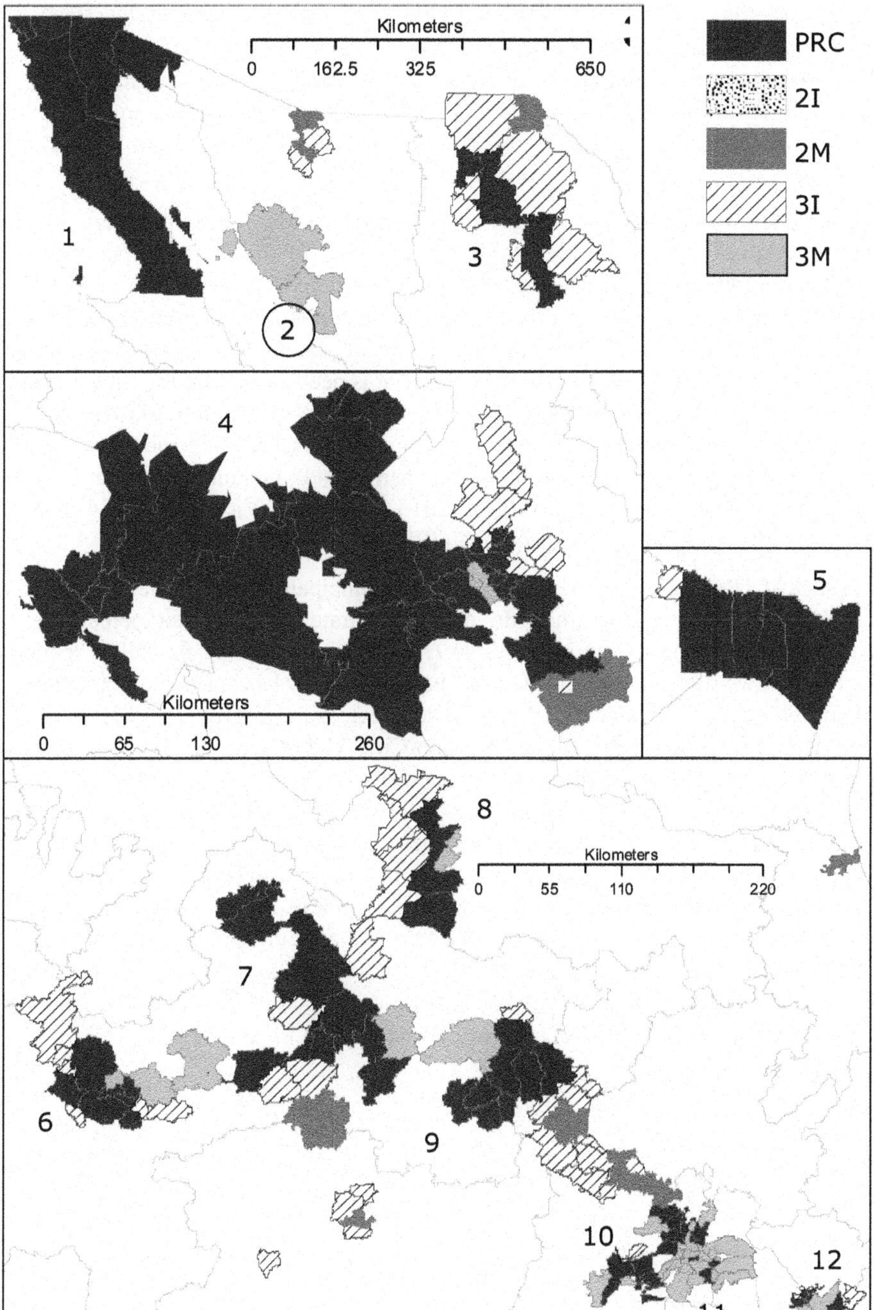

Fig. 6 PRC and spatial hierarchy of the municipalities surrounding them, 2013. *Source*: Elaboration by the author. Note: The map includes the spatial hierarchy of municipalities around PRC-2, identified in 1998 but vanished in 2013. The explanation is in the text

Level 2 M There are 16 areas that have a high global value of magnitude (HGV-M) and are located in a conglomerate of intensity (CI). They are part of the CI. The HGV-M guarantees a critical mass in areas of important specialization. Usually, although not always, 2 M areas are HGV-M adjacent to specialized areas of small economies (3I-values). Examples of 2 M-municipalities in 2013 are San Juan del Rio (Qro), Linares (NL), Nogales (Son), and Juarez (Chi).

Level 3I (Rest of the CI) There are 68 high concentration areas that may also be called "enablers"[9] because their high concentration of the national manufactures implies that they provide the required local conditions (whatever they are) for the existence and predominance of this activity. Industrial employment in these areas is important in relative terms although not necessarily in absolute terms. Since manufactures may dominate very small economies, it is necessary to be sure that enablers are not an illusion of the intensity effect, as in the cases of Santa Maria Atzompa or San Agustin Yatareni, located in the mountains of Oaxaca. They should always be reviewed in the context of both intensity and magnitude. Examples of 3I-municipalities adjacent to a PRC in 2013 are Salinas Victoria (PRC-4 in NL), Tequila (PRC-6 in Jal), y Tequisquiapan (PRC-9, Qro).

Level 3 M (Rest of the CM) There are 35 municipalities that have a significant number of employees but they do not concentrate an important percentage of national manufactures (low or negative H_{ij} values). They may be called "generators"[10] for two different reasons. On one hand, they may be central municipalities of metropolitan areas affected by a "magnitude effect," such as Monterrey, Guadalajara or delegaciones (mayoralties) from Mexico City. The magnitude effect in this case refers to diversified economies, usually specialized in services rather than in industry.[11] These areas, although they have a considerable pool of industrial employment, are not dominated by manufactures. These 3 M-municipalities are generators because they originally contained a significant volume of industrial employment that selectively relocated to the less congested periphery. 3 M-municipalities may be generators if their have a firm industrial base and a significant volume of employment but their economic structure is not specialized in manufactures. Examples of these 3 M-muncipios in 1993 are Hermosillo (Son.), Guaymas (Son.), Guanajuato (Gto.), Tepatitlan de Morelos (Jal.), Ixtapaluca (Mex.)

[9]This term is adapted from Brantingham and Brantingham (1995).

[10]Term adapted from Brantingham and Brantingham (1995).

[11]It is argued that an important proportion of services depends on industry and, therefore, estimations do not provide a fair relevance of industry. This point is not discussed in this research.

4.4 Analytic Scrutiny of PRC and their Spatial Dynamics, 1998–2013

Municipalities integrating PRC at the beginning year are not exactly the same at the end of the period. PRC mainly locate in the Northern and Central regions of Mexico.

Northern Mexico (PRC-1 to 5) It noted that some PRC expand by incorporating surrounding municipalities, such as PRC-1 (BC), PRC-4 (NL), and PRC-5 (TAM); and others are stable (PRC-3 in Coa) or vanish (PRC-2 in Son). It should be mentioned, however, that a detailed analysis shows that the disappearance of the PRC-2 is apparent. It is due to the conformation of the "Cajeme-Nogales corridor" in Sonora rather than the local fading out of the industrial activity. Data on the spatial shift of industrial occupation show an increase in both manufacturing (86,200) and total (356,532) employment in this industrial corridor that enlarged from six to eight municipalities in 1998–2013. This illusory fading out of the PRC-2 centered in Empalme shows that there is no infallible methodology to detect PRC or replace the analytical scrutiny in the spatial pattern analysis.

Central Mexico (PRC-6 to 12) These PRC include the metropolitan areas located at the El Bajio region, the Valley of Mexico and Puebla. In the period of study, three aspects stand out: a) Consolidation of the industrial corridor of Central Mexico. When all levels of the spatial hierarchy are included, as suggested in the methodology, a continuous industrial corridor emerges connecting seven PRC (numbered from 6 through 12 in Fig. 5), located in the states of Jalisco, Aguascalientes, Guanajuato, San Luis Potosi, Queretaro, Michoacan, Estado de Mexico, Hidalgo, and Puebla. b) Creation of the PRC-8 as a result of the transition of SLP from a 2 M municipality in 1998 to a PRC in 2013. And c) Expansion of PRC detected in 1998, especially the PRC-6 (Guadalajara region), PRC-9 (Queretaro region), PRC-10 (municipalities in the State of Mexico adjacent to Mexico City), and PRC-12 (Puebla, surrounding the capital city).

4.5 Other Industrial Zones

PRC are the most important industrial areas but they are not the only ones. To the previously identified PRC it may be added an "industrial promissory zone" in Yucatan. It is "promissory" because there is a 2 M-municipality (Izamal) and a bunch of 2I-municipalities (mainly Tixkokob, Kanasin, and Acanceh) surrounding Merida (the capital city with 34,737 employees in manufactures). Based on their physical nearness and the important number of employees in manufactures in the whole area, this set of municipalities may be called "the promissory industrial corridor of Merida."[12]

5 Discussion

This research presents and applies a new procedure to identify industrial conglomerates and set up its spatial hierarchy by simultaneously combining concentration and agglomeration of magnitude and intensity of industrial employment. The study first focuses on intensity. It identifies concentrations of industry and integrates them with agglomerations (cores) to form conglomerates of intensity (cores and peripheries). In the case study, concentration refers to the location of high global values in some municipalities of Mexico, regardless of their geographic location. Agglomeration, on the other hand, refers to the localization of high local values in contiguous municipalities, without considering the general distribution, order or hierarchy of values. High global values, identified by resampling, can be located anywhere. They create conglomerates when they are contiguous to agglomerations, identified by spatial autocorrelation. On the other hand, considering that size matters, conglomerates of magnitude are obtained by repeating the same methodological steps to create conglomerates of intensity.

Every value, every spatial unit, is analyzed under four interpretations: two for the geographical process of agglomeration or concentration; and two for the structural (intensity) or numeric (magnitude) nature of the variable. These interpretations lead to two problems addressed in this methodology: a) discrepancy between high global values and high local values and b) intensity effect (overvaluation of small economies and sub-valuation of big ones) and magnitude effect (exclusion of important small areas highly specialized, especially those close to PRC). The suggested methodology, besides addressing these two problems, partially deals with the MAUP and checkerboard problems by aggregating areas, and with physical characteristics of polygons (shape, location and size) by using row-standardized matrices of contiguity, and eliminates zeros to avoid jumps in values.

5.1 Summary and Lessons from the Case Study

The relevant spatial pattern of manufactures in this research can be summarized as follows:

[12]Merida (Yuc) has the greatest number of employees in manufactures in the area, but it is not in any conglomerate, either of intensity or magnitude. As in the case of Empalme (Son), this case shows that analytical scrutiny cannot be replaced by statistical techniques or methodological procedures.

- Industries mainly located in conglomerates of intensity and magnitude that may be overlaid to set up their internal spatial hierarchy. These conglomerates and their hierarchy are identified with a new spatial approach. Potential Regional Conglomerates (PRC) are the most important industrial areas in this hierarchy.
- Most PRC are stable in industrial employment during the period.
- Invariably, PRC are located and expanded selectively in the same locations. These localities are metropolitan areas located in the Central and Northern Region of the country. This result supports the New Economic Geography (NGE) argument that free trade reinforces regional inequalities if regions and cities with initial advantages continue receiving benefits (greater employment in manufactures, in this case). It still needs to be tested whether the Northern region receives the greatest economic benefit, as the NGE asserts.
- The South does not exist for industry, although PRC are perceived in the Southeast, in Merida and its surroundings, in Yucatan.
- The industrial corridor of the Central region stands out. Taking as reference the west, the corridor advances from the Metropolitan Area of Guadalajara to the municipalities of Guanajuato where it bifurcates to north and south. To the north, the corridor climbs up to Aguascalientes and, to south, it goes down to CdMx, reaching Puebla, near Tlaxcala. This corridor has access to the domestic markets of the two main metropolitan areas of Central Mexico, Guadalajara and Mexico City, as well as metropolises of the Bajio region. In 2013, SLP becomes a PRC, located between the corridors of Central Mexico and La Laguna-Metropolitan Area of Monterrey. Both corridors, including SLP, head up towards the international market through the nearest border in the Northeast of the country. This border directly connects cities of the South, Southeast, Middle, and Northeastern US, as well as Eastern and Southeastern Canada (the so-called Heartland).

The case study confirms that there is no statistical technique fully replacing the analytical inspection of results. The explanation of the apparent disappearance of PRC and the detection of promissory industrial zones is possible thanks to the comparative analysis of spatial data in the period (e.g., spatial reconfiguration and change of the economic structure in Empalme), a detailed review of the matrix of neighbors and values of the variable in all surrounding areas (e.g., the matrix of contiguities in the case of Merida), analysis of surrounding areas (Empalme, Sonora), assessment of magnitude in high intensity areas (e.g., municipalities of Oaxaca and Chiapas), and of intensity in areas of high magnitude (e.g., municipalities surrounding the metropolitan areas of Mexico city or Monterrey).

6 Concluding Remarks

The methodology of this research underlines the necessity of simultaneously including intensity and magnitude to compensate or counterbalance their negative effects and reinforce their positive effects, which include enhancement of comparative advantages (measured by specialization) in areas with agglomeration economies (measured by magnitude). While intensity overestimates manufactures in small economies and underestimates them in large and diversified economies, magnitude may neglect important specialized areas, especially those located in the vicinity of potential regional conglomerates (PRC). This same argument is also valid for the conglomerates of intensity and magnitude: each PRC must be analyzed simultaneously considering relative concentration (H_{ij} values) and absolute concentration (number of employments). Otherwise, agglomerations of small economies located high in the mountains of Oaxaca and Guerrero could mistakenly be considered important conglomerates of intensity. In a similar way, agglomerations of well known industrial areas could be neglected because highly diversified environments are usually low relative concentration areas.

The possibility of having agglomerations of small economies with high relative concentrations, on one side, and omissions of agglomerations of highly diversified areas with a significant number of employees, on the other, force us to simultaneously consider both conglomerates of intensity and magnitude to analyze, not only to detect, PRC.

As with any method, the spatial hierarchy in this research has its own limitations:

- It depends on the disaggregation and exactitude of the spatial unit of analysis (e.g., municipalities or AGEB in the Mexican case study).
- It does not provide a spatial hierarchy for not-conglomerated industries.
- It does not include transport networks and natural characteristics of the landscape.
- It requires analytic scrutiny of the results to distinguish real from illusory vanishing of CPR. Scrutiny and field study is also necessary to confirm promissory industrial zones.

Main results in this research are not comparable with those reported by similar studies in Mexico or the rest of the world because there is no background on the methodology suggested. In general, the present study invites scholars to reconsider or evaluate previous studies on the spatial pattern of social problems (e.g., sexually transmitted diseases, criminality, poverty, social backwardness) or economic activities only based on spatial statistics or only on non-spatial statistics. The same invitation is extended for future research on these topics.

Future studies may confront results in this research with those obtained by increasing distances in the matrix of contiguity or expanding the criteria of vicinity to include areas in the second crown of the focal area. Optional results may also be obtained if input variables are smoothed, standardized or transformed.

References

Aiginger K, Rossi-Hansberg E (2006) Specialization and concentration: a note on theory and evidence. Empirica 33(4):255–266. https://doi.org/10.1007/s10663-006-9023-y

Anselin L (1995) Local indicators of spatial association-LISA. Geogr Anal 27(2):93–115

Anselin L (1996) The Moran scatterplot as an ESDA tool to assess local instability in spatial association. In: Fischer MM, Scholten HJ, Unwin D (eds) Spatial analytical perspectives on GIS. Taylor y Francis, London, pp 111–125

Anselin L, Kim YW, Syabri I (2004) Web-based analytical tools for the exploration of spatial data. J Geogr Syst. https://doi.org/10.1007/s10109-004-0132-5

Anselin L, Murray AT, Rey SJ (2013) Spatial analysis. In: Little TD (ed) The Oxford handbook of quantitative methods, vol 2. Oxford: University Press, Oxford

Anselin L, Sridharan S, Gholston S (2007) Using exploratory spatial data analysis to leverage social Indicator databases: the discovery of interesting patterns. Soc Indic Res 82(2):287–309. https://doi.org/10.1007/s11205-006-9034-x

Arbia G (2001) The role of spatial effects in the empirical analysis of regional concentration. J Geogr Syst 3:271–281. https://doi.org/10.1007/PL00011480

Aroca P, Bosch M, Maloney WF (2005) Spatial dimensions of trade liberalization and economic convergence: Mexico 1985-2002. Policy Research Working Papers https://doi.org/10.1596/1813-9450-3744

Arribas-Bel D, Sanz-Gracia F (2014) The validity of the monocentric city model in a polycentric age: US metropolitan areas in 1990, 2000 and 2010. Urban Geogr 35(7):980–997. https://doi.org/10.1080/02723638.2014.940693

Atkins MT, Tonts M (2015) Exploring cities through a population ageing matrix: a spatial and temporal analysis of older adult population trends in Perth, Australia. Aust Geogr 47(1):65–87. https://doi.org/10.1080/00049182.2015.1110087

Baumont C, Ertur C, Gallo JL (2004) Spatial analysis of employment and population density: the case of the agglomeration of Dijon 1999. Geogr Anal 36(2):146–176. https://doi.org/10.1353/geo.2004.0001

Becattini G (2002) Del distrito industrial marshalliano a la «teoría del distrito» contemporánea. Una breve reconstrucción crítica. Investigaciones Regionales 1:9–32. Retrieved from http://www.redalyc.org/articulo.oa?id=28900101

Brantingham P, Brantingham P (1995) Criminality and place: crime generators and crime attractors. Eur J Crim Policy Res 3(3):5–26

Brenner T (2004) Local industrial cluster. Existence, emergence and evolution. Routledge, London

Burt JE, Barber GM, Rigby DL (2009) Elementary statistics for geographers, 3rd edn. Guilford Press, New York

Carroll MC, Reid N, Smith BW (2008) Location quotients versus spatial autocorrelation in identifying potential cluster regions. Ann Reg Sci 42:449–463

Chihara L, Hesterberg T (2011) Mathematical statistics with resampling and R. Wiley, Hoboken

Choudhury NY, Räder C (2014) Targeting the poorest and most vulnerable: examples from Bangladesh. In: Von Braun J, Gatzweiler FW (eds) Marginality: addressing the Nexus of poverty, exclusion and ecology. Springer, Dordrecht

De Dominicis L, Arbia G, De Groot HL (2013) Concentration of manufacturing and service sector activities in Italy: accounting for spatial dependence and firm size distribution. Reg Stud 47(3):405–418. https://doi.org/10.1080/00343404.2011.579593

Feser E, Sweeney S, Renski H (2005) A descriptive analysis of discrete U.S. industrial complexes. J Reg Sci 45(2):395–419. https://doi.org/10.1111/j.0022-4146.2005.00376.x

Fingleton B, Igliori DC, Moore B, Odedra R (2007) Employment growth and clusters dynamics of creative industries in Great Britain. In: Polenske KR (ed) The economic geography of innovation. Cambridge University Press, Cambridge, pp 60–84

Fracasso A, Vittucci Marzetti G (2018) Estimating dynamic localization economies: the inadvertent success of the specialization index and the location quotient. Reg Stud 52(1):119–132. https://doi.org/10.1080/00343404.2017.1281388

Frizado J, Smith BW, Carroll MC, Reid N (2009) Impact of polygon geometry on the identification of economic clusters. Lett Spat Resour Sci 2(1):31–44. https://doi.org/10.1007/s12076-008-0020-6

Goodchild MF, Lam NS (1980) Areal interpolation: A variant of the traditional spatial problem. Geo-Processing, 1: 297–312. http://www.geog.ucsb.edu/~good/papers/46.pdf. Accessed 25 Jan 2016.
Griffith DA (1996) Some guidelines for specifying the geographic weights matrix contained in spatial statistical models. In: Arlinghaus SL, Griffith DA (eds) Practical handbook of spatial statistics. CRC Press, Boca Raton
Hesterberg T, Moore DS, Monaghan S, Clipson A, Epstein R, Craig BA, McCabe GP (2010) Bootstrap methods and permutation tests. In: Moore DS, McCabe GP, Craig BA (eds) Introduction to the practice of statistics, 7th edn. W. H. Freeman, New York
Jiang B (2014) Geospatial analysis requires a different way of thinking: the problem of spatial heterogeneity. GeoJournal. https://doi.org/10.1007/s10708-014-9537-y
Jing N, Cai W (2010) Analysis on the spatial distribution of logistics industry in the developed East Coast area in China. Ann Reg Sci 45(2):331–350. https://doi.org/10.1007/s00168-009-0307-6
Kaygalak I, Reid N (2016) The geographical evolution of manufacturing and industrial policies in Turkey. Appl Geogr 70:37–48. https://doi.org/10.1016/j.apgeog.2016.01.001
Ketels C and Sölvell Ö (2005) Clusters in the EU 10 new member countries. Europe INNOVA. http://www.europe-innova.eu. Accessed 15 Sept 2014
Li Y, Monzur T (2017) The spatial structure of employment in the metropolitan region of Tokyo: a scale-view. Urban Geogr:1–27. https://doi.org/10.1080/02723638.2017.1308182
May W, Mason C, Pinch S (2001) Explaining industrial agglomeration: the case of the British high-fidelity industry. Geoforum 32(3):363–376. https://doi.org/10.1016/s0016-7185(01)00004-5
Moro FN, Villa M (2016) The new geography of mafia activity. The case of a Northern Italian region. Eu Soc Rev:1–13. https://doi.org/10.1093/esr/jcw046
North B, Curtis D, Sham P (2002) A note on the calculation of empirical p values from Monte Carlo procedures. Am J Hum Genet 71(2):439–441. https://doi.org/10.1086/341527
Paez A, Scott DM (2004) Spatial statistics for urban analysis: a review of techniques with examples. GeoJournal 61(1):53–67. https://doi.org/10.1007/s10708-004-0877-x
Parajuli J, Haynes KE (2012) Patterns of broadband efficiency in the U.S. Growth Chang 43 (4):590–614. https://doi.org/10.1111/j.1468-2257.2012.00599.x
Paunero Amigo FX, Sanchez Daza G, Corona Treviño L (2007) Sistemas productivos locales en México. Tipología desde la perspectiva europea Economía Informa 345:216–337. April 18, 2017
Porter ME (1990) The competitive advantage of nations. Free Press, New York
Riguelle F, Thomas I, Verhetsel A (2007) Measuring urban polycentrism: a European case study and its implications. J Econ Geogr 7:193–215. https://doi.org/10.1093/jeg/lbl025
Rogerson P, Yamada I (2009) Statistical detection and surveillance of geographic clusters. Chapman & Hall/CRC, Boca Raton
Shiode N, Morita M, Shiode S, Okunuki K (2014) Urban and rural geographies of aging: a local spatial correlation analysis of aging population measures. Urban Geogr 35(4):608–628. https://doi.org/10.1080/02723638.2014.905256
Szanyi M, Iwasaki I, Csizmadia P, Illésy M, Makó C (2010) 5 cluster development in Hungary: searching for a 'critical mass' of business via cluster mapping. In: Dallago B, Guglielmetti C (eds) Local economies and global competitiveness. Palgrave Macmillan, London
Treviño CJA (2016) Mapa y jerarquía espacial de la pobreza en México. Un nuevo procedimiento para identificar el patrón espacial de los problemas sociales. El Trimestre Económico 83 (332):679–723. https://doi.org/10.20430/ete.v83i332.236
Treviño CJA (2017) Patrón interurbano de la industria en México, 1998-2008. In: Ojeda A, Treviño CJA (eds) Asuntos urbanos en México [PDF], Mexico, pp 167–212. Retrieved from http://www.ameditores.com/asuntos-urbanos-en-mexico

Van den Heuvel FP, De Langen PW, Van Donselaar KH, Fransoo JC (2012) Identification of employment concentration areas. Eur Plan Stud. https://doi.org/10.1080/09654313.2012.741573

Wong DW, Lee J (2005) Statistical analysis of geographic information with ArcView GIS and ArcGIS. John Wiley & Sons, Hoboken

Zhang C (2008) An analysis of urban spatial structure using comprehensive prominence of irregular areas. Int J Geogr Inf Sci 22(6):675–686. https://doi.org/10.1080/13658810701602245

Zhang C, Luo L, Xu W, Ledwith V (2008) Use of local Moran's I and GIS to identify pollution hotspots of Pb in urban soils of Galway, Ireland. Sci Total Environ 398:212–221. https://doi.org/10.1016/j.scitotenv.2008.03.011

Regional Characteristics of Labor Productivity in Mexico's Manufacturing Sector

Jorge Eduardo Mendoza-Cota

Abstract The chapter studies labor productivity in the manufacturing sector of Mexico for the period 2007–2020/01. An analysis of the structure and trends of labor productivity at the state level is studied. Labor productivity at the regional level has shown an uneven growth. In addition, the study discusses the determinants of labor productivity in Mexico and establishes an econometric model to estimate the impact of the determinants of labor productivity. The results suggest that foreign direct investment, schooling, and gross capital formation have positive effects on labor productivity growth.

Keywords Labor productivity · Regional economics · Foreign direct investment · Exports · Schooling

1 Introduction

Labor productivity is an important determinant of the level of economic development because it increases both output and income. Therefore, understanding the determinants of labor productivity is an important basis for promoting policies that encourage economic growth and development. At the international level, there has been an extensive discussion regarding the determinants of productivity of the factors of production. The literature on productivity have considered diverse factors such as foreign direct investment, education, and trade liberalization, among others.

Regarding FDI, the presence of large multinational enterprises could increase productivity by expanding the economies of scale and encouraging the adoption of more efficient technologies. Nevertheless, there are constraints for the process of innovation that are related to the level of education of the workforce. Also, it has been argued that FDI could have an economic efficiency spillover effect by

J. E. Mendoza-Cota (✉)
El Colegio de la Frontera Norte, Departamento de Estudios Económicos, Tijuana, Mexico
e-mail: emendoza@colef.mx

A. de León-Arias, P. Aroca (eds.), *NAFTA's Impact on Mexico's Regional Development*, New Frontiers in Regional Science: Asian Perspectives 51,
https://doi.org/10.1007/978-981-16-3168-9_5

supplementing the lack of financial resources for local firms and adapting new technologies (Toppalova and Khandelwal 2011). Decreuse and Maarek (2015) established a model to address the impact of FDI on labor productivity in developing countries. This approach analyzes productive heterogeneity between firms, in a frictional labor market. According to the authors, FDI has two opposite effects. One the one hand, it increases productivity, due to technological developments, and, on the other hand, encourages labor market competition between firms. Clegg and Wang (2004) studied the multinational firm's effects on the Chinese economy using cross-section data for the year 1995. The results found the existence of technological and labor productivity spillovers within the high-tech foreign firms, which contributed to the upgrading of the Chinese manufacturing sector.

Regarding the role of education in the expansion of labor productivity, Lucas (1988) and Romer (1990) pointed out the importance of human capital for sustained economic growth. However, since the Mexican economy has exhibited a relatively low level of schooling and labor skills, this has limited the impacts of FDI on labor productivity.

With respect to the effect of exports on labor productivity, several papers have indicated that exports and trade could encourage the transmission of ideas and knowledge such as, for example, Grossman and Elhan Helpman (1991), who indicated that trade promotes specialization and therefore allows for "learning by doing" and faster productivity growth.

After the establishment of the North American Free Trade Agreement (NAFTA), the Mexican economy significantly expanded its exports, predominantly in the manufacturing sector. Since the decade of the eighties, the growth of the Mexican economy has been based on a strategy of economic liberalization. One of the arguments used to implement this policy has to do with the importance of foreign direct investment (FDI). It has been proposed that FDI encourages a better allocation of resources and greater productivity in the economy. However, the dynamics of trade have not been able to encourage the rapid growth of labor productivity in the manufacturing sector.

De Hoyos and Iacovone (2013) used a microeconometric approach to estimate the impact of trade integration on the productivity of manufacturing plants in Mexico. The results of the paper underlined the importance of import competition resulting from trade openness. They indicated that trade reform has benefited international trading companies by reducing intermediate input costs, although they do not find exports to be a source of higher productivity. The authors also pointed out that foreign direct investment has been a factor in the growth of productivity in plants acquired by multinationals.

However, Mexico continues to be characterized as an economy with low labor productivity and low wages. The trend of Mexican labor productivity indicates that, at the sectorial and regional level, growth has been rather slow and heterogeneous. Multiple factors have been considered as likely determinants of this stagnant behavior, such as low levels of schooling, and a lack of capital. Furthermore, the establishment of the United States, Mexico, and Canada Agreement (USMCA) has caused a readaptation of the industries engaged in trade to the new rules of origin.

As a result, since 2019, the Mexican economy has experienced a very poor performance. Moreover, with the emergence of the Covid 19 pandemic, the GDP of the Mexican economy presented negative rates of growth. In addition, the recessionary impact has had an adverse effect on labor productivity growth.

One of the main obstacles for Mexico's economic development has been the sluggish growth of labor productivity, both at the sectorial and regional level (Krozer et al. 2015). The long run impact of labor productivity is related to its role in generating higher wages and capital gains. As a result, growth in labor productivity raises consumption and investment, increasing the welfare of the economy (Sprague 2014).

The effects of trade liberalization on efficiency and labor productivity have been discussed extensively. The arguments are, among others, that trade and sound investment decisions will encourage efficiency in production and consumption, greater competitiveness, and the use of internal and external economies of scale. However, in the case of Mexico, it has been claimed that trade expansion could have negative effects on economic growth and productivity by reducing the firms' innovation activities, since they can acquire inputs and technology from external markets (Lopez-Cordova et al. 2003).

The empirical research on labor productivity has produced mixed results. Blomström and Wolff (1994) analyzed the Mexican manufacturing sector with data from year 1970 and encountered that the output per worker was two times higher in multinational corporations than in domestic plants, although total factor productivity was lower due to the effect of greater intensity of capital in the multinational enterprises. Aravena and Fuentes (2013) estimated the total factor productivity and extended it to include human capital. They found that in the Mexican case, productivity growth was related to the intensity of capital. Also, the result showed that the labor skills of workers, measured as the weighted average of schooling, were a relevant factor for explaining the evolution of labor productivity.

An important determinant of labor productivity expansion has to do with labor skills. Both schooling and training increase the productivity of labor, promoting economic growth and the income of the factors of production. Mendoza and Pereyra (2014) studied the impact of highly skilled labor on total workers income for the period 2001–2009. They used a mixpanel model applied to the manufacturing subsectors of Mexico located in the urban areas of the northern border states of Mexico. The results indicated that the productivity of workers with more years of schooling grew at a rate of 4.6% in the period considered, suggesting that labor productivity increases faster in the presence of positive capital flows and FDI. In spite of these results, the authors indicated that the largest share of the employed population showed a low level of education, at the elementary or high school level.

In addition, the specialization of production and FDI positively impacted the wages of urban workers with higher levels of education. The outcome suggests that urban and economic infrastructure generates positive externalities that multiply the positive effects of technological innovation created by FDI and increase the productivity of workers with higher levels of schooling in the manufacturing sector.

Ramirez (2002) analyzed the impact of public infrastructure investment on economic growth and labor productivity for the period 1954–1994 in Mexico. By estimating a cointegration model, they presented a dynamic labor productivity function, including as explanatory variables the stock of public and private capital and the economically active population. The findings indicated that a drastic reduction of public investment could be a factor in decreasing labor productivity. In addition, Castro (2006) and Machuca and Mendoza (2017) estimated econometric models which produced evidence that labor productivity is not improving wages in the manufacturing sector.

Brown and Dominguez (1999) estimated total factor productivity indices in the manufacturing sector. They pointed out that, starting in 1994, the Mexican economy has experienced an increase in labor productivity; however, there was a noticeable heterogeneity in the manufacturing sector. In a second paper, Brown and Dominguez (1999) estimated an econometric model to analyze the impact of microeconomic variables (technology, advertisement, etc.) and macroeconomic variables (GDP, imports, and exports) on manufacturing productivity. The results suggested that there are heterogeneous impacts of the explanatory variables, depending on the intensity of capital and the location of the manufacturing industries.

The characteristics of productivity growth were studied by De Leon (1995). According to the author's estimations, up to the early nineties, the large urban areas of Mexico were leading the productivity increases, while the northern border of Mexico exhibited lower growth rates than the national average. This result changed after the decade of the nineties and the northern border region started to experience more rapid rates of productivity growth. Mendoza (2004) pointed out that in the in-bond assembly plants (maquiladoras) there are different levels of technological endowments, size, and labor training, creating diverse levels of labor productivity both at the national level and in the northern Border States. Appling a growth model with panel data to the maquiladora industry for the period 1991–1999, he found that the central states of Mexico experienced higher levels of labor productivity than those of the northern Border States. The subsectors that showed higher labor productivity were metallic products, machinery and equipment, chemical products, and rubber and plastics industries. Therefore, both theoretical and empirical studies on labor productivity have shown that capital, schooling, and labor training are important factors for encouraging labor productivity.

Within this context, the present paper seeks to analyze labor productivity growth in the manufacturing sector of Mexico and the determinants of that growth at the regional level. The analysis considers information for the period 2007–2020/1 in order to capture recent historic developments in labor productivity. The variables used are FDI, manufacturing exports, technical schooling, labor training, and gross capital formation at the state level.

In order to assess the determinants of labor productivity in Mexico, a fixed panel data econometric model was developed. The estimations indicated that FDI and fixed capital formation and labor training positively impacted labor productivity. Also, the results exhibited positive effects of schooling and public infrastructure, which underline the importance of regional manufacturing interconnections at the state level.

The document is structured as follows. The introduction, which included a review of the theoretical empirical findings on the contributing factors of labor productivity; the second section analyzes the structure and trends of labor productivity in the manufacturing sector at the regional level; the third section describes the methodological strategy and databases; in the fourth section the results of the fixed panel econometric model are discussed, and section five presents the conclusions of the paper.

2 Trends of Labor Productivity in Mexico

2.1 Labor Productivity in the Mexican Economy

There are several causes of the lack of dynamism of labor productivity in Mexico. Hanson (2010) pointed out that the high proportion of the labor force employed in the informal sector partially explained the slow growth of labor productivity. The author argues that both the low level of returns of labor experience in the informal markets and the existence of government social programs have constrained the incentives for human capital accumulation. Another aspect is related to the poor success of the Mexican education system, as shown by the poor test results in the PISA (Programme for International Student Assessment) test results, and which has negatively impacted economic growth (Arias et al. 2010).

According to information from the National Institute of Statistics and Geography (INEGI), the global labor index of the Mexican economy, measured using the quarterly real GDP and the number of occupied workers and hours worked[1], showed limited growth during the period 2005–2017, where it increased from 97.6 the first quarter of 2005 to 106.6 in the third quarter of 2017, representing a quarterly average growth rate of 0.2%. (Fig. 1).

It is important to note that trends in labor productivity indices, measured by the number of workers employed and the number of hours worked, differ only during economic recessions. Thus, between the first and third quarters of 2009 there was a smaller drop in the productivity of labor measured by hours worked, due to a smaller decrease in hours worked than the occupied workers. Similarly, in the first three quarters of 2020, the labor productivity measured by the hours worked increased markedly in relation to the labor productivity measured by the occupation of workers. In any case, both trends can be used as general indicators of labor

[1]The global labor productivity rates of the economy are calculated based on two benchmarks: the number of workers employed, and hours worked. This index results from the division of the real GDP index, and the index of the occupied population and hours worked, and is presented quarterly.

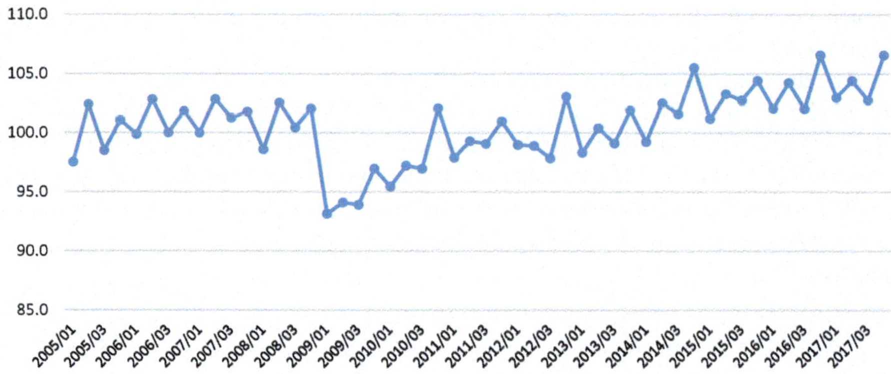

Fig. 1 The Global Labor Productivity Index 2005/1–2017/3. Source: Own elaboration with data from Global Index of Labor Productivity in Mexico published by the National Institute of Statistics, Geography, and Informatics (INEGI)

Fig. 2 Annual Percentage Change of Labor Productivity Based on Hours Worked and Occupied Workers, 2005–2020. Source: Own elaboration with data from Global Index of Labor Productivity in Mexico published by the National Institute of Statistics, Geography, and Informatics (INEGI)

productivity in Mexico over a long-term horizon and during periods of economic expansion (Fig. 2).

In addition, the labor productivity performance of the Mexican economy exhibited irregular growth. From 2006 to 2009, the average annual rate of growth was negative, at −1.32%; this was the result of the negative impact on productivity generated by the recession of 2008 and 2009. The period also exhibited a great volatility, given the positive productivity growth of 2006 and 2007 (Table 1).

Table 1 Global index of labor productivity in Mexico. Quarterly percentage change

2006–2009	% change	2010–2013	% change	2014–2017	% change	2018–2020	% change
2006/01	2.4	2010/01	2.5	2014/01	0.9	2018/01	−0.5
2006/02	0.4	2010/02	3.3	2014/02	2.1	2018/02	0.2
2006/03	1.5	2010/03	3.3	2014/03	2.5	2018/03	−0.2
2006/04	0.7	2010/04	5.2	2014/04	3.5	2018/04	−1.4
2007/01	0.1	2011/01	2.5	2015/01	2	2019/01	−1.3
2007/02	0	2011/02	2.1	2015/02	0.8	2019/02	−3.2
2007/03	1.3	2011/03	2.2	2015/03	1.2	2019/03	−2.6
2007/04	0	2011/04	−1.1	2015/04	−1	2019/04	−3.4
2008/01	−1.4	2012/01	1.1	2016/01	0.9	2020/01	−3.4
2008/02	−0.3	2012/02	−0.4	2016/02	0.9	2020/02	0.9
2008/03	−0.8	2012/03	−1.2	2016/03	−0.7		
2008/04	0.2	2012/04	2.1	2016/04	2.1		
2009/01	−5.5	2013/01	−0.7	2017/01	0.9		
2009/02	−8.2	2013/02	1.5	2017/02	0.2		
2009/03	−6.5	2013/03	1.3	2017/03	0.7		
2009/04	−5	2013/04	−1.1	2017/04	0		
Mean	−1.3		1.4		1.1		−1.5
Standard deviation	3.2		1.9		1.2		1.6

Source: Own elaboration with data from INEGI, National Accounting System of Mexico

2.2 *Labor Productivity in the Mexican Manufacturing Sector*

The labor market of the Mexican manufacturing exhibited three characteristics with respect to labor productivity and the share of wages to value added in that sector. The first aspect is that, according to the Economic Census, between 2004 and 2014, the average labor productivity, as measured by the manufacturing sector value added in dollars divided by the number of hours worked, showed a slightly higher growth than the national level with 4.9% and 2.5%, respectively. However, when estimating the average rate of growth for the period 2004–2019, a drop in the rate of growth is observed, falling to 0.7% at the national level and to 4.7% for the manufacturing sector (Table 2). It is important to underline that this measure of average labor productivity is higher than that presented in the last section because it is denominated in dollars and, therefore, captures the competitive effect of the Mexican peso depreciation. This difference in the rhythm of growth of the manufacturing sector is partially explained by the presence of exporting firms in the automotive and electronic sectors, which have enhanced the production and productivity of the economy.

The second characteristic of the manufacturing labor market is that workers' income rose at a lower rate than labor productivity. As a result, the share of workers' income in the total value added decreased from 24.8% to 21.2% at the national level

Table 2 Labor productivity and share of workers' income in the value added (dollars)

	Productivity rates of growth			Workers' income share of value added	
	National	Manufactures		National	Manufactures
2004–2009	1.2%	3.1%	2004	24.8%	30.6%
2009–2014	1.3%	1.8%	2009	21.2%	24.8%
2014–2019	−1.8%	−0.2%	2014	23.3%	21.2%
2004–2014	2.5%	4.9%	2019	14.0%	14.8%
2004–2019	0.7%	4.7%			

Source: Own elaboration with data from the Mexican Economic Census 2004, 2009, and 2014, INEGI and exchange rates from Bank of Mexico

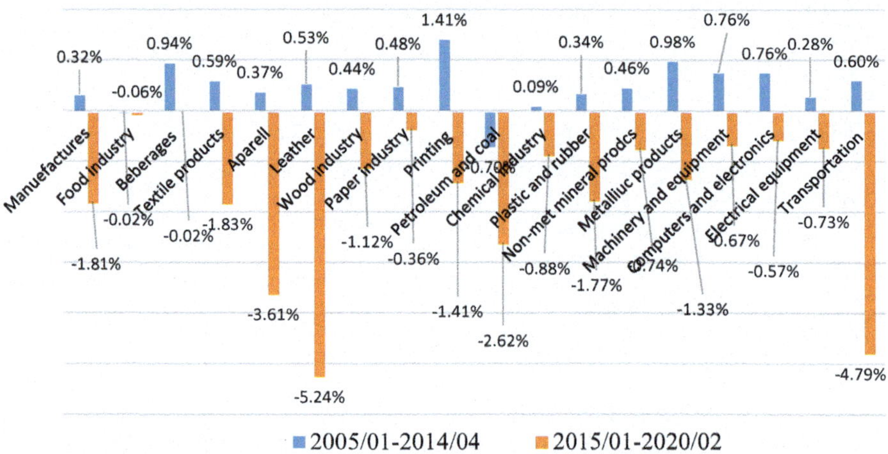

Fig. 3 Labor productivity in the manufacturing sector, 2005–2014 and 2015–2020/2. Source: Own elaboration with data from Monthly manufacturing Industry Survey, INEGI

from 2004 to 2009, and from 30.6% to 24.8% in the manufacturing sector during the same period. In 2019, labor productivity fell dramatically due to the large depreciation of the peso against the dollar.

Finally, within the manufacturing subsectors there is great heterogeneity. During the period 2005–2014, the fastest average rates of growth of labor productivity were experienced in the basic metallic industry, machinery and equipment, and printing, among others. In contrast, paper industry, electric equipment, and plastic and rubber industries exhibited moderate rates of growth. In fact, several manufacturing industries experienced negative rates of growth, such as the food industry, and petroleum and coal. However, during the period 2015/1 to 2020/2 there was an evident decline in labor productivity, which was heavily impacted by the drop in production derived from the Covid 19 pandemic (Fig. 3).

2.3 *Regional Characteristics of Labor Productivity Growth*

Besides the heterogeneity of labor productivity growth experienced within the manufacturing sector, there was also a high heterogeneity at the regional level. This diverse rhythm of labor productivity growth of the Mexican states was related to the re-localization of the manufacturing production process that expanded the exporting industries with higher technology and efficient methods of production (Mendoza 2004).

The manufacturing labor productivity at the state level shows that most of the states presented different levels of labor productivity. Between 2007/1 and 2020/1 Jalisco, Queretaro, and Puebla showed the fastest quarterly average rate of growth in the manufacturing sector. The determinant of this relatively rapid labor productivity growth could be related to the FDI in the electronic and automobile industries in those states. They were followed by the states of Chihuahua, and Baja California, which are characterized by their proximity to the USA and the localization of the in-bond assembly plants (maquiladoras) within those states (Fig. 4). In addition, Mexico City, the state of Mexico, and the central states of San Luis Potosi and Guanajuato showed rapid labor productivity growth, possibly because of a higher level of technology and capital endowments in the plants localized in that region.

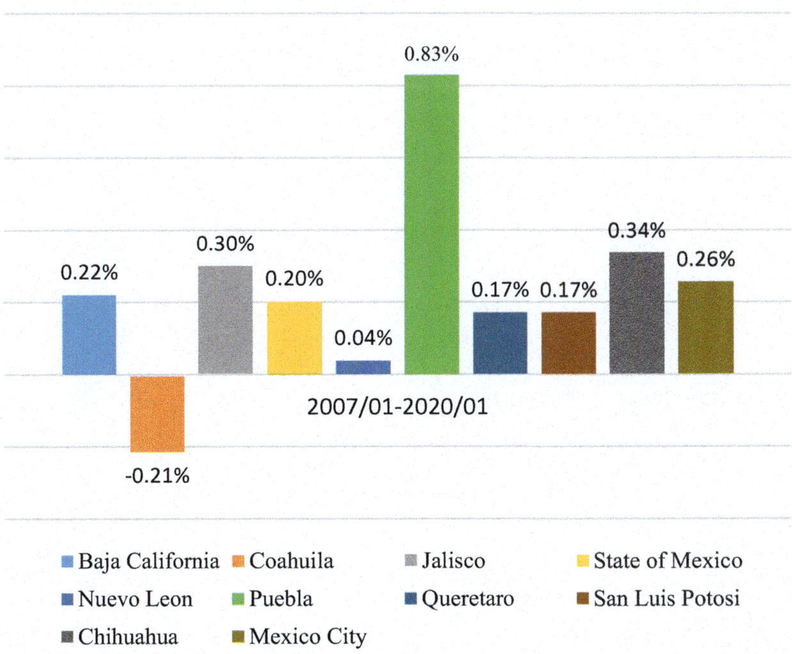

Fig. 4 Quaterly average rate of labor productivity growth of the major states of Mexico, 2007/01–2020/1. Source: Own elaboration with data from the Bank of Economic Information of INEGI. AARG = annual average rate of growth. 1. Value added divided per hours worked

3 Determinants of Labor Productivity in Mexico

In order to analyze the most significant determinants of Mexican labor productivity an econometric panel model was estimated. This methodology was applied to solve the correlation of statistical errors associated with non-observable effects. The period considered was from 2007 to 2016 for the 32 states of Mexico. The variables analyzed in the model included labor productivity and value added, which were obtained from the Mexican Industry Monthly Survey (EMIM for its acronym in Spanish). The variables of gross capital formation, FDI, and manufacturing exports, at the state level, were obtained from the Economic Information Bank (BIE) from the National Institute of Geography and Statistics (INEGI). Labor training and technical high school were gathered from the Interactive System of Educational Statistics of Mexico.

The estimation of the model presented mixed results. The FDI and technical schooling coefficients were positive and statistically significant (Table 3). This outcome supports the results of previous literature regarding labor productivity. The presence of FDI encourages the development of labor skills because it incorporates productive processes that require higher labor abilities and schooling. Also, the results agree with previous papers that have found a positive effect of schooling on the GDP per capita growth in several economies, such as Barro (1991) and

Table 3 Fixed panel model with random perturbations AR(1)

Number of groups	32			
Number of observations	287			
R squared				
Total	0.1805			
Corr(u_i, Xb)	= 0.2910	F(5,250)	= 8.60	
		Prob > F	= 0.00	
LPl	Coef.	Std. err.	t	P > |t|
FGKF	0.1175	0.2456	0.479	0
EXP	−0.0316	0.0332	−0.95	0.342
LTR	−0.0104	0.0408	−0.26	0.799
TS	0.2887	0.0688	3.03	0.003
FDI	0.0186	0.0111	1.68	0.094
Cons	0.4673	0.4363	1.07	0.285
Rho	0.3254			
sigma_u	1.0817			
sigma_e	0.1796			
rho_fov	0.9731			
F test u_i = 0				
Prob > F = 0.0000				

Source: Own elaboration. *LP* Labor productivity, *FGKF* Fixed gross capital formation, *Exp* Manufacturing exports, *LTR* Labor training, *TS* Students with technical high school, *FDI* Foreign direct investment

Sala-i-Martin (1997), among others. In addition, FDI encourages greater productivity by creating incentives for firms to expand production and exports to foreign markets (Helpman et al. 2004). In contrast, the coefficient of labor training was negative. This result is the opposite of the expected effect, which considers that labor training should increase labor skills and, therefore, labor productivity. Probably, the effect of labor training in the model is imprecise, since the variable encompasses the total amount of workers at the national level, not only in the manufacturing sector.

The negative sign of the coefficient of manufacturing exports at the state level could be explained by the way exports are registered in Mexico by the exporting firms. Typically, the firms with administrative offices in Mexico City register that locality as the origin of the state exports, which distorts the econometric estimations.

Overall, the estimation of the panel model corroborates two significant aspects: the role of FDI as a mechanism to transmit more efficient methods of production that could drive up labor productivity and the importance of increasing the level of education of workers in order to be able to implement technological innovations within the production process. In this regard, the positive impact of technical training at the high school level substantiates the significance of schooling and labor training in encouraging the increase of labor productivity. Finally, the state gross capital formation coefficient indicates the importance of private and public investment for promoting labor productivity.

4 Concluding Remarks

The moderate growth of labor productivity has been an obstacle for its Mexico's rapid economic growth and for wage increases. During the period studied, both labor income and labor productivity in the manufacturing sector experienced rather slow growth. Three important characteristics of labor productivity in the manufacturing sector stand out. First, labor productivity in the manufacturing sector increased at a slightly faster rate than the national average. Second, labor productivity grew faster than wages, possibly determined by institutional factors constraining wage expansion. A third aspect has to do with the heterogeneity of the speed of growth of the manufacturing sector labor productivity, both at the sectoral and state level. At the regional level, labor productivity was lower in the northern Border States, which reflect the low labor skills required in the maquiladora industry; whereas central states such as Guanajuato and Queretaro experienced important increases in productivity. At the sectoral level, the subsector of metallic industries exhibited higher labor productivity, whereas light industries like food and beverages exhibited lower labor productivity.

As mentioned above, several authors have presented a variety of possible determinants of labor productivity. In this chapter, the analysis of labor productivity is approached from a macroeconomic perspective. The econometric model includes variables that have been used in theoretical and empirical studies. The results of the estimations provide evidence that FDI boosts labor productivity by promoting technological innovation at the production level. However, the positive effects of FDI are constrained by certain structural problems of the Mexican economy, such as low levels of education and low public spending on infrastructure. Although the coefficient suggests positive effects of these two variables on labor productivity, the comparatively low levels of schooling and the lack of public infrastructure provide an explanation of the rather stagnant growth of labor productivity in Mexico.

From the results, it can be concluded that it is important to improve the quality and facilitate the access to technical and higher education, as well as training courses to increase the added value generated by the labor factor. Additionally, policies to promote infrastructure investments aimed at increasing trade and reducing costs should be implemented to encourage an overall productivity expansion.

Finally, it is important to mention that the Covid-19 pandemic has had an adverse effect on labor productivity growth, given that the recessionary phase of the business cycle has reduced the levels of production and employment in the Mexican economy and its manufacturing sector. Further development of labor productivity will depend on the recovery time of the pandemic and on the upturn of Mexican production, and on trade and investment within the USMCA.

References

Aravena C, Fuentes JA (2013) El desempeño mediocre de la productividad laboral en América Latina: una interpretación neoclásica. In: Serie Macroeconomía del Desarrollo, vol 140. Cepal, Santiago

Arias J, Azuara O, Bernal P, Heckman J and Villarreal C (2010) Policies to promote growth and economic efficiency in Mexico. Institute for the Study of labor. Discussion paper 4740

Barro RJ (1991) Economic growth in a cross section of countries. Q J Econ 2(106):407–444

Blomström M and Wolff EW (1994) Multinational Corporations and Productivity Convergence in Mexico. In W. Baumol, R. Nelson and E. Wolff (eds.) Convergence of Productivity: Cross-national Studies and Historical Evidence, Oxford: Oxford University Press

Brown G, Dominguez L (1999) Dinámica de la productividad manufacturera. In Brown F and Dominguez L, L (Comps.), Productividad: desafío de la industria mexicana, Jus/UNAM, México

Castro D (2006) Curva salarial: una aplicación para el caso de México, 1993-2002. Estudios Económicos 21(2):233–273

Clegg J, Wang C (2004) The impact of inward FDI on the performance of Chinese manufacturing firms. The challenge of international business. Palgrave Macmillan, London

De Hoyos RE, Iacovone L (2013) Economic performance under NAFTA: a firm-level analysis of the trade-productivity linkages. World Dev 44:180–193

De Leon A (1995) Cambio regional y productividad en México. In: Arroyo J, De Leon A (eds) Ajustes y desajustes regionales. Universidad de Guadalajara/UCLA, programa sobre México, Guadalajara

Decreuse B, Maarek P (2015) FDI and the labor share in developing countries: a theory and some evidence. Ann Econom Stat/Annales d'Économie et de Statistique 119/120:289–319

Grossman G, Elhan Helpman E (1991) Innovation and growth in the global economy. MIT Press, Cambridge

Hanson G (2010) Why Isn't Mexico rich? J Econ Lit 48(4):987–1004

Helpman E, Melitz M, Yeaple S (2004) Exports versus FDI with heterogeneous firms. Am Econ Rev 94:300–316

Krozer A, Moreno JC, Rubio JC (2015) Inequality and minimum wage policy: not even talking, much less walking in Mexico. Investigación Económica 74(293):3–26

Lopez-Cordova E, Esquivel G, Monge A (2003) NAFTA and manufacturing productivity in Mexico. Economía 4(1):55–98

Lucas RE (1988) On the mechanics of economic development. J Monet Econ 22(1):3–42

Machuca JA, Mendoza JE (2017) Salarios, desempleo y productividad laboral en la industria manufacturera mexicana. Ensayos 36(2):185–228

Mendoza JE (2004) Productividad del trabajo en la industria maquiladora del norte de México: un análisis de convergencia. EconoQuantum I(1):57–81

Mendoza JE, Pereyra JA (2014) Trabajo calificado, especialización y productividad laboral urbana en la frontera norte de México: un análisis de panel de efectos mixtos. Investigación Económica LXXIII(287):89–119

Ramirez MD (2002) Public capital formation and labor productivity growth in Mexico. Atl Econ J 30(4):366–379

Romer PM (1990) Endogenous technological change. J Polit Econ 98(5):S71–S102

Sala-I-Martin X (1997) I Just Ran Four Million Regressions. National Bureau of Economic Research, Working Paper 6252

Sprague S (2014) What Can Labor Productivity Tell Us About the U.S. Economy? Bureau Labor Statistics 3(12) https://stats.bls.gov/opub/btn/volume-3/pdf/what-can-labor-productivity-tell-us-about-the-us-economy.pdf

Toppalova P, Khandelwal A (2011) Trade liberalization and firm productivity: the case of India. Rev Econ Stat 93(3):995–1009

Value Added in Exports Under NAFTA: A Binational Input–Output Model

Noé Arón Fuentes, Alejandro Brugués, and Gabriel González-König

Abstract The work highlights the stylized fact that Mexico has had a significant gross trade surplus with the USA during the NAFTA period, proving the existence of a notable deficit for Mexico in terms of the added value incorporated in this trade. The value-added flow in Mexico's gross exports to the USA only reaches 164.4 billion dollars, while the domestic content of the USA gross exports is 188.7 billion dollars. In the disaggregation of added value, the great difference between domestic and foreign components incorporated in exports stands out, while for the USA the foreign added value in its exports reaches 2.5 billion dollars for the case of Mexico, this concept is 50.2 billion dollars, which is more than 20 times the amount it represents for the USA. A conclusion that derives directly from this last aspect is that during NAFTA an important part of the income from Mexican exports goes to remunerate productive factors used in the USA.

Keywords Value added in gross exports · Global value chains · NAFTA · Bilateral product input

1 Introduction

Perhaps the most important result during the period of the North American Free Trade Agreement (NAFTA) is the drastic change in the trade relationship between the USA and Mexico, turning Mexico's trade deficit into a surplus. This caused former President Donald Trump to decide to renegotiate or cancel it.

As an example of this stylized fact is that between 2013 and 2016, the commercial flow between both countries was more than 500 billion dollars annually. Of these, US imports originating in Mexico reached values close to 300 billion dollars and exports to Mexico showed figures around 240 billion dollars. Consequently, the

N. A. Fuentes · A. Brugués (✉) · G. González-König
El Colegio de la Frontera Norte, Tijuana, Mexico
e-mail: afuentes@colef.mx; abrugues@colef.mx; ggkoning@colef.mx

A. de León-Arias, P. Aroca (eds.), *NAFTA's Impact on Mexico's Regional Development*, New Frontiers in Regional Science: Asian Perspectives 51,
https://doi.org/10.1007/978-981-16-3168-9_6

gross trade deficit of the USA with Mexico, according to official statistics, was around 60 billion dollars for this period (Chiñas 2017).

However, during NAFTA both countries have maintained an intense flow of trade in intermediate inputs in respect of which an overestimation of the values recorded by their double counting is recognized as they are incorporated into the products that use them (Lalanne 2016). Moreover, it is known that the higher the content of intermediate input imports in Mexican exports, the lower the added value generated in Mexico and, therefore, a greater part of the export revenue is used to remunerate productive factors used in USA (De La Cruz et al. 2011; Fujii Gambero and Cervantes 2013). Hence, a correct measurement of the added value contained in exports between these two countries is a basic starting point for the net quantification of the trade balance and for assessing the relevance or effects of a change in the bilateral trade policy.

The present work carries out a binational and sectoral analysis for the study of the added value incorporated in trade between the USA and Mexico for 2013. The objective is to apply a methodology that allows us to characterize the commercial integration between both countries during NAFTA and investigate the breakdown of the content of the bilateral value added by making a comparative analysis between countries and sectors. To this end, a bi-regional (or binational) input-output table is used as an analytical framework, allowing, among other advantages, to analyze the interregional and intersectoral links of both countries (Miller and Blair 2009).

It is also important to mention some publications related to this current work. Boundi-Chraki analyzes the dependence and integration in NAFTA, especially the inter-relationship of Mexico with the USA and Canada by calculating the backward linkages, the forward linkages, and the interregional feedbacks generated by the three countries (Boundi-Chraki 2017). Torre, Chapa, and González estimate Mexico's gross output and its value added linked to the economic activity of the USA by sectors and regions (Torre et al. 2020). Lastly, Aroche and Marquez hypothesized that changes in the level of integration affect the ability an economy has to provide welfare opportunities to its population. They also show that a reduction in the degree of integration of an economy weakens its ability to achieve steady growth, because of the loss of the propagating effects of an expanding demand, even if exports expand at high rates. This might explain the disappointing performance of the Mexican economy in regard to these issues even after structural reforms have been adopted and exports growth has become a central component of the development strategy (Aroche and Marquez 2012).

The work is structured in such a way that Sect. 1 reviews the literature on vertical productive specialization and the measurement of added value contained in foreign trade. Section 2 presents the methodology for the breakdown of the added value of bilateral trade and its limits. Section 3 shows the database used and the estimation of the binational product input model for 2013. Section 4 shows the estimates of the value-added breakdown and a comparison of the sectoral results between the two countries. Finally, Section 5 indicates the relevance of the exercise for the USA and Mexico case.

2 Literature Review

NAFTA has been consistent with the increase in cross-border trade between countries, which is a dominant feature today and is a challenge for measuring world trade volumes. In particular, during this period, vertically integrated global production chains have emerged.

There is international literature that studies patterns of productive specializations from the perspective of the vertical integration of productive processes that employ a structural framework of product input. This highlights the seminal work of (Hummels et al. 2001), which adopts a global inter-country input–output (GICIO) and provides a formulation for the calculation of content in intermediate imports in exports, variable that they call vertical specialization (VS).

Additionally, there is literature that quantifies the content of value added in world trade using a multi-country input-output table (Trefler and Zhu 2010; Daudin et al. 2011; Johnson and Noguera 2012a, b; Koopman et al. 2012, 2014), which employs a GICIO and others like (Timmer et al. 2013; Baldwin and Lopez-Gonzalez 2015; Johnson 2014; Solaz 2016), which uses the World Input Output Database (WIOD). It is important to point out that the work of (Koopman et al. 2012) integrates vertical specialization measures and the breakdown of value added in international trade into a multi-country conceptual framework.

Torre et al. (2020) based their work on the World Input-Output Database 2016 and using the Hypothetical Extraction Method to estimate Mexico's gross output and value added linked to the economic activity of the USA and then the gross output and value added of the USA linked to Mexico's economic activity as well as the Ghosh Regional Model to estimate how the value added of Mexico linked to the economic activity in the USA is allocated among its sectors and regions. The authors capture the strong economic linkage between both economies at the aggregate level, as well as its sectoral concentration. The results also indicate that the Northern and Central regions of Mexico are those with the strongest link to the USA, followed by the Southern region, where the largest share of the oil industry is located (Torre et al. 2020). While Boundi-Chraki (2017) analyzes the dependence and integration in NAFTA, especially the inter-relationship of Mexico with the USA and Canada by calculating the backward linkages, the forward linkages, and the interregional feedbacks generated by the three countries (Boundi-Chraki 2017). And Aroche and Márquez (2012) employ the "important coefficients" of the input–output table as indicators of the level of integration between the industries in an economic structure. An economic structure is defined as a set of interdependent sectors linked by a set of intermediate demand flows. Such flows define the character of the aforementioned structure. It is hypothesized that changes in the level of integration affect the ability an economy has to provide welfare opportunities to its population. The article also shows that a reduction in the degree of integration of an economy weakens its ability to achieve steady growth, because of the loss of the propagating effects of an expanding demand, even if exports expand at high rates.

In addition, there is some international literature that addresses the national content of intermediate inputs in exports from the USA and Mexico during the NAFTA period. The most direct works by their scope and methodology are those of (De La Cruz et al. 2011) and (Fujii Gambero and Cervantes 2013). Both are based on the input-output table for Mexico, prepared by the National Institute of Statistics and Geography (Instituto Nacional de Estadística y Geografía—INEGI in Spanish) with data from 2003 and make estimates separately for the export maquiladora industry and for the rest of the activities exporters included in what INEGI calls the internal economy, both estimates used in the national model.[1]

They apply the methodology of (Koopman et al. 2012) that seeks to discriminate the information of companies in special foreign trade regimes in order to improve the estimation of the imported component of imports, under the premise that these companies have greater relative use of imported inputs than traditional companies do. The estimation strategy was to create new rows and columns in the single country model for these specific companies. The estimated single country model assumes that the companies (or rather the operations) that carry out *processing exports* allocate all their product to the final demand abroad, so that the intermediate use of these industries is zero. Thus, the national added value contained in exports is broken down into two parts: a fraction generated by maquiladora industry exports and, the other, by internal economy exports. In turn, each of these subdivides the direct and indirect added value contained in exports that estimated from the multipliers derived from the table of added value coefficients contained in IME and EI exports.

(De La Cruz et al. 2011) conclude that more than 85% of its exports are operations of global value chains. In addition, their estimates suggest that, on average, Mexican manufacturing exports have a share in the domestic added value of around 34%. Industries that have a national content of less than 50% represent approximately 80% of the country's manufacturing exports. The low internal value-added industries include computer and peripheral equipment, audio and video equipment, semiconductors and electronics. Industries with content greater than 65% represent only 5.1% of total exports of manufactured goods from Mexico. They also point out that the export industries that tend to use the IME program, for example, electronics, have a low domestic added value, while the industries that export under PITEX—the automobile and machinery industry—have a relatively higher domestic content.

Meanwhile (Fujii Gambero and Cervantes 2013) point out that the EMI with 62% of manufacturing exports contribute only 33% of the domestic added value contained in them. For its part, EI, which has 38% of exports, contributes 67% of the internal added value contained in exports. In the manufacturing sector, the added value of national origin represents 42% of the value of manufactured exports. This

[1]De La Cruz et al. (2011) makes the observation that INEGI reports information only on IME, but not on PITEX (Programa de Importación Temporal para Exportación), so Mexican imports from the US might be underestimated. They include data from both IME and PITEX.

proportion is significantly higher in EI exports (75%) than in IME (22%). Finally, the electronics (29% of the total), transportation (28%), and electrical equipment (9% of the total) sectors together contribute 66% of the value of the country's manufacturing exports.

The single country approach used by the last authors allows estimating the added value of exports without having to resort to multi-country input-output models, but to work directly with the domestic input-output table. However, single country models suffer from certain limitations when they are used to estimate the imports contained in exports: existence of the domestic and imported utilization table and their official availability.

3 Value-Added Methodology in Binational Trade

(Koopman et al. 2012) synthesize the conceptual framework that allows the complete breakdown of the origin of the added value contained in exports. In addition, they developed a general formulation and include the particular case of two countries (1 and 2). In the latter case, the partition of the input–output matrices balance equation for both countries is formally expressed by

$$\begin{bmatrix} x_1 \\ x_2 \end{bmatrix} = \begin{bmatrix} a_{11} & a_{12} \\ a_{21} & a_{22} \end{bmatrix} \begin{bmatrix} x_1 \\ x_2 \end{bmatrix} + \begin{bmatrix} y_{11} + y_{12} \\ y_{21} + y_{22} \end{bmatrix} \quad (1)$$

where x_1 is total gross production of country 1 used as an intermediate or final input, internally or externally; y_{12} is the final demand in country 2 of final goods of country 1; and a_{ij} are the technical coefficients or direct coefficients. The same interpretation will be for x_2 denoting country 2.

Rearranging the previous terms we have

$$\begin{bmatrix} x_1 \\ x_2 \end{bmatrix} = \begin{bmatrix} I - a_{11} & a_{12} \\ a_{21} & I - a_{22} \end{bmatrix}^{-1} \begin{bmatrix} y_{11} + y_{12} \\ y_{21} + y_{22} \end{bmatrix} = \begin{bmatrix} b_{11} & b_{12} \\ b_{21} & b_{22} \end{bmatrix} \begin{bmatrix} y_1 \\ y_2 \end{bmatrix} \quad (2)$$

where b_{ij} are the Leontief inverse or total coefficients, likewise, $y_1 = y_{11} + y_{12}$, and $y_2 = y_{21} + y_{22}$.

Defining the direct coefficients of added value (v_i) as the division of the added value (VA_i) between the production for each sector (X_i) and expressing it in a matrix way (although having no interaction they are treated as independent vectors), we have the following:

$$V = \begin{bmatrix} v_1 & 0 \\ 0 & v_2 \end{bmatrix} \quad (3)$$

Pre-multiplying Eq. (2) by Eq. (3) results in the internal and external value-added participation of country 1 and country 2, respectively. Following (Koopman et al. 2012) and without loss of generality, we can only work with the gross exports of country 1 to define the conceptual framework of value-added decomposition:

$$\begin{aligned} e_{12} &= y_{12} + a_{12}x_2 = [v_1b_{11}e_{12} + v_2b_{21}e_{12}] \\ &= [v_1b_{11}y_{12} + v_1b_{12}y_{22}] + \left[v_1b_{12}y_{21} + v_1b_{21}a_{12}(1 - a_{11})^{-1}y_{11}\right] \\ &\quad + v_1b_{21}a_{21}(1 - a_{11})^{-1}e_{12} + \left[v_2b_{21}y_{12} + v_2b_{21}a_{12}(1 - a_{22})^{-1}y_{22}\right] \\ &\quad + v_2b_{21}a_{12}(1 - a_{22})^{-1}e_{21} \end{aligned} \tag{4}$$

Equation (4) says that the gross exports of country 1 consist of final and intermediate goods and is made up of eight terms. Of these, the first two represent the domestic added value absorbed by the foreign economy, being in the case of the first through the final demand served directly by the domestic country and in the second by the final demand of the foreigner satisfied from abroad, the formulations would be expressed as:

$$\boldsymbol{v}_1 = v_1b_{11}y_{12} \tag{5}$$

$$\boldsymbol{v}_2 = v_1b_{12}y_{22} \tag{6}$$

The third term is domestic added value that is initially exported as an intermediate input but is returned to the domestic country as part of the final imports of the domestic country, being expressed as:

$$\boldsymbol{v}_3 = v_1b_{12}y_{21} \tag{7}$$

The following term also represents the value added initially exported as an intermediate input but which in this case is returned to the country as part of the intermediate imports of the foreign country that are integrated into the final domestic products consumed in the domestic country:

$$\boldsymbol{v}_4 = v_1b_{12}a_{21}(1 - a_{11})^{-1}y_{11} \tag{8}$$

The following term represents pure double counting and occurs when both countries export intermediate consumer goods back and forth that are absorbed by new exports of intermediate goods from the domestic country:

$$\boldsymbol{v}_5 = v_1b_{12}a_{21}(1 - a_{11})^{-1}e_{12} \tag{9}$$

The sixth term is the foreign value added in the gross exports of the domestic country:

$$v_6 = v_2 b_{21} y_{12} \quad (10)$$

The next term is part together with the previous one to the value added abroad that returns to it, in this case as part of the consumption of final goods in that country:

$$v_7 = v_2 b_{21} a_{12} (1 - a_{22})^{-1} y_{22} \quad (11)$$

The last term is the one that represents the trade in both directions of intermediate goods that are returned abroad as intermediate goods and represent together with $\mathbf{v}_5$ the double counting in international trade although in this case the one that returns abroad.

$$v_8 = v_2 b_{21} a_{12} (1 - a_{22})^{-1} e_{21} \quad (12)$$

The application developed for the economies of the USA and Mexico needs to consider a modification of the original model. By not having the rest of the world included in the binational model, it is not possible to determine the Mexican added value in extraregional intermediate inputs. This assumption implies that exports from the rest of the world behave as if they were of final goods. Thus, the VS[2] is overestimated and the VS1[3] will be underestimated. It is also important to recognize that according to the authors of the methodology in countries with high participation in global production chains, the added value that returns could be important.

4 Binational Input-Output Table

(Koopman et al. 2012) develop a conceptual framework based on a multi-country input–output model and its decomposition into a matrix of technical coefficients, a matrix of global and country total requirements, production vectors, final demand both internal and by country, exports and domestic and by country added value. Based on this, they make an analytical derivation of the previous eight components that are then able to combine to reproduce different measures of vertical specialization (previously used by others) and the measurement of sources of added value in international trade.

[2]VS measures the direct and indirect content of imports and is a measure for their foreign content. This is based on the assumption that imports have been produced completely abroad, without any domestic content, which is hardly true when the good is produced in more than two stages and there is intermediate good trade between both economies; that is, when the country trades intermediate goods in both directions Hummels et al. (2001).

[3]*VS1* generalizes the concept of VS proposed by (Hummels et al. 2001) by eliminating the assumption of no intermediate good trade in three directions. It adds value added indirect exports, the domestic content exported for third countries to produce intermediate good exports, and the domestic value added that returns as imports from third countries.

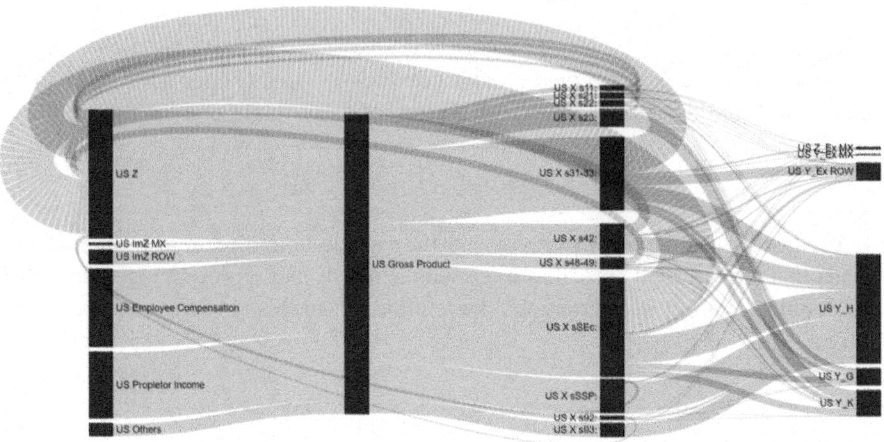

Fig. 1 Structural Relation of Transaction Flow of the US Economy. Source: based on IMPLAN 2013 IO model

Here we use an alternative methodology for immersion in foreign trade figures in the USA and Mexico. That is, we elaborate a binational input-output table. In assuming this task, it was considered appropriate that the level of sector aggregation had the highest level of detail possible. For the USA, the model contained in the IMPLAN (Minnesota Implan Group -MIG- 2017) was used for 2013 with a sector structure of 526 sectors. In the case of Mexico, the table built by INEGI for 2013 (INEGI 2014) was used at the four-digit level of the North American Industrial Classification System (NAICS) composed of 261 sectors.

Those models represented as the structural relation of transaction flows between the economic agents are shown in Figs. 1 and 2. Initially, we can see how in the US economy the production sectoral composition has a large share of the services sector and secondly the industrial sector, also in both cases half of its product is destined to productive inputs within the USA. In contrast, in the Mexican economy, the main sector is the industrial sector, followed by the services sector. In both, only 30% are productive inputs and in the industrial sector another 30% is exported to other countries mainly the USA.

In both economies, value added accounts for more than half of the gross product and is even somewhat higher in the Mexican economy compared with the USA. However, the internal composition in Mexico has a low proportion corresponding to employee compensation—30%—when this proportion for the USA is around 50%. It is also notable how the share of imports in production inputs is much more significant for the Mexican economy, where, in addition, about 60% comes from the USA, while for the US economy, imports from Mexico are around 5%. Something similar occurs with exports, which are relatively more important as a destination for production for the Mexican economy than for the USA and the main destination of those exports is the USA.

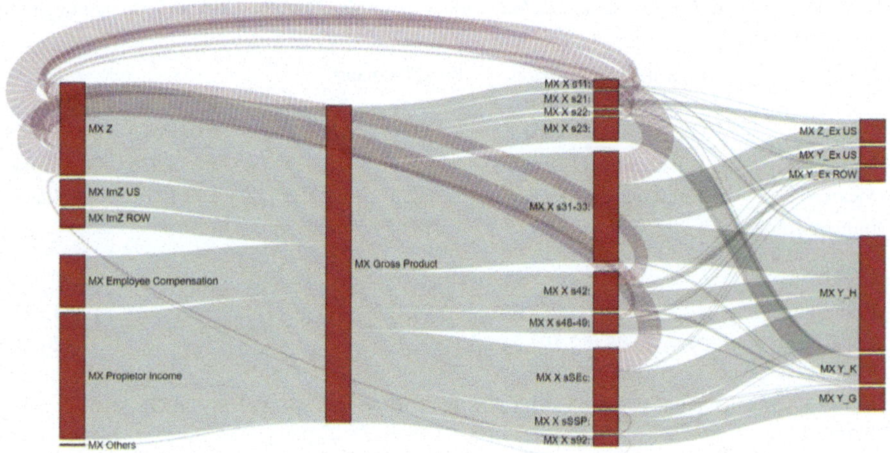

Fig. 2 Structural Relation of Transaction Flow of the US Economy. Source: based on INEGI 2013 IO model

The first step in the generation of the integrated model of the USA–Mexico was the sectorial compatibility of the individual models. Of the 526 sectors, a total of 488 had total correspondence at the four-digit level of the NAICS and the remaining 38 combined activities from various sectors which were assigned according to a weighting based on their relative participation in their aggregate using data from economic censuses This process resulted in 259 sectors. Finally, the compatibility of the activities between both models required minor adjustments in the classifications, which resulted in 247 economic sectors.

With the national models reconfigured to a compatible classification, the second step is the construction of the integrated model required for the estimation of trade flows between both countries at the level of interaction of individual sectors for which we have the specific aggregate flows of trade USA–Mexico and as part of the matrix of import flows at the level of sector interaction and aggregates of total exports by sector, a problem similar to that faced for the estimation of multiregional models referred to in (Canning and Wang 2005).

The reasoning that supports the estimation of foreign trade matrices begins by considering that trade between both countries is already part of the aggregates of imports and exports of the matrices of each country and therefore its incorporation into the matrix initially considers subtracting the values of trade flows of total imports and exports of the matrices of both countries, as appropriate. With this procedure, we can already incorporate these amounts to the trade matrices by making an initial distribution based on the structural composition of the import matrices for each country as appropriate. The consistency of the aggregates is achieved considering that the sum by rows of the trade flows between the USA and Mexico and the exports must coincide with the exports by sector of the individual models and the sum by columns of the trade flows between the USA and Mexico and the imports of

Table 1 Aggregate Representation of the Product Input Model of the USA and Mexico (Millions of US Dollars)

	Intermediate Demand		Final Demand			
	US	Mexico	US	Mexico	RM Exports	Total availability
US	12,165,962	178,532	14,377,515	56,799	1,658,836	28,437,643
Mexico	166,098	589,306	120,855	1,128,118	100,167	2,104,544
Imports from the rest of the world	1,207,596	128,716	1,068,879	48,138		
Primary factors	14,897,988	1,207,991	1,884,123			1,884,123
Total production	28,437,643	2,104,544	1,884,123			32,426,310

Source: Own calculation based on IMPLAN 2013 IO model (USA) and INEGI 2013 IO model (Mexico)

the rest of the countries must add up by sector the total imports of the individual models. Finally, the adjustment of trade values and of the imports and exports of the rest of the countries will be achieved using the RAS method (Lahr & De Mesnard 2004), which knowing the aggregates of a matrix performs an iterative procedure that adjusts the sum of the internal values to totals added by row and column.

The integrated model of the economies of the USA and Mexico, as can be seen in the following table, is a combination of economic interactions and the main aggregates of the economy for each economy and includes a record of trade flows. The above is an aggregate representation of the model where the rows identified as the USA and Mexico are composed of the integration of the values of the 247 economic sectors already mentioned and the columns of the intermediate demand block also identified as the USA and Mexico are also composed of the integration of the values of the 247 sectors of economic activity (Table 1).

The exposed binational model by rows is a representation of the production destinations that can be dedicated to meet the requirements of intermediate demand when its consumption involves the incorporation of a new product or as final consumption when consumers extract the production of the flow of productive interactions of the economy. By columns, the model represents the way in which production is generated and can be associated to a production function where inputs from other sectors of the economy are combined with primary factors such as labor and capital to generate the production. In the biregional model we can also identify the main aggregates of the national accounts system as gross domestic product—by consolidating the added value—household consumption, government consumption, intermediate demand, demand final, exports, among others.

5 Results

The results of the decomposition of the origin of the added value contained in the gross exports of the USA and Mexico in 2013 were calculated using the "decompr" module developed by (Quast and Kummritz 2015) that is integrated into the R software (R Core Team 2018) and is presented in Table 2.

For 2013, out of the 236 billion dollars exported by the USA to Mexico there were 120.2 billion dollars directly added value in the USA and another 62.1 billion dollars that were added in the USA, but exported as intermediate inputs and returned to USA to become part of exports again. Additionally, 6.4 billion dollars were part of a duplicate accounting, but which were part of the 188.7 billion dollars domestic product. The other components of exports from the USA to Mexico are 2.5 billion dollars of value added in Mexico and 1.4 billion dollars of duplicate accounting generated in Mexico. Finally, 43.3 billion dollars are integrated that are imported by the USA from other nations to be integrated into exports to Mexico.

In addition, the results show that out of the 287 billion dollars of exports from Mexico to the USA, the direct added value in Mexico included in them reaches 140.5 billion dollars to which we must add 22.5 billion dollars of added value that returns to Mexico and 1.5 billion dollars of accounting double that integrate the 164.4 billion dollars of domestic production contained in the exports. The rest is made up of 50.2 billion dollars value added in the USA and a double accounting from the USA that reaches the amount of 6.4 billion dollars, and the 65.9 billion dollars imports from third countries.

We can highlight the fact that in terms of domestic added value the content in the gross exports of the USA reaches 188.7 billion dollars, while the domestic content of

Table 2 Results of the Value-Added Breakdown of Trade Between the USA and Mexico

Component	USA (1)	Mexico (2)
Domestic added value in final exports	46,358.1	61,712.4
Domestic added value in intermediate exports absorbed by direct importers	73,797.4	78,753.4
Domestic added value in intermediate exports re-exported to third countries	11,858.8	19,933.9
Domestic added value that returns as final goods	29,722.9	882.4
Domestic added value that returns home as intermediate goods	20,532.7	1666.0
Double counting of domestic origin	6426.0	1470.9
Foreign added value in exports of final products from the direct importer	882.4	29,722.9
Foreign added value in exports of intermediate goods from the from the direct importer	1666.0	20,532.7
Double counting of foreign origin due to the production of direct importer exports	1470.9	6426.0
Trade with the participation of third countries	43,309.5	65,852.5
Total gross bilateral trade	236,024.7	286,953.0

Source: Own elaboration, based on (Koopman et al. 2012) model

Table 3 Breakdown of Value Added and Relative Indicators of Trade between the USA and Mexico

Value-added breakdown	USA to Mexico	Mexico to USA
Value added in exports	120,155.5	140,465.8
National value added	161,737.2	161,282.0
Foreign value added	2548.4	50,255.6
National content in gross exports	188,695.9	164,418.9
Pure double count of national origin	6426.0	1470.9
Pure double count of foreign origin	1470.9	6426.0
Trade with the participation of third countries	43,309.5	65,852.5
Relative indicators		
Value added to export ratio (Johnson and Noguera)	0.5091	0.4895
Export value added	0.6853	0.5621
National export content	0.7995	0.5730
Total gross bilateral trade	236,024.7	286,953.0

Source: Own elaboration, based on (Koopman et al. 2012) model

the gross exports of Mexico is around 164.4 billion dollars. This is a result with great implications because it means that when we take into account the imported contents of the gross exports, the domestic content of the USA exceeds that of Mexico. In terms of trade between the two countries, this implies that it would be the USA who would maintain a surplus relationship in the balance trade with Mexico as opposed to the conclusions derived from the analysis of gross foreign trade between both countries.

Additionally, the difference between the domestic and foreign components of the added value incorporated in exports can be observed because for the USA the foreign added value in its exports reaches 2.5 billion dollars for the case of Mexico, this concept is around 50.2 billion dollars that is more than 20 times the amount that it represents for the USA.

Finally, imports from third countries are larger for the Mexican economy where they reach 65.9 billion dollars than its equivalent for the USA economy where they account for 43.3 billion dollars.

Conversely, the analysis of these figures in aggregate terms by concept and in relative terms can be done by calculating the indices used by other authors referred to by (Koopman et al. 2012) who had previously researched the value-added content in exports. These results are presented in Table 3.

The table shows how both in the domestic value-added content and in the total domestic content the commercial relationship favors the USA which in terms of trade means that it is a surplus—it has an export value that exceeds that of its imports. Also notable is the differences in the content of foreign added value in the exports of each country. In terms of the proportion of added value proposed by Johnson and Noguera (VAX ratio) applied to US–Mexico trade figures, the value reaches 51% for the USA while in the case of Mexico it is 50%. In the case of the domestic value added and domestic content ratios in relation to gross exports, they reach values close to 80% in the case of the USA and 57.3% in the case of Mexico.

The results of the relative indices show how when considering trade volumes in terms of added value, they only partially account for the participation of countries in international trade and how to integrate the return value added the position of countries in terms of trade may change, as in the case of the US–Mexico trade relationship. In addition to this, it is also important to recognize how imports from the rest of the countries explain part of the trade in gross terms between countries and that their integration allows identification closer to the contributions of each country and third parties in international trade relations.

The findings by sectors show in Table 4. The information contained in the table shows how trade between the two countries is highly concentrated, because of the total of 247 sectors; the 15 main exporters accumulate more than 58% of exports. In terms of added value, these are sectors where the percentage of the same is for the majority of the cases below the average but which stand out as being inputs of a great variety of processes. In that sense, as you will remember the great difference we can place it as part of the intermediate products that return to the US economy as intermediate products that are then integrated into products of the USA that are exported. This is the case, for example, of sector 3344 Manufacture of electronic components were the DVA is more than 14 billions and 60% is returned DVA a production first made in the US and then exported to México, returned as imports to be incorporated again to US production finally exported to México.

In contrast, the sectors such as *3363 Manufacture of parts for motor vehicles* have low added value but a strong sectorial link with the rest of the sectors of the economy. In that case, the sector has 7.3 billion dollars of the 16.8 billion exported as domestic added value and an additional 5.9 billion as return value added. Taking all this into account, the sector will have a high domestic product content as part of exports.

In summary, the volume of exports from the USA to Mexico shows how among the main exporters we have sectors that generally do not stand out as high value-added sectors. Instead, the main exporters include a variety of industrial processes in some cases highlighting by the magnitude of the return value added as part of the trade in intermediate products that are exported and imported to be integrated back into exported products.

For the by sectors exports from Mexico to the USA it is noted that among the main exporters, the high aggregate sectors do not stand out again. Futhermore, the returned DVA in México is mainly return as finals products, unlike those of the USA exports. That makes the added value of return not very significant and in this case the added value abroad has an important proportion of Mexico's gross exports.

Table 4 Results of the Value-Added Breakdown in the US and Mexico Trade by Main Sectors

		Domestic content						Foreign content				
		Domestic value added (DVA)					Double count	Foreign value added (FVA)		Double count	Rest of the world	Gross bilateral trade
		Value added in export		DVA re-exported	Returned DVA							
NAICS	Description	DVA_FIN	DVA_INT	DVA_INTrex	RDV_FIN	RDV_INT	DDC	MVA_FIN	MVA_INT	MDC		
3344	Manufacture of electronic components	678	2841	2136	5518	2949	818	13	55	227	2983	18,220
3241	Manufacture of petroleum and coal products	0	8784	701	543	725	191	0	600	149	6381	18,073
3363	Manufacture of parts for motor vehicles	286	5996	971	4630	1226	370	6	128	155	3065	16,832
3251	Manufacture of basic chemical products	316	6283	564	691	1326	328	7	131	61	2377	12,083
3252	Manufacture of synthetic resins and rubber and chemical fibers	0	3152	524	1229	1366	313	0	64	71	1856	8574
3361	Manufacture of cars and trucks	5660	39	8	50	7	2	251	2	3	1914	7937
3342	Manufacture of communication equipment	2551	530	432	1294	587	180	51	11	51	1978	7665
3341	Manufacture of computer and peripheral equipment	2302	1511	441	995	561	154	48	31	45	1466	7554

3339	Manufacture of other machinery and equipment for the industry in general	3162	1323	182	303	410	112	62	26	20	1169	6771
3345	Manufacture of measuring, control, navigation, and electronic medical equipment	2227	889	336	891	609	176	33	13	30	1006	6208
3336	Manufacture of internal combustion engines, turbines, and transmissions	263	2129	413	957	640	249	8	62	67	1267	6055
3261	Plastic products manufacturing	605	2008	347	868	621	158	9	28	28	914	5587
3353	Manufacture of electricity generation and distribution equipment	676	1219	379	815	961	274	19	34	68	994	5441
3329	Manufacture of other metal products	150	1867	334	848	932	263	2	29	37	779	5240
3359	Manufacture of other electronical equipment and accessories	470	1144	376	981	816	235	14	34	73	1040	5183

Source: Own elaboration, based on (Koopman et al. 2012) model

6 Conclusions

From the study, we highlight the fact that even though Mexico officially has a significant gross trade surplus with the USA during the NAFTA period, there is a notable deficit for the former in terms of the added value incorporated in this trade. Thus, the flow of added value in the gross exports of Mexico to the USA only reaches 164.4 billion dollars, while the domestic content of the gross exports of the USA is 188.7 billion dollars. In the disaggregation of added value, the main difference between the domestic and foreign components of the added value incorporated in exports is that while for the USA the foreign added value in its exports reaches 2.5 billion dollars for the case of Mexico, this concept is of around 50.2 billion dollars which is more than 20 times the amount that it represents for the USA. A conclusion that derives directly from this last aspect is that, as a result of NAFTA, an important part of Mexican export revenues is used to remunerate productive factors used in the USA.

In the sector disaggregation, the result that stands out mainly due to its importance is that of the Electronic Component Manufacturing sector is 46.5% and for which of the 18 billion gross exports 5.7 are domestic added value, 8.5 billion are added value of return and 3 more are imports from third countries so that these sources manage to explain 17 of the 18 billion dollars traded. In addition to the sector of Manufacture of parts for motor vehicles whose 7.3 billion dollars of the 16.8 billion exported are domestic added value and only 5.9 billion are return value added, because it has a high content of domestic product as part of exports gross. The conclusion derived from this aspect is the difference and importance between the consumption of intermediate goods of both countries and their consequences in the generation of added value in certain sectors of activity.

Therefore, a correct measurement of the added value contained in exports between these two countries should be a basic starting point for the net quantification of the trade balance and to assess the suitability or effects of a change in the bilateral trade policy.

Finally, an important limitation to take into account in future works that try to estimate the added value incorporated in the commercial interrelations between both countries is the need to incorporate the impact of the rest of the world endogenously in the net balance of the distribution of the added value at the level as disaggregated as we present. In the case of the countries considered here, the importance of this is really evident and, in the end, it cannot be said that third countries are taking advantage of the commercial agreements without taking into account their impact. Ultimately, its estimate is really complex.

References

Aroche F, Marquez MA (2012) Structural integration, exports and growth in Mexico: an input-output approach. Estados Unidos: Rev Polit Econ, Northampton 24(1):87–101

Baldwin R, Lopez-Gonzalez J (2015) Supply-chain trade: A portrait of global patterns and several testable hypotheses. World Econ 38(11):1682–1721

Boundi-Chraki F (2017) Análisis Insumo-Producto Multirregional e Integración Económica del TLCAN. In: Una Aplicación del Método de Extracción Hipotética. Cuadernos de Economia, Colombia

Canning P, Wang Z (2005) A flexible mathematical programming model to estimate interregional input–output accounts. J Reg Sci 45(3):539–563

Chiñas C (2017) Perspectivas del Comercio México-Estados Unidos ante el resurgimiento del proteccionismo y la renegociación del Tratado de Libre Comercio de América del Norte (TLCAN). Cimexus 12(1):81–100

Daudin G, Rifflart C, Schweisguth D (2011) Who produces for whom in the world economy? Canadian J Econ/Revue canadienne d'économique 44(4):1403–1437

De La Cruz J, Koopman RB, Wang Z, Wei SJ (2011) Estimating foreign value-added in Mexico's manufacturing exports. US International Trade Commission Working Paper, 04A.

Fujii Gambero G, Cervantes MR (2013) México: valor agregado en las exportaciones manufactureras. CEPAL, Santiago

Hummels D, Ishii J, Yi KM (2001) The nature and growth of vertical specialization in world trade. J Int Econ 54(1):75–96

INEGI (2014) Sistema de Cuentas Nacionales de México. Desarrollo de la matriz de insumo producto 2012: Fuentes y Metodología. Obtenido de Instituto Nacional de Estadística Geografía e Informática. http://www.inegi.org.mx/est/contenidos/proyectos/cn/mip12/doc/SCNM_Metodologia_28.pdf

Johnson RC (2014) Five facts about value-added exports and implications for macroeconomics and trade research. J Econ Perspect 28(2):119–142

Johnson RC, Noguera G (2012a) Accounting for intermediates: production sharing and trade in value added. J Int Econ 86(2):224–236

Johnson RC, Noguera G (2012b) Proximity and production fragmentation. Am Econ Rev 201 (3):407–411

Koopman R, Wang Z, Wei SJ (2014) Tracing value-added and double counting in gross exports. Am Econ Rev 104(2):459–494

Koopman R, Wang Z, Wei S-J (2012) Tracing Value-Added and Doubled Counting in Gross Exports. NAtional BUreau of Economic Research Working Paper Series(18579).

Lahr M, De Mesnard L (June 2004) Biproportional Techniques in Input–Output Analysis: Table Updating and Structural Analysis. Econ Syst Res 16(2):115–134

Lalanne A (2016) Medición de las exportaciones de Uruguay en valor agregado doméstico en presencia de regímenes especiales de comercio. Revista de economía 23(2):101–139

Miller RE, Blair PD (2009) Input–Output Analysis: Foundations and Extensions, 2nd edn. Cambridge University Press, Cambridge

Minnesota Implan Group MIG (2017) United States 2013 lmplan data. Minnesota Implan Group, Stillwater

Quast B, Kummritz V (2015) decompr: Global Value Chain decomposition in R. CTEI Working Papers, 1.

R Core Team (2018) R: A language and environment for statistical computing. R Foundation for Statistical Computing. Vienna, Austria. Obtenido de https://www.R-project.org

Solaz M (2016) Cadenas globales de valor y generación de valor añadido: el caso de la economía española. WP-EC (IVIE) 1

Timmer MP, Los B, Stehrer R, De Vries GJ (2013) Fragmentation, incomes and jobs: an analysis of European competitiveness. Econ Policy 28(76):613–661

Torre LE, Chapa JC, González EE (2020) La integración económica México-Estados Unidos y su aprovechamiento regional en México: un análisis de extracción hipotética y matrices regionales. Serie de Documentos de Investigación N 2020-06, Banco de México

Trefler D, Zhu SC (2010) The structure of factor content predictions. J Int Econ 82(2):195–207

Structural Change in the Exports and Foreign Direct Investment of the Southeast Gulf Mexican States

Edgardo Arturo Ayala Gaytán and Joana Cecilia Chapa Cantú

Abstract It is commonly stated that NAFTA has only beneficiated northern states in Mexico, with no absolute gain for the south region of Mexico. In this research, a combination of econometric and multi-sectoral techniques is employed to show this is probably not true. A structural break in manufacturing exports and foreign direct investment is found in the Southeast Gulf of Mexico, which encompass the states of Veracruz, Tabasco, Campeche, Quintana Roo, and Yucatán, most likely caused by those major liberalization reforms. Manufacturing exports might increase by 48.3% of pre-NAFTA levels, whereas FDI rose by 71.6%. The increment in manufacturing exports is linked to a rise of 1.0% in gross value added and 1.7% in employment of the region. Meanwhile, FDI expansion likely contributed with an additional increment of value added and employment of 1%.

Keywords Structural change · Regional economics · Trade · Foreign direct investment · Accounting multipliers

1 Introduction

The Southeast Gulf region of Mexico is encompassed by the states of Veracruz, Campeche, Tabasco, Quintana Roo, and Yucatán, their geographical location is shown in Fig. 1. The region has a population of 15 million of inhabitants and represents 14% of the Mexico's Gross Domestic Product (GDP). The Southeast Gulf zone presents a salient economic specialization: 98% of the Mexico's oil

E. A. Ayala Gaytán (✉)
Instituto Tecnológico y de Estudios Superiores de Monterrey, Departamento de Economía, Monterrey, Mexico
e-mail: edgardo@tec.mx

J. C. Chapa Cantú
Universidad Autónoma de Nuevo León, Facultad de Economía, Monterrey, Mexico
e-mail: joana.chapacn@uanl.edu.mx

A. de León-Arias, P. Aroca (eds.), *NAFTA's Impact on Mexico's Regional Development*, New Frontiers in Regional Science: Asian Perspectives 51,
https://doi.org/10.1007/978-981-16-3168-9_7

Fig. 1 Southeast Gulf of Mexico. Source: own elaboration

production is originated in Veracruz, Campeche, and Tabasco, whereas the main beach tourist sites of the country are located in Quintana Roo (e.g. Cancún) and Yucatán.

As historically Oil and Tourism are free of important barriers to trade worldwide, it is natural to think that the Southeast Gulf region should have not benefited from the commercial and foreign investment liberalization wave Mexico took since the 90s. This is the question we approach in this chapter, as we show, even when the manufacturing exports and the foreign direct investment (FDI) incoming to the region were small at the beginning of the 90s, during the three decades that followed the Mexico reforms liberalizing trade and deregulating FDI, they grew significantly producing important collateral effects for the region value added and employment.

We provide evidence that manufacturing exports and FDI had experienced a structural change in this region employing the Markov Switching Regime technique, we also assess the size of the change comparing the percentage change of the estimated coefficients. To assess the impact of this structural change on the region GDP, value added and employment, we build a regional Social Accounting Matrix (SAM) to form a counterfactual, that is what would had happened to this region if there has been no structural change in the manufacturing exports and the incoming FDI.

The next section briefly describes the main economic structure of the region, Sect. 3 presents the econometric methodology employed, the way data of exports and FDI was assembled and the estimations of the structural change occurred during the period 1993–2019. The details of the construction of the regional SAM are discussed in Sect. 4, whereas the effects in the main socioeconomic variables of the counterfactual simulation (extraction exercise) are presented in Sect. 5. The chapter ends with some final comments.

2 Structure of the Southeast Gulf Region

The Southeast Gulf economy took off in the 70s, during this decade the GDP of the region grew up at rates of almost 11%, driven by the petroleum bonanza after the discovery of the major oil well, Cantarell. Even though neither Quintana Roo nor Yucatán have oil, their economy also grew rapidly, at rates of more than 8%, thanks to the development of Cancún and other tourist sites (see Ayala et al. 2015a, b).

During the 80s the growth of the sub-region of the Gulf, Veracruz, Tabasco y Campeche, still reached a modest 2%, but afterwards, practically disappeared. In the last 10 years, the GDP of this sub-region has contracted due to the exhaustion of the reserves of the Cantarell well. In contrast, the Southeast states GDP steadily grow at rates of –5% (Ayala and Chapa 2019).

The economic activity of the region is still very concentrated in petroleum and activities related with Tourism. Ayala and Chapa (2019) estimated that the only activities with a simple location quotient[1] larger than one in 2016 were Extraction of petroleum (6.7), Manufacturing of derivatives of petroleum, chemicals and plastics (1.4), and Hotels (1.6). Although there is some evidence suggesting a small reversion toward a more diversification structure in last years, for example, in 2003 the Coefficient of Gini was 0.766 and the Herfindahl Hirschman index[2] (IHH) was 2590, whereas in 2016 they declined to 0.701 and 1511, respectively.

The economic structure is also reflected in the exports of the region by industry. Table 1 presents the exports for 3 years, 2007, 2011 (year where oil exports began to decline), and 2018 (the last year available). During this period region's oil exports declined 11 billion dollars, whereas non-oil increased short less 1 billion. Among the non-oil exports, Food, Chemical, Primary Metal and Apparel Manufacturing represent the 70%. Food and Primary Metal Manufacturing have been steadily growing, in contrast Chemicals and Apparel Manufacturing are persistently declining.

[1]The simple location quotient is defined as the ratio of the share of the activity in the region and the share in the nation, if it is larger than one, then it is evidence that the region is more specialized in that activity.

[2]The coefficient of Gini takes the values of 0 to 1, 0 is all activities have the same weight and 1 when one activity produces all the region output. On the other hand, the IHH is an index of concentration, it takes the value of 0 if total region output is produced by a very large amount of activities, and 10,000 when is produced by just one activity.

Table 1 Southeast Gulf exports (millions of US dollars)

				Mean annual growth rate			Export weight		
	2007	2011	2018	2007–2011	2011–2018	2007–2018	2007	2011	2018
Total exports	42,781.3	55,053.7	32,315.9	6.5%	−7.3%	−2.5%	100.0%	100.0%	100.0%
211 oil and gas extraction	37,178.4	47,899.2	26,122.0	6.5%	−8.3%	−3.2%	86.9%	87.0%	80.8%
Non-oil and gas exports	5602.9	7154.5	6193.9	6.3%	−2.0%	0.9%	13.1%	13.0%	19.2%
311 food manufacturing	540.8	1094.1	1178.8	19.3%	1.1%	7.3%	9.7%	15.3%	19.0%
312 beverage and tobacco product manufacturing	3.0	100.5	206.2	140.5%	10.8%	46.9%	0.1%	1.4%	3.3%
315 apparel manufacturing	621.5	527.7	398.0	−4.0%	−4.0%	−4.0%	11.1%	7.4%	6.4%
325 chemical manufacturing	2077.7	2407.0	1611.7	3.7%	−5.6%	−2.3%	37.1%	33.6%	26.0%
326 plastics and rubber products manufacturing	57.0	111.4	129.3	18.2%	2.1%	7.7%	1.0%	1.6%	2.1%
327 nonmetallic mineral product manufacturing	35.9	40.2	47.2	2.9%	2.3%	2.5%	0.6%	0.6%	0.8%
331 primary metal manufacturing	1048.5	1122.0	1433.7	1.7%	3.6%	2.9%	18.7%	15.7%	23.1%
332 fabricated metal product manufacturing	33.6	49.9	159.3	10.4%	18.0%	15.2%	0.6%	0.7%	2.6%
333 machinery manufacturing	164.4	189.7	87.9	3.6%	−10.4%	−5.5%	2.9%	2.7%	1.4%
336 transportation equipment manufacturing	-	199.4	216.5	Nd	1.2%	Nd	0.0%	2.8%	3.5%
339 miscellaneous manufacturing	471.5	567.5	341.2	4.7%	−7.0%	−2.9%	8.4%	7.9%	5.5%
Other non-oil exports	89.5	111.2	74.0	5.6%	−5.6%	−1.7%	1.6%	1.6%	1.2%

Note: Export weight of the NAICS industries 311–339 are expressed as proportions of total non-oil exports
Source: National Institute of Statistics and Geography (known as INEGI)

3 Estimation of the Structural Change in Exports and FDI

One of the goals of this work is to assess if the liberalizing policies in trade and foreign investment that Mexico has taken have had any effect in the Southeast Gulf states of Mexico. To accomplish this is necessary to prove that a change in the trajectory of the main variables related with commerce and investment in the region had occurred. It is also fundamental to find a simple way of estimating the size of the change. For this motive we took the strategy employed by Ayala et al. (2015c) in a former study assessing the impact of the North American Free Trade Agreement (NAFTA) in the economy of the Northeast states of Mexico (Coahuila, Nuevo León y Tamaulipas).

The method consists of two steps. In the first one a Markov Switching Regime model is applied to the region manufacturing exports and incoming FDI to test for structural change and estimate the size in the difference of the means of those variables between both regimes, the one of low level of exports and FDI and the high export and FDI regime. The second step consisted in building a contrafactual extracting these structural changes in exports and FDI to the regional economy employing a SAM, with the objective to observe the corresponding variations in value added and employment. In this section we described the procedure we followed in the first phase.

A Markov Switching Regime is a popular time series model developed by Hamilton (1989). It assumes the Markov property that the variable of interest, say y_t, follows a probability distribution that depends on what happened with y_{t-1} only, but not with any other further lag. In any period, the variable is one of the m regimes designed, for our case $m = 2$ and correspond to a low- and high-level regime. The process is determined by an unobserved random variable s_t, that can take the value of any regime, for example, if $s_t = j$, then the process is in the j regime.

Assuming a normal distribution function, given y is in the regime 1, then the process is governed by the mean μ_1, and the variance σ_1^2, if y is in regime 2, then the mean and variance are μ_2 and σ_2^2, respectively. The conjoint probability of observing y_t in a regime s_j, in our case j = 1 or 2, is

$$p(y_t, s_t = j) = \phi_j \left(2\pi\sigma_j^2\right)^{-0.5} exp \frac{(y_t - \mu_j)^2}{2\sigma_j^2} \quad (1)$$

where ϕ_j is the non-conditional probability that the process is governed by regime j. Thus, the non-conditional density for y_t, is.

$$f\left(y_t; \mu_j, \sigma_j^2\right) = \sum_{j=1}^{m} p(y_t, s_t = j) \quad (2)$$

Following the construction of the probability distribution we can form a log-likelihood function and obtain the parameters, in this case μ_j, σ_j^2 for $j = 1...$m that maximize the likelihood of obtaining the process y_t. From the maximum likelihood estimators, fixed transition probabilities can be obtained, for instance, the probability that the variable stays in regime 1 given it was in this regime, and from these transition probabilities the unconditional probability that the variable is in each of the regimes.

The annual export data by state is published by the National Institute of Statistics and Geography (INEGI, by the acronym in Spanish) since 2007–2018, in our case. Before that, there are estimations realized by the Ministry of Economy for the period 1993–2004. The INEGI figures correspond to the non-agricultural industries and we remove the oil exports, while the Ministry of Economy series corresponds to the exports of manufactures. We form a whole export by state series back poling the all-states exports from 1993 to 2006 using the growth rate of the national manufacturing exports, then we interpolate the state share in the all-states exports between 2004 and 2007, obtaining a gross estimation for 2005 and 2006. Finally, we applied the export shares of the Ministry of Economy figures for 1993 to 2006 to the all-state exports to get a nominal estimate. We find this simple method feasible once we test that the export shares by state of the two series are actually very similar, indeed the shares of 2004 and the one of 2007 have a correlation of 0.947, and only in two states the difference was larger to one percentage point (pp), none of them of our region of interest.

In the case of the FDI, the source is the Ministry of Economy. There is a long series of FDI by state with the current methodology from 1999 to 2019, there are also available estimations from 1994 to 1999 with and older methodology. Taking the advantage that 1999 is included in both series, we estimate a correction factor just dividing the FDI with the current methodology by the one with the older methodology for each state of the region and corrected the FDI shares by this correction factor.

We applied the Markov Switching Regime to all-states and Southeast Gulf states manufacturing exports and FDI, allowing for just two regimes, heterogeneous variances across regimes and controlling by a linear trend. Figures 2 and 3 show the actual export series along with the probability of being in the high-level regime for all states and the Southeast Gulf states. Both series are increasing in time, but after the 90s exports and FDI presents an apparently jump in the Southeast Gulf states.

Table 2 presents the estimation of the Markov Switching Regime for the manufacturing exports for two specifications: in column one there is only a constant, whereas in the second column a linear trend is included to capture the non-stationarity of the manufacturing exports of the region. The figures at the Regime Change line present the estimation of the change in the export between both regimes, for the only constant specification it represents the difference in the constants of the regimes, for the linear trend model it corresponds to the difference of the estimated expected values of both regimes for 2013, that is our benchmark year. The estimation of the gains in manufacturing exports are of the order of 4.3 billion dollars for the constant model but when a trend is included, they diminish to 2.4 billion. In both specifications the probability of being in the High-Level Regime in 2013 is almost one.

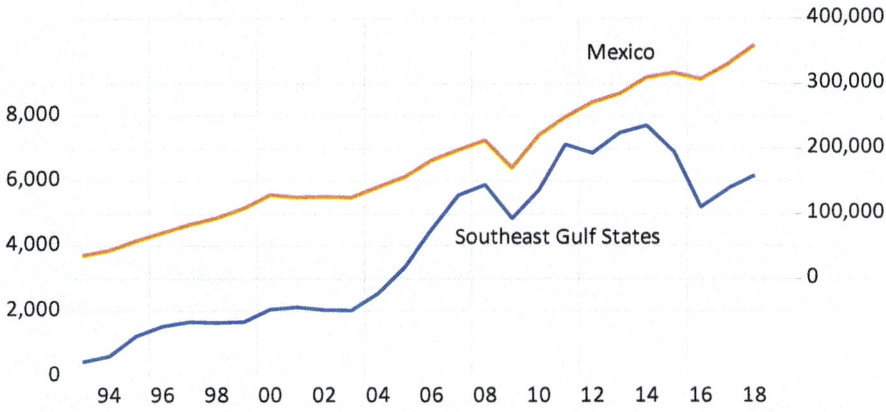

Fig. 2 Mexico's (Right Axe) and Southeast Gulf States (Left Axe) Manufacturing Exports (Millions of US dollars). Source: Estimated by the authors with information of INEGI and Ministry of Economy

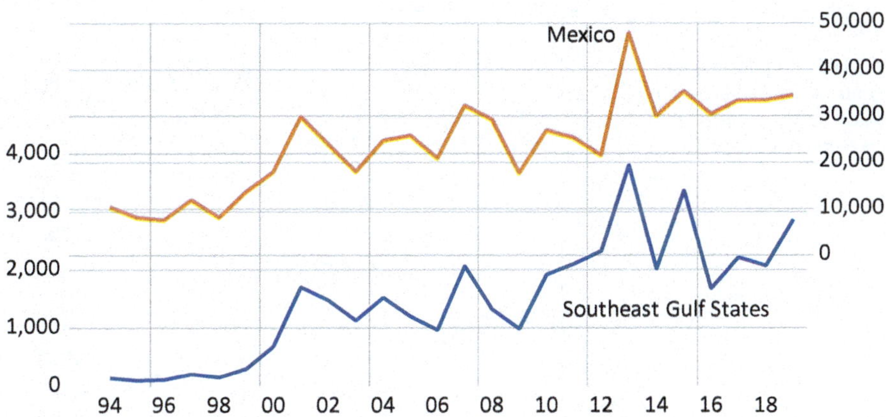

Fig. 3 Mexico's (Right Axe) and Southeast Gulf States (Left Axe) Foreign Direct Investment (Millions of US dollars). Source: Estimated by the authors with information of INEGI and Ministry of Economy

Table 3 presents the Markov Switching models for FDI in the Southeast region. As in the case of manufacturing exports, the FDI series in the region presents a structural change after the 90s. In this case both models deliver an estimated gain of 1.5 billion dollars in 2013, year in which the probably of being in the High-level regime is 99%.

The estimations of the econometric models prove that indeed a structural change in manufacturing exports and FDI in the Southeast Gulf states occurred, and that the gains in both variables are not minor, triple digit figures. Of course, before the Mexico trade and investment liberalization the levels of these variables were small, but any way, the evidence is consistent with the fact that even highly specialized

Table 2 Estimated Coefficients of the Southeast Gulf States Manufacturing Exports Markov Switching Regime Models

		Manufacturing exports	
		(1)	(2)
Low-level régime	Constant	1777.5***	535.9***
		(242.9)	(141.1)
	Trend		212.9***
			(11.2)
	Log(σ)	6.6***	5.6***
		(0.3)	(0.2)
High-level regime	Constant	6120.6***	536.7
		(353.0)	(904.6)
	Trend		328.1***
			(51.4)
	Log(σ)	6.4	6.3***
		(0.3)	(0.3)
Regime change		4349.1	2420.2

Note: ***$p < 0.01$. **$p < 0.05$ and *$p < 0.1$
Source: Estimated by the authors with information of INEGI and Ministry of Economy

Table 3 Estimated coefficients of the Southeast Gulf States Foreign Direct Investment Markov

		Foreign direct investment	
		(1)	(2)
Low-level regime	Constant	900.0***	22.9
		(205.0)	(172.0)
	Trend		96.4***
			(10.9)
	Log(σ)	6.5***	5.9***
		(0.2)	(0.2)
High-level regime	Constant	2414.4***	−302.8
		(309.7)	(447.4)
	Trend		181.7***
			(30.7)
	Log(σ)	6.5***	5.9***
		(0.3)	(0.3)
Regime change		1514.4	1465.3

Note: ***$p < 0.01$. **$p < 0.05$ and *$p < 0.1$
Source: Estimated by the authors with information of INEGI and Ministry of Economy

regions can benefit from an institutional framework that incentive free commerce of goods and assets.[3]

[3]A note of caution is pertinent. Indeed, the econometric approach employed in this exercise allows us to identify a structural change in the variables of interest, the likely period delimiting both regimens and gives us an estimate of the probable impact (i.e., difference between the regimens); however, it does not test formally for a specific cause of the structural change. In this chapter we

4 Impact of Exports and FDI on Mexico's Southeast Gulf

The accounting multiplier model is specified to quantify the effect on the value added and employment in the Southeast Gulf region of Mexico associated to the expansion in manufacturing exports and FDI. Next, the model and the database that was used to calibrate it are described.

4.1 Accounting Multiplier Model

The Accounting Multiplier Model, developed by Pyatt and Round (1979), is static. It involves fixed average expenditure propensities, linear production relations (complementarity between intermediate goods, imports, and primary factors), and fixed prices or an economy with idle capacity.

Households, economic sectors, and productive factors are the accounts that will be considered as endogenous since it is desired to explain their level of income in the face of a change in the demand of exports and in FDI (foreign investors' expenses in capital goods). These last two variables correspond to the external sector and investment, respectively, which are the accounts conceived as exogenous and that can be used as instruments of economic policy. In addition, the government sector also remains exogenous.

Table 4 contains the relationships between endogenous and exogenous accounts. The matrix T_{nn} is that of transactions between endogenous accounts, T_{nx} includes injections of exogenous to endogenous accounts, T_{xn} contains the payments from endogenous to exogenous accounts, and T_{xx} is the matrix of residuals, that is, of exchanges between the exogenous institutional sectors. It should be noted that N denotes the number of endogenous accounts and X the number of exogenous accounts.

The matrix T_{nn} can be expressed as a function of a matrix of fixed average propensities to spend (A_n):

$$T_{nn} = A_n Y_n \tag{3}$$

where Y_n is a diagonal matrix of order (NxN) that in its main diagonal contains the total income of each endogenous account y_n, and the other elements are zeros.

address the structural change as a consequence of the trade and foreign liberalization measures adopted at the light of NAFTA and other commercial agreements, but also other major reforms were undertaking in those years in agriculture, finance, telecommunications, and competence. Moreover, a major world recession occurred in the second regime years, probably underestimating the difference between regimens.

Table 4 Schematic Representation of Endogenous and Exogenous Accounts in the Linear Model of the Circular Flow of Income

		Expenditures				
		Endogenous	Sum	Exogenous	Sum	Total
Incomes	Endogenous	Tnn	n	Tnx	x	y_n
	Exogenous	Txn	1	Txx	t	y_x
Total		$y_n{}'$		$y_x{}'$		

n = column vector of order (Nx1) that contains the income of the endogenous accounts coming from themselves
l = column vector of order (Xx1) containing the income of the exogenous accounts coming from the endogenous accounts
x = column vector of order (Nx1) that contains the income of the endogenous accounts coming from the exogenous accounts
t = column vector of order (Xx1) that contains the income of the exogenous accounts coming from the exogenous accounts
y_n = column vector of order (Nx1) containing the total income of the endogenous accounts
y_x = column vector of order (Xx1) containing the total income of exogenous accounts
Source: Defourny and Thorbecke (1984)

Starting from the relationships by row of the social accounting matrix, and applying the aforementioned assumptions, the accounting multipliers are obtained as follows:

$$y_n = n + x = A_n y_n + x \tag{4}$$

$$y_n = (I - A_n)^{-1} x \tag{5}$$

$$y_n = Mx \tag{6}$$

M is a square matrix of order (NxN) that contains the accounting multipliers, the M_{ij} element of the matrix represents the increase in the income of account *i* when account *j* receives a unit injection of income from one of the exogenous accounts.

The exogenous injections analyzed in this investigation are directed to the economic sectors; note that, we analyze the effects of an increase in manufacturing exports and also the one in the demand for capital goods by foreign investors. In this sense, it is assumed that foreign investors decide to stock up on capital goods that can be provided regionally, as laid by the SAM Southeast Gulf of Mexico.

Given the above, work will be carried out with a part of the matrix of accounting multipliers, called call M_{ES}, which accounts for the income expansions of the *N* accounts as results of the injections of income in the N_{ES} accounts corresponding to the economic sectors, so that its dimension will be (N x N_{ES}).

The M_{ES} matrix can be specified in terms of value added and employment per unit of income, through the following operations:

$$MVA = VA * M_{ES} \tag{7}$$

$$ML = L * M_{ES} \tag{8}$$

where *VA* is a diagonal matrix that includes the value added per unit of income for each sector *j*, in the case of the rest of the accounts (primary factors and households) there are zeros in the main diagonal. Similarly, *ML* is a diagonal matrix that includes the employees per unit of income for each sector *j*, in the case of the rest of the accounts (productive factors and households) the main diagonal contains zeros. Both matrices are of dimension (*NxN*).

The va_{ij} element of the *MVA* matrix indicates the value added of the economic sector *i* associated with the injection of income into the economic sector *j*. While the l_{ij} element of the matrix *ML* is interpreted as the direct and indirect contracted employment by sector *i* to supply the income injection of sector *j*.

4.2 Database: Social Accounting Matrix of the Southeast Gulf Region of Mexico

The model is specified based on the relationships of the Social Accounting Matrix of the Southeast Gulf Region of Mexico of 2013 (SAM Southeast Gulf) built by Dávila (2019). The SAM Southeast Gulf reflects the income-expenditure relationships of 32 economic sectors, ten types of households differentiated by the decile of income to which they belong, two primary factors (work and capital), an aggregate level of government (local and federal), a sector of the rest of the country, a sector of the rest of the world, the identity of saving-investment (collects the identity that the sum of household savings, government and from the external sector must equal the aggregate investment), and a statistical discrepancy account (considered by construction by INEGI). The matrix contains the origin and destination of the income of each of the economic agents of the Southeast Gulf region; therefore, for each economic agent or institutional sector, the income (sum of the elements of its corresponding row) equals the expenses (sum of the elements of its corresponding column), so the matrix fits perfectly. Table 5 contains the SAM in aggregate format.[4]

Below, some distinctive features about the generation and distribution of income in the Southeast Gulf region are commented. The interested reader can see a deeper analysis in Ayala and Chapa (2019):

- Due to the presence of Petroleos Mexicanos (PEMEX), just over half of the gross output of the economic sectors (51.2%) is used to pay rent of capital. 44.4% of the total gross operating surplus or capital payment from the Southeast Gulf comes from the oil sector. This is a reflection of the change in the treatment of oil rights in the System of National Accounts, which began from the 2008 methodological

[4]The SAM in its disaggregated format is available upon express request to the authors.

Table 5 Aggregate Social Accounting Matrix of the Southeast Gulf region, 2013. (Million Pesos of 2013)

	Economic sectors	Labor	Capital	Households	Government	Saving-Investment	Rest of the states	Rest of the world	Statistical discrepancy	Income
Economic sectors	571,496	0	0	1,035,071	100,047	532,735	915,365	707,895	0	3,862,609
Labor	519,595	0	0	0	0	0	0	1404	0	520,999
Capital	1,976,252	0	0	0	0	0	0	0	0	1,976,252
Households	0	520,999	868,549	0	97,981	0	0	14,994	14,553	1,517,076
Government	6654	0	93,321	70,104	8980	2944	0	0	0	182,003
Saving-investment	0	0	991,426	192,290	−47,094	0	−287,607	−194,334	0	654,681
Rest of the states	452,648	0	0	135,435	22,323	17,352	0	0	0	627,758
Rest of the world	336,010	0	22,909	84,176	−233	87,097	0	25,504	0	555,463
Statistical discrepancy	−46	0	46	0	0	14,553	0	0	0	14,553
Expenditure	3,862,609	520,999	1,976,252	1,517,076	182,003.2	654,681	627,758	555,463	14,553	

Source: authors elaboration base on Ayala and Chapa (2019)

base, since then the rights are recorded as gross operating surplus and were previously accounted as taxes on production.

- Southeast Gulf households obtain most of their income from the profit income (57.3%), followed by remunerations (34.3%), government transfers (6.5%), remittances (1.0%) and unreported income (1.0%). The 82.7% of its income goes to the purchase of goods and services either produced locally, from another federal entity or imported from the rest of the world. A 4.6% of their income is used to pay taxes at the three levels of government and the remaining 12.7% goes to savings.
- Households in this region allocate most of their income to the acquisition of retail trade services (11.5%); real estate services (10.6%); food industry products (9.4%); transport, mail and storage services (7.9%); petroleum and coal derivatives, chemical, plastic, and rubber industries (4.8%); health services (4.5%); and educational services (4.3%).
- Gross savings reach 26.2% of the region's GDP. Household, capital factor, government, and foreign savings finance investment in the Southeast Gulf region. Within the capital factor savings, part of the income from the oil activity is registered. Thus, the Southeast Gulf is a net provider of resources for the rest of the country, the rest of the world and the government, because it is an oil producer and that an important part of the income from such activity does not remain in the region.

4.3 Empirical Strategy

The SAM Southeast Gulf portrays the productive structure and income-expenditure relations of the Southeast Gulf of Mexico from 2013, which belongs to the period of high regime of manufacturing exports and FDI. Given the above, in order to quantify the economic impact of structural change in manufacturing exports and FDI, the situation of the low regime is generated, reducing manufacturing exports by 48.3% and FDI by 71.6% in the region of 2013, and the change of high regime compared to the low one is introduced in the accounting multiplier model to quantify the impact:

$$\Delta VA_i^{Exp} = \sum_{j=1}^{N_{ES}} \Delta Exp_j * va_{ij} \tag{9}$$

$$\Delta \mathrm{VA}_{\mathrm{i}}^{\mathrm{FDI}} = \sum_{\mathrm{j=1}}^{\mathrm{N_{ES}}} \Delta \mathrm{FDI}_{\mathrm{j}} * \mathrm{va}_{\mathrm{ij}} \tag{10}$$

$$\Delta L_i^{Exp} = \sum_{j=1}^{N_{ES}} \Delta Exp_j * l_{ij} \tag{11}$$

$$\Delta L_i^{FDI} = \sum_{j=1}^{N_{ES}} \Delta FDI_j * l_{ij} \tag{12}$$

where ΔExp_j is the change in exports of the economic sector j, ΔFDI_j is the change in the demand for capital goods provided by sector j, ΔVA_i^{Exp} is the effect on the value added of sector i generated by the expansion in exports of all manufacturing industries, and ΔVA_i^{FDI} is the value added linked to the expansion in demand for all sectors that provide investment goods. Similarly, ΔL_i^{Exp} and ΔL_i^{FDI} capture the impacts on employment.

In addition, the calculation of the impact multipliers is performed, which summarizes the aggregate effect on the economic indicators (value added and employment) in the event of an exogenous shock or public policy, in this case, given the increase in manufacturing exports and in FDI:

$$IMVA^{EXP} = \frac{\sum_{i=1}^{N} \Delta VA_i^{EXP}}{\sum_{j=1}^{N_{ES}} \Delta EXP_j} \tag{13}$$

$$IMVA^{FDI} = \frac{\sum_{i=1}^{N} \Delta VA_i^{FDI}}{\sum_{j=1}^{N_{ES}} \Delta FDI_j} \tag{14}$$

$$IML^{EXP} = \frac{\sum_{i=1}^{N} \Delta L_i^{EXP}}{\sum_{j=1}^{N_{ES}} \Delta EXP_j} \tag{15}$$

$$IML^{FDI} = \frac{\sum_{i=1}^{N} \Delta L_i^{FDI}}{\sum_{j=1}^{N_{ES}} \Delta FDI_j} \tag{16}$$

where $IMVA^{EXP}$ and IML^{EXP} are the impact multipliers on value added and employment linked to the increase in exports. Similarly, $IMVA^{FDI}$ and IML^{FDI} are those corresponding to the expansion in foreign direct investment.

4.4 *Results*

4.4.1 Impact of the Structural Change in Manufacturing Exports

The 48.3% increase in manufacturing exports is linked to an expansion in the value added of 25,097.3 million pesos and a generation of 100,465.6 jobs. These are equivalent to 1.0% in value added and 1.7% in employment in the region (see Table 6).

In addition to the manufacturing sector, all other economic sectors are expanding, because the model captures the increase in demand for intermediate inputs and services required to supply the increase in manufacturing exports. Furthermore, the model captures the increase in the demand for goods and services because households have more income since the demand of labor and capital raises. Thus, the productive activities that expand the most in terms of value added are manufacturing (5.6%); agriculture, livestock, forestry, hunting, and fishing (1.8%); and electricity, gas, and water (1.4%). The arrangement is mostly similar in the case of employment; only this one is significantly higher.

The impact multiplier of manufacturing exports on value added is 0.74, this is interpreted as follows: for each peso that exports increase, it causes an increase in value added of 74 cents in the region. In the case of employment, the impact multiplier is 3.0, that is, to an increase of a peso in manufacturing exports, approximately 3 jobs are involved.

4.4.2 Impact of the Structural Change in Foreign Investment

It is assumed that 84.0% of FDI is spent on goods and services that can be provided by the economy of the region, the rest is supplied from abroad or used to pay taxes. Thus, the increase in 71.6% of FDI translates into an increase in 25,991.6 million pesos of value added and 64,397.8 jobs. In proportional terms, it represents increases of about 1.0% in the two economic indicators at a regional level (Table 7).

Given the increase in FDI, the sectors that most expand their value added and employment are construction, transport, and commerce. This is because the construction sector (64.4%) and commerce (4.7%) are the main suppliers of goods and services for investors.

The value added impact multiplier of FDI is 0.86, that is, an increase of a peso in FDI, causes an increase in the value added of 86 cents in the Southeast Gulf region. Regarding employment, the multiplier is 2.1, which implies that two jobs are associated with each FDI peso.

Table 6 Exports´ Impact on Value Added and Employment in the Southeast Gulf of Mexico

	Structural Change	Value added initial	Value added impact	Value added impact	Employment initial	Employment impact	Employment impact
Sectors	Millions of Mexican pesos at constant prices of 2013			%	Number of jobs		%
Agriculture, livestock, forestry, hunting and fishing	0.0	58,894.1	1033.6	1.8%	1158,976.0	20,339.5	1.8%
Mining	0.0	925,216.5	3475.1	0.4%	74,004.0	1492.7	2.1%
Electricity, gas and water	0.0	29,603.4	423.1	1.4%	31,624.0	452.0	1.4%
Construction	0.0	220,745.3	48.5	0.0%	498,313.0	109.4	0.0%
Manufacture	33,823.1	215,910.2	11,517.3	5.6%	631,109.0	49,438.2	8.5%
Commerce	0.0	286,175.7	2970.7	1.0%	1,090,838.0	10,769.0	1.0%
Transport, storage and post	0.0	109,287.9	978.6	0.9%	283,573.0	2539.2	0.9%
Services	0.0	658,994.0	4650.4	0.7%	2,326,491.0	15,325.6	0.7%
Total	33,823.1	2,504,827.1	25,097.3	1.0%	6,094,928.0	100,465.6	1.7%

Source: authors elaboration

Table 7 FDI's Impact on Value Added and Employment in the Southeast Gulf of Mexico

Sectors	Structural Change		Value added initial	Value added impact	Value added impact	Employment initial	Employment impact	Employment impact
	Millions of Mexican pesos at constant prices of 2013	Distribution %	Millions of Mexican pesos at constant prices of 2013		%	Number of jobs		%
Agriculture, livestock, forestry, hunting and fishing	211.4	0.8%	58,894.1	410.4	0.7%	1158,976.0	8077.0	0.7%
Mining	6181.8	24.5%	925,216.5	5528.3	0.6%	74,004.0	750.6	1.0%
Electricity, gas and water	0.0	0.0%	29,603.4	163.9	0.6%	31,624.0	175.1	0.6%
Construction	16,244.6	64.4%	220,745.3	9949.4	4.7%	498,313.0	22,459.9	4.7%
Manufacture	773.4	3.1%	215,910.2	1514.5	0.7%	631,109.0	4964.4	0.8%
Commerce	1190.1	4.7%	286,175.7	2859.6	1.0%	1,090,838.0	10,473.0	1.0%
Transport, storage and post	540.0	2.1%	109,287.9	1158.5	1.1%	283,573.0	3006.0	1.1%
Services	96.4	0.4%	658,994.0	4406.9	0.7%	2,326,491.0	14,491.8	0.6%
Total	25,237.8	100.0%	2,504,827.1	25,991.6	1.0%	6,094,928.0	64,397.8	1.1%

Source: authors elaboration

5 Conclusions

In the 90s Mexico took under way several aggressive trade and foreign investment measures, most of them contained in the trade agreement that created the north American free trade zone. It is commonly stated that NAFTA has only beneficiated northern states in Mexico, with no absolute gain for the south region of Mexico. In this research, a combination of econometric and multi-sectoral techniques is employed to show this is probably not true. A structural break in non-petroleum exports and foreign direct investment is found during the last 30 years in the Southeast Gulf of Mexico, which encompass the states of Veracruz, Tabasco, Campeche, Quintana Roo, and Yucatán, most likely caused by those major liberalization reforms.

Non-manufacturing exports and FDI showed a significant structural change, according to the Markov Switching Regime model estimates. Manufacturing exports are 48.3% higher in the high regime compared to the low regime, and FDI is 71.6% higher in the high regime than in the low regime.

Introducing these changes into an accounting multiplier model, increases in the added value and employment of the region were estimated, taking into account the income-expenditure relationships between households, primary factors, and economic sectors. The model estimates indicate that the increment in manufacturing exports is linked to a rise of 1.0% in gross added value and 1.7% in employment. The sectors most favored by expansion, in addition to manufacturing, are agriculture, livestock, forestry, hunting, and fishing; and electricity, gas, and water.

In the case of FDI, its expansion is associated with an increase equivalent to 1.0% of the added value and employment in the region. In this case, the most favored economic sectors are construction, commerce, and transport, storage, and post.

In this way, it is concluded that trade liberalization and investment deregulation had significant impacts in the Southeast Gulf of Mexico economy despite its sharp specialization in natural resources, its remoteness from the USA (see Fig. 1) and its lack of public and technological infrastructure to attract FDI. Indeed, the Centro de Investigaciones Económicas (2021) technology absorption index ranked the Southeastern Mexico below the 12th place, and three of them are in the lowest positions: Tabasco (27 out of 32), Campeche (28), and Quintana Roo (31).

It is important to alert the reader that this exercise represents a first approach to quantifying the economic impact of the structural reforms of the 1990s at the regional level, since the exercise assumes that the productive structure does not change. Furthermore, in the case of the impact of FDI, only the effects of the increase in the demand for capital goods are being considered.

One line of future research is to build a general equilibrium model of the region to be able to analyze the resources reallocation caused by the increase in exports and FDI, in fact, this type of models was widely used to analyze the impact of NAFTA at the country level (Francois and Shiells 1994; Chapa 2003). Also, another line of research consists of studying the effects of the increase in FDI on the supply-side, for which, it is considered to explore the relationship between FDI and TFP (total factor productivity) in the region and introduce the change in TFP caused by the impact of FDI, in the general equilibrium model and quantify the effects throughout the economic system of the Southeast Gulf region.

Even when the employed models might be improved, this research is rigorous enough to prove that early trade liberalization measures had some significant impact in the of the Southeast Gulf region. Nevertheless, the magnitude of the total impacts in value added and employment are relatively small compared with those in the Northeast region of Mexico (Ayala et al. 2015). Clearly, the sustained progress of the region involves more and better investment in education, public infrastructure, and private capital in order to get more benefits out of the trade and capital market liberalization.

References

Ayala E, Chapa J (2019) Efectos del declive de la producción petrolera en la región Golfo-Sureste: Un Análisis con la Matriz de Contabilidad Social. In: Dávila A (ed) Modelos económicos de las regiones de México. Miguel Angel Porrúa, México, pp 213–247

Ayala E, Chapa J, Treviño L (2015a) Modelo interregional de insumo producto de la región Golfo-Sureste. In: Dávila A (ed) Modelos interregionales de insumo producto de la economía mexicana. MA Porrúa, México, pp 61–102

Ayala E, Chapa J, Treviño L (2015b) Análisis estructural de la región petrolera del Golfo-Sureste de México, en un contexto interregional. Equilibrio Económico 11(2):135–168

Ayala E, Chapa J, Treviño L, Genna G, Peréz F (2015c) Efectos regionales del libre comercio. In: El caso del noreste de México. Pearson, Ciudad de México

Centro de Investigaciones Económicas (2021) Determinantes de la competitividad del estado de Nuevo León. Facultad de Economía, Universidad Autónoma de Nuevo León, Monterrey. forthcoming

Chapa J (2003) Análisis de la apertura comercial en México mediante modelos multisectoriales, 1970–1993. Universitat de Barcelona, España, Tesis de doctorado. http://diposit.ub.edu/dspace/handle/2445/43021

Dávila A (2019) Modelos económicos multisectoriales elaborados con matrices de contabilidad social. In: Dávila A (ed) Modelos económicos de las regiones de México. Miguel Angel Porrúa, México, pp 7–30

Defourny J, Thorbecke E (1984) Structural path analysis and multiplier decomposition within a social accounting matrix framework. Econ J 94(373):111–136. https://doi.org/10.2307/2232220

Francois J, Shiells C (1994) Modeling trade policy: applied general equilibrium assessments of north American free trade. Cambridge University Press, Cambridge

Pyatt G, Round J (1979) Accounting and fixed Price multipliers in a social accounting matrix framework. Econ J 89(356):850–873. https://doi.org/10.2307/2231503

The manufacturer's authorised representative in the EU is Springer Nature Customer Service Centre GmbH, Europaplatz 3, 69115 Heidelberg, Germany. If you have any concerns regarding our products, please contact ProductSafety@springernature.com

Printed and bound by CPI Group (UK) Ltd, Croydon, CR0 4YY
30/09/2026
02225265-0012